JACK AUBREY COMMANDS

JACK AUBREY COMMANDS

AN HISTORICAL COMPANION TO THE NAVAL WORLD
OF
PATRICK O'BRIAN

BRIAN LAVERY

Foreword by Peter Weir

Naval Institute Press
Annapolis, Maryland

AUTHOR'S ACKNOWLEDGEMENTS

This book is the result of many years working in the subject, and I have had the benefit of ideas from many sources, including those who have attended lectures at the Open Museum in Greenwich, and other places.

Particular thanks are due to John Lee, Martin Robson and Stuart Robertson for encouraging the idea and Robert Gardiner, formerly of Conway Maritime Press, who set me on the track which led to *Nelson's Navy* and ultimately the present book; Frank Nowosielski and Peter Goodwin of HMS *Victory*; Robert Prescott, Colin Martin and Martin Deane of St Andrews University; Andrew Lambert of Kings College, London and N A M Rodger of Exeter University; past colleagues at the National Maritime Museum including Roger Knight, David Cordingly, Alan Pearsall and Roger Morriss; present colleagues including Colin White, Margarette Lincoln, Nigel Rigby, Simon Stephens and Robert Blyth; the library and manuscripts departments, including Jill Davies, Daphne Knott and Liza Verity; staff of the Royal Naval Museum including Campbell MacMurray and Matthew Sheldon; David Syrett of New York and Dan Baugh of Cornell. Thanks to the staffs of the Public Record Office, The British Library Manuscripts department and the London Library. The National Maritime Museum Picture Library, especially Eleanor Heron and David Taylor, has been very helpful in tracing images.

In home life, Sarah and Alice Lavery have been tolerant and supportive of my efforts. In the wider world, I was much encouraged by contact with Patrick O'Brian during his lifetime, and with Peter Weir while making the film *Master and Commander: The Far Side of the World*. I must also thank Peter for kindly writing the Foreword for this book and also his help, along with his assistant, Andy Weltman, in providing images to accompany the Foreword.

The largest single acknowledgement is due to my late colleague David Lyon, who over many yeras helped form my thinking on naval history and on Patrick O'Brian. He will always be missed as a friend and as a critic.

Brian Lavery, Greenwich, July 2003

First published in Great Britain in 2003 by
Conway Maritime Press
The Chrysalis Building
Bramley Road
London, W10 6SP

Published and distributed in the United States and Canada by Naval Institute Press,
291 Wood Road, Annapolis, MD 21402-5034
Library of Congress Control No 2003106249

ISBN 1-59114-403-5

Project Editor: Martin Robson
Design and typesetting: Champion Design
Printed and bound in Spain

FRONTISPIECE: 'HMS *Sophie* leaving Port Mahon' by Geoff Hunt RSMA. The subject is taken from Patrick O'Brian's novel *Master and Commander*. (Reproduced by kind permission of the artist)

CONTENTS

FOREWORD

1. 'What's Lavery got to say about it?'
2. 'He agrees.'
3. 'No, I'm sure he disagrees.'

1. 'Go and get the Lavery.'

Any or all of the above dialogue might have been heard in my office in Baja, Mexico, during the early months of 2002. We were preparing to shoot a film based on the novels of Patrick O'Brian, and the book in question was Brian Lavery's *Nelson's Navy*, a prime source for all departments, as it crossed the spectrum from buttons to boomkins. The book held a prominent place in our growing library alongside Jean Boudriot's *The 74-Gun Ship* and Peter Goodwin's *The Construction and Fitting of the English Man of War*, and hundreds of other titles.

Outside the office, the concrete apron surrounding the studio tank resembled an 18th-Century dockyard in time of war. Marines drilled to one side, while gun-crews practiced beating to quarters and swords flashed in the sun, as coils of rope and chords of timber were stacked at hand for the riggers and construction crews.

All the while in the middle of our pond, the *Surprise*, Jack Aubrey's favourite command, rose up into the Mexican skyline, an ant's nest of activity. At times, it seemed as if we were actually going to set sail for the Horn in some bizarre recreation, and at any moment you expected to bump into Thor Heyerdahl.

The 20-volume opus of O'Brian's was our touchstone. His books reflect a lifetime of research, and co-writer John Collee and I began by marking up each of the books under appropriate headings: 'Divisions,' 'Gunnery,' 'Crew,' 'Jack and Stephen Dialogue,' and so on. These references were in turn photocopied and turned into books themselves, handy cribs for cast and crew.

I had two years to write the script and prepare for the shoot, and given such little time, the possibility of making a serious error was ever present. There's an ocean of books out there and I had little hope of doing much more than a superficial survey. To help me I had a wonderful team of experts. On the set: Gordon Laco, historian and tall-ship captain; Leon Poindexter, shipwright and historian; and Andy Reay-Ellers, also a tall-ship captain who had the difficult job of planning our sail pattern as we journeyed around the world in our tank. On the end of a telephone a patient Brian Lavery, Peter Goodwin, Keeper and Curator of HMS *Victory*, Chuck Fithian, Curator of Archaeology at the University of Delaware, and for help with Stephen Maturin, Mick Crumplin of the Royal College of Surgeons. At sea, two tall-ship captains, Richard Bailey of the *Rose*, and Chris Blake of the *Endeavour* Replica, the finest recreation vessel afloat.

Before starting the script, I joined Captain Blake for a cruise on the *Endeavour*. The attention to detail in bringing this famous vessel of Captain Cook's to life is astonishing. Not that I was thinking of anything more than trying to avoid falling and breaking my neck as I struggled up and over the futtock-shrouds at five past midnight, to take in sail as we began a cruise off the New South Wales coastline in late 2000. What's unique about the *Endeavour* Replica is that not only her spar-deck is museum accurate, so too is the berth-deck below. This makes it almost impossible for even the dullest imagination not to be jolted back to the 18th Century.

Time expanded, a day a week, a night endless. The words of Charles Dickens came to mind: 'It was the best of times, it was the worst of times.'

This was the first of two cruises on the *Endeavour*. I went back with my producers and cameraman, to be sure they too would have the experience stored in their bones when it came time for our 'voyage.'

Visits to HMS *Victory* and the *Trincomalee* in Britain, and the USS *Constitution* in Boston were part of this early preparation. At the time, I recalled a quote of film director Sergei Eisenstein's when surveying Nishnynovgorod, a setting for his famous film *Alexander Nevsky*. Looking at the walls of that ancient city, the same walls that centuries before witnessed the invasion he was to film, he said, 'If these stones could speak.' So I felt, as I ran my hand over the deck-timbers of HMS *Victory*. You can become obsessed. I was aware that these three ships had been rebuilt over the years, and on the *Constitution* I crawled behind a young naval officer deep down in the orlop-deck so I could touch the wood he assured me was 'original.' I remember Chuck Fithian showing me a collection of some 130 odd shoes brought up from the wreck of the British brig HMS *De Braak*, sunk off the Delaware coast in 1812. There was something so touching about those well-preserved shoes, some of which had crude lace-holes punched in them. 'Laces were just coming in,' he said. 'Perhaps they belonged to the younger men, taking up the latest fashion.'

I surrounded myself with artifacts of the period as I worked on the script, swords, belt-buckles, maps, hoping to draw down the muse. Music was another aid, as I groped in the dark, trying to find my way back in time. Patrick O'Brian was so successful at this that in his rare interviews he came across as a time-traveler. Dr Maturin himself, it was tempting to think.

The casting of the crew, some 130 men, received as much attention as did that of the principals. Searching for '18th Century faces' was left to Judy Bouley, and, incredibly, she saw

The *Rose*, a replica of a British frigate, had to undergo extensive alterations to prepare her for the role of the 28-gun HMS *Surprise*.

vii

more than 7,000 hopefuls. As a guide, we had reproductions of paintings and sketches of the period and most importantly a rare set of photographs, taken in the mid-1840s of English fishermen, shot by David Octavius Hill and Robert Adamson. I also had friends casting in Poland to get us as far away as possible from people raised on a western diet, with Kodak-ready smiles and expressions of world-weary cynicism.

'Guileless.' I read that word often from those writing at the time, when they described the typical foremast-jack, and that was a quality we looked for. Judy often found this in the young crews of the tall-ships of today, and they became our most valuable extras.

Russell Crowe, in preparing for the role of Jack Aubrey, sailed through tempest-tossed waters in the Fijian Island Group, coincidentally in a boat named the *Surprise*, the skipper a fan of the books. Meanwhile in London, Paul Bettany was doing research for Dr Maturin. In between running his hands across his cello, he was clamping my arm in preparation for an amputation or preparing my skull for a trepanning under the watchful eye of Mick Crumplin.

The *Surprise* was a key member of our cast, and to play her we chose the *Rose*, a replica of a British frigate, active off the coast of Newport, Rhode Island during the Revolutionary War. She was a little smaller than the 28-gun *Surprise*, and although a Coast Guard-rated sail-training vessel, there was much to be done to prepare her to play the *Surprise*. To work with our American shipwrights, I called on three men key to building the *Endeavour*: Bill Leonard, Master Shipwright; Nick Truelove, Carpenter; and Igor Bjorksten, Rigger.

Captain Bailey had the job of installing new engines and preparing to sail the *Rose* through the Panama Canal and up to San Diego. There the Art Department anxiously awaited them. They had built everything from spacecraft to medieval castles, but never a ship of His Majesty's Navy nor with shipwrights and historians determined on accuracy. They had a few short months to not only convert the *Rose* and have her ready for Second Unit work at sea, but also build an identical *Rose/Surprise*, fully-rigged, to be placed on a gimble in the tank, where she would be rocked and rolled from Brazil to the Galapagos Islands. This was the finest hour of our Construction Coordinator, Gary Deaton, and the Art Department as a whole.

The *Rose*'s rigging had to be either replaced or 'thickened,' her rig was fine for sailing today but not heavy enough, nor enough of it for the period. Her bow and stern were to be altered, her deck-timbers 'disguised' as they were too narrow, a wale added to her hull, and dozens of alterations including extra gun-ports. Apart from that, new sails had to be ordered and made, and all of this duplicated for our tank vessel. At the same time, Weta Workshop in New Zealand, part of the wonderful *Lord of the Rings* team, were to build miniatures in complete detail, their *Surprise* alone was over 25 feet in length. While all this was going on, complete 'models' were created inside the computers at Asylum, our digital effects house. At Baja, the interior sets were started, gun-deck, berth-deck, orlop-deck, all to be fitted out and aged.

Here our library of books came into play. We had plans kindly made available by the National Maritime Museum, Greenwich of both the *Rose* and the *Surprise* but inevitably not in enough detail, and despite books and advisors, many an educated guess was made. There was a considerable degree of individuality expressed in the work of the shipwrights of the day. The *Surprise*, originally a French vessel, *L'Unité*, had been altered in the British yards following her capture, so who knew exactly what she finally looked like?

Throughout the process, I managed to keep reading, and there was no shortage of material, with the exception of first-hand accounts. These are few, and mostly written by officers. The world of the crew is the hardest to penetrate. This applied to the Wardrobe

Department, who with gloved hands could study an officer's coat at Greenwich but not crew clothing. Seamen did not have uniforms at this period so they turned to visual material as well as trying to interpret from lists of slop-clothing in the records of individual ships, or from the rare mention of clothing in the first-hand accounts. Although talking of the American Navy, Herman Melville's *White Jacket* was a wonderful source if seen through a veil of biting sarcasm. That's also true of Tobias Smollett, one of the first to write from first-hand experience in *Roderick Random*. It wasn't until I hit Frederick Marryat that I felt on safer ground. I'd read his *Midshipman Easy* as a boy and he, along with James Anthony Gardner (*Above and Under Hatches*) and Samuel Leech (*A Voice from the Main Deck*) I found most helpful, and my notebook began to fill up.

Leech on the mood of battle: '...a strange noise, such as I had never heard before, next arrested my attention; it sounded like the tearing of sails, just over our heads. This was the wind of our enemy's shot.'[1] And this after battle and a burial at sea: '...the men brushed away their tears, muttered "It's no use to fret," and things once more wore their wonted aspect.'

Dudley Pope's *Life in Nelson's Navy* is an excellent contemporary work, giving a social and political background to naval matters, invaluable for the cast.

There have been many analogies constructed by nervous filmmakers to cover their translation of book to screen. A 'portrait painter' comes to mind, the book the subject, the resulting painting the film. When the work is finally shown some will say it's nothing at all like the subject. Others might say the artist caught the 'spirit' of the sitter. Time will tell, but I hope the O'Brian fans will feel the latter.

Inevitably there will be inaccuracies, and for that, none of my advisors, including Brian Lavery, are to blame. Even the enjoyment of reading the manuscript of *Jack Aubrey Commands* was occasionally disturbed by mention of books I'd not read, or worse, facts that disputed some aspect of what we'd done. These were momentary, however, and I was overwhelmed by the experience, once again, of 'time-travel' – back to the wooden world. For the reader, a sea of pleasure lies ahead.

Peter Weir
June 2003

Peter Weir, director of *Master and Commander: The Far Side of the World*, on the deck of *Surprise*.

Patrick O'Brian in his study at his home in Colliure in the south of France. On the bookshelf can be seen copies of David White's *Anatomy of the Ship – Diana* and Brian Lavery's book on the *Bellona* in the same series - the book which gave O'Brian the idea for Jack Aubrey's main ship in *The Commodore*.
(*The Sunday Times*/Wist Thorpe)

INTRODUCTION

NAVAL FACT AND NAVAL FICTION

The Royal Navy of 1793-1815 still has an enormous hold on the public imagination. It produced many heroes at the time, and Horatio Nelson (1758-1805) was not alone in a pantheon which included Thomas Cochrane (1775-1860) and Sir Sidney Smith (1764-1840). It produced just as many heroes in twentieth century fiction, including Horatio Hornblower, Nathaniel Drinkwater and Jack Aubrey. It is not the acclaim of critics or historians which has sustained this public interest; the historical novel as a genre has been unfashionable for a century or so. It is not the attention of the mass media, for until recently film and television have tended to ignore maritime matters of all kinds. Naval fiction has tended to gain a market slowly, often against the tide of intellectual opinion.

The founder of naval fiction is usually taken as Captain Frederick Marryat (1792-1848), who entered the Royal Navy under Lord Cochrane in 1806. Marryat's books are clearly fiction, and contain some fantastic incidents. In *Mr Midshipman Easy* (1836) for example, a young and inexperienced midshipman, with the help of a black cook and a few disaffected seamen, navigates and maintains a ship for several weeks in unfriendly waters. But Marryat's books give a very good impression of the culture and attitudes which pervaded the navy of the age. Sometimes words are put into the mouth of his characters which are obviously not his own views, but give an idea of what is believed at the time. Captain Frederick Chamier (1796-1870), a contemporary of Marryat, wrote autobiography rather than fiction in his *Life of a Sailor*. Basil Hall (1788-1844) too described the navy as it really was. At the same time there were many men of the lower deck, such as William Robinson, William Spavens, David Hay and John Nicol, who wrote with perhaps less literary skill but no less authority on what they found in a life at sea.

Nearly a century after the death of most of the protagonists, the genre was revived by authors who had no personal knowledge of the age of sail. Modern naval fiction is as believable as possible, but based on research rather than the author's personal experience. Mistakes can be made, for example in C S Forester's Hornblower books the hero often steps from his cabin in a frigate direct to the steering wheel, which could only be done on a ship of the line; the author is mistaken about the nature of the press gang in the first book of the sequence,

Captain Frederick Marryat,
(1792-1848) who served in the
Royal Navy under Cochrane
from 1806, and published his
first naval novel, *The Naval
Officer*, in 1829. Painted by E
Dixon between 1835 and
1839. (NMM BHC 2851)

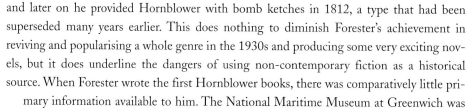

and later on he provided Hornblower with bomb ketches in 1812, a type that had been superseded many years earlier. This does nothing to diminish Forester's achievement in reviving and popularising a whole genre in the 1930s and producing some very exciting novels, but it does underline the dangers of using non-contemporary fiction as a historical source. When Forester wrote the first Hornblower books, there was comparatively little primary information available to him. The National Maritime Museum at Greenwich was just about to open its doors and its huge collection of warship plans was not yet accessible, while the Public Record Office was comparatively little used. The standard work on social history was John Masefield's superficial and rather biased *Sea Life in Nelson's Time*, written in a hurry and published in 1905.

More recently, Patrick O'Brian had the advantage of a deeper level of historical information, in view of the greater body of primary source material that was available in his time. He seems to have been more thorough in his research, and had extensive correspondence with many experts, for example in the National Maritime Museum. He was also far more prone to use real ships, incidents and people in his books, for example Lord Cochrane in *Master and Commander* and the sinking of the *Guardian* in *Desolation Island*. But O'Brian's writings on naval intelligence, though based on at least one real character and several real incidents, is much more fictional than the purely naval parts of his stories.

There are many and varied sources for naval history, including the collections of the Public Record Office and the National Maritime Museum, the second of which had only been fully available since 1945. The Navy Records Society has published many volumes of edited documents since the Hornblower series started, some of which are highly relevant to the social history of the period. These include *Five Naval Journals*, *The Health of Seamen* and *Manning Pamphlets*. One might modestly mention one's own effort, *Shipboard Life and Organisation* of 1998.[1] Departments of maritime history have been set up in the Universities of Greenwich, Exeter and more recently the Laughton Naval History Unit at King's College London, and even more research effort is likely to be devoted to the subject, which is healthier than it has ever been. After a gap of several decades, it seems that radio and television are taking more interest in maritime history and archaeology than ever before; the *Hornblower* series on television is highly popular; not to mention the new audience which will be opened by Peter Weir's film, and the forthcoming bicentennial of Trafalgar in 2005. Captain Marryat might be disappointed at how little his books are read today, but he would be pleasantly surprised at how the movement he started continues to flourish and expand through other media.

It is interesting to see how staggeringly popular naval fiction has been in the past, far beyond the cult status enjoyed by Patrick O'Brian in his later lifetime. Captain Frederick Marryat, it has been said, was recognised as 'the most celebrated English novelist between Jane Austen and Charles Dickens'[2] for several decades after his death. More recently, C S Forester was a literary superstar from the 1930s to the 1950s. 'Not until Ian Fleming's James Bond crashed into the literary consciousness of the Anglo-American reading public in the 1950s was Hornblower's primacy in escapist fiction challenged and finally superceded.'[3] The comparison with Bond is an interesting one. His origins are also naval and he, like his creator, was a commander in the Royal Navy. He is even described by his enemies as a 'man of war.' His esteemed superior, Admiral Sir Miles Messervy or 'M', was modelled on the Director of Naval Intelligence during the early years of the Second World War, Admiral John Godfrey, who has a 'keen sailor's face' and a house full of naval prints and relics, and tells stories of 'battles, tornadoes, bizarre happenings, courts-martial, eccentric officers, neat-

ly worded signals.' Bond has enjoyed an afterlife since the death of his creator in 1964, which has been fantastic in every sense of the term. While 'serious' critics have tended to ignore naval fiction, they have dissected the Bond myth from many angles. If naval fiction is unfashionable because it is nationalistic, masculine and involves violence, then this is far more so for the Bond stories, which almost revel in being full of 'sex, snobbery and sadism.' Only the ironic tone of the films, and their indulgence in high technology, allows them to be culturally acceptable. The secret agent formula is infinitely adaptable throughout the decades and hints at the idea that Britain, though clearly declining by normal economic and military standards, might have some secret powers which maintains her position as a player in global affairs.

In contrast, the naval officer of the age of sail was rooted in a particular period, a time when the Royal Navy was stretched to the utmost but usually victorious and the individual captains have independence of action well beyond the dreams of a modern captain, who is constantly at the end of a radio link with headquarters. Scientific interests are pursued by well-educated gentlemen, and the class system is rigid enough to let everyone know his place, but flexible enough to allow them to rise in British society through prize money and good marriages. The ship of war is a well-honed weapon and skilfully deployed by a navy which has operated them on the same principles for a century and a half. The steam power which will supersede it is barely on the horizon, though Hornblower for one was aware of it. The fictional secret agent, like some fictional naval officers, is in many senses a man alone, but between times of great danger and activity the agent lives in a world of luxury hotels, good food and glamorous women. The naval officer spends most of his time in a very mas-

Geoff Hunt's painting 'HMS *Surprise* off Cap Pilar' was originally created to illustrate the cover of Patrick O'Brian's novel *Blue at the Mizzen*. (Artist: Geoff Hunt RSMA)

culine environment, and even the captain's cabin is cramped and Spartan by any standards of shore life. He lives most of his life in a very intense world. 'Men are nowhere crowded in so small a space as in a man of war. The individuals of which the company is composed may literally be said to live in public. Actions can never be concealed, even whispers may be heard.'[4] It is a world so different from today's experiences, a world so filled with exotic travels, dangers, hardships and triumphs that it might also be compared with the novel and film fantasies of the modern age – *Lord of the Rings* and *Harry Potter*. But unlike these works naval fiction is firmly rooted in historical fact.

Naval fact and naval fiction continue to feed on one another. More than thirty years ago I was intrigued by the writings of Forester and the unknown Patrick O'Brian, and this has led me, like many others, to a lifelong interest in naval history. It has caused me to learn to sail in many types of ship, to seek work at Chatham Historic Dockyard and the National Maritime Museum at Greenwich, and to advise on the restoration of HMS *Victory* and the reconstruction of Captain Cook's ship *Endeavour*. Like many other published naval historians I can claim to have some slight impact on the O'Brian novels, specifically in my case in the ship *Bellona* used in *The Commodore*. Patrick O'Brian was kind enough to write the foreword for my *Nelson's Navy*, and we have shared a cover artist in the magnificent paintings of Geoff Hunt. *Nelson's Navy*, in turn, has been used as a standard textbook in the research for Peter Weir's film *Master and Commander: The Far Side of the World*, and so the cycle continues.

Naval fiction presents a portrait of a great armed force at the height of its powers, a force which ranged all over the world and delivered victory in many different circumstances. The Royal Navy of Hornblower and Aubrey was not just the largest in the world; it was also the best, ship for ship and man for man (even against the Americans, when the forces were genuinely even). For a British readership, it provides a very satisfying glimpse of what their ancestors were capable of two centuries ago; for the Americans, it gives an example of what they would like their own armed forces to be. Historically, one would have to go back two millennia, to the Roman army, to find a force which was quite so pre-eminent in the Western world. That needs a great leap of the imagination, and fiction about that period is not likely to become widespread. Some armies in the last two centuries, notably those of Napoleon and Hitler, have been as successful as the Royal Navy in the short term, but both were ultimately defeated, because their authoritarian leaders over-reached themselves; and Hitler's army, in particular, was associated with some of the greatest war crimes in history. The Royal Navy, on the other hand, was mostly associated with causes which are very acceptable today: national independence; parliamentary (if not democratic) politics; anti-slavery (at least after 1807) and technological progress. It was also a great defender of imperialism, which is a deeply unpopular concept today, but that is passed over. It was not engaged in any war crimes on a large scale, or in repression (except perhaps of its own seamen and pressed men). It operated mainly on the sea so it did not act against civilian populations, except, indirectly through bombarding Copenhagen in 1807 and in the occasional raid. It treated fellow seamen, merchant or naval, of whatever nationality, with respect and in general it did not ill-treat its prisoners. It is not difficult for the modern reader to identify with the aims and the people of the navy of Horatio Hornblower or Jack Aubrey.

CHAPTER 1

THE WORLD OF THE SEAMAN

As Patrick O'Brian wrote as the very first words of his great naval opus, 'When one is writing about the Royal Navy of the eighteenth and early nineteenth centuries it is difficult to do full justice to one's subject, for so very often the improbable reality outruns fiction.'[1] The Royal Navy was highly successful during two decades of war with France between 1793 and 1815. It fought and won six major fleet battles, several important squadron actions and countless fights between single ships on each side. It generally expected to win against odds of up to three to two, except when fighting the Americans. When fleet action was not possible, it blockaded the enemy fleets in ports. It protected British trade and attacked that of the enemy. It launched numerous seaborne invasions of enemy-held colonies, and one major opposed landing in Egypt in 1801. It landed and supported Wellington's army in the Peninsula and nurtured a force which would win the land war in Europe. Though its main strength was in European waters, it operated in all the seas of the world, and there were notable successes in the Caribbean, Indian Ocean and East Indies. It had its share of problems, notably in its archaic administrative system and the recruitment and management of its seamen, but it rose above them to triumph. It remains one of the most popular subjects, both for historical research and historical fiction and its greatest hero, Nelson, is still considered one of the greatest Britons of all time.

The sailors who fought in these wars lived in an introverted world on board ship and had only tenuous contacts with the shore. Shipboard society of the period was more self-contained than almost anything one could think of. After the conquest of scurvy in the late eighteenth century ships could stay continuously at sea for several months, while the global nature of the wars caused them to make very long voyages, away from their home bases for years at a time. They were not hampered by the steamship's need for frequent refuelling, or constrained by orders received by radio. Even in port the lower-deck seamen often stayed on board ship and shore leave was by no means a right. It could be the same at the other end of the chain of command, for example Nelson, in an extreme case, spent two years from 1803 to 1805 without leaving the decks of the *Victory*.

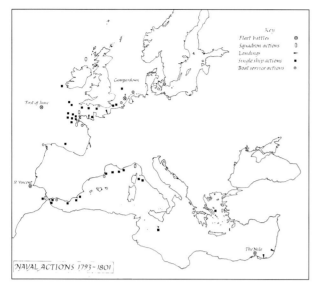

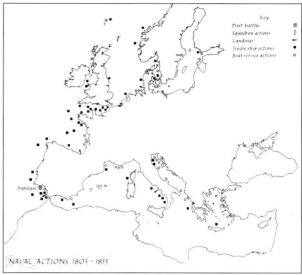

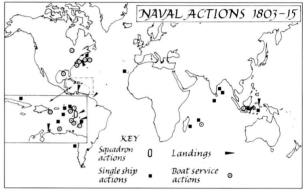

The actions between 1793 and 1815 for which the Naval General Service Medal was eventually issued in 1840. Though it only shows actions that were regarded as reasonably successful by the British, it gives a good indication of the range and scope of the naval wars. Based on Kenneth Douglas-Morris, *The Naval General Service Medal Roll*, 1982.

But against this, sailors saw far more of the world than their shore-based fellows and their wives could ever dream of. An exception to the belief that women did not go to sea is Jane Austen's Mrs Croft, the wife of an admiral:

"What a great traveller you must have been, ma'am!" said Mrs Musgrove to Mrs Croft.

"Pretty well, ma'am, in the fifteen years of marriage; though many women have done more. I have crossed the Atlantic four times, and have been once to the East Indies and back again; and only once, besides being in different places about home – Cork, Lisbon and Gibraltar. But I never went beyond the Streights – and was never in the West Indies. We do not call Bermuda or Bahama, you know, the West Indies."

Mrs. Musgrove had not a word to say in dissent; she could not accuse herself of having ever called them any thing in the whole course of her life.[2]

The great novelist herself was never bitten by the travel bug, and did not completely understand it in others. She wrote to her brother, a naval captain:

It must be real enjoyment to you, since you are obliged to leave England, to be where you are, seeing something of a new Country, & one that has been so distinguished as Sweden – You must have great pleasure in that....So zealous as it always was for Protestantism [sic] – And I have always fancied it more like England than many other Countries.[3]

There is a striking contrast between the enclosed, overcrowded setting of the ship itself, and the vast, empty world of sea just outside it – between the dark, fetid environment of the lower deck, and the wide horizons that could be seen from the masthead. As a vehicle the ship was far more mobile than anything else of the age; as Admiral Patton put it, 'ships, which are of great value and great importance, may be with ease transferred, with all their tackle and ammunition, from one state to another'. Authority was usually rigid on board ship, but that was mitigated by the need to respect the skills of experts, and the hierarchy was undermined by the physical layout of the vessel. 'The apartments of the officers are always open to those immediately under them in rank and must often be exposed to the access of the whole company. Nothing private can be transacted in such a community; even a sudden gust of passion is incapable of being concealed.' According to a modern critic it had much in common with the far more domestic world of other writers. 'Like Jane Austen, O'Brian is really happiest working on two or three inches of ivory and turning to art the daily lives of three or four families in a locality – except that the village happens to be a wooden ship of war at the apogee of a great Navy's world sea-power in the days of sail…'[4]

THE WORLD
OF THE SEAMAN

THE FRENCH REVOLUTIONARY WAR

The Royal Navy already had a long and largely successful history by the time war with France broke out in 1793. It had risen and fallen in medieval times according to the king's inclinations and needs. It was firmly established by the Tudors, notably Henry VIII, as a means of defending the English kingdom. It fought the Spanish Armada under Queen Elizabeth, with help from armed merchant ships and the weather. Its character was formed during a series of intensely-fought battles with the Dutch in the third quarter of the seventeenth century, and these battles were still cited as examples more than a hundred years later. From 1689 it took part in five wars against the French, with other conflicts against the Spanish, Dutch and Americans. When the French Revolution began in 1789, it was almost a century after the start of a long series of wars between Britain and France – five in all, lasting for 38 years out of a hundred. They had started mainly as European wars but in the second phase, after the British declared war on the Spanish in the War of Jenkins Ear in 1739, they had largely been concerned with the fight for colonial empire, especially after 1778 when the French joined the American War of Independence in support of the colonial revolt. The Royal Navy was increasingly successful during these wars, beginning with defeat by the French at Beachy Head in 1690, to victory in a great fleet battle off the Saintes in the West Indies in 1782, which saved much of the British Empire after the loss of America to the colonists.

The Great Wars between Britain and France from 1793 to 1815 were not simple on any level. Britain's enemy changed slightly over two decades of war; from the French Revolution and its excesses during the Reign of Terror, to the diminutive but terrifying figure of Napoleon Bonaparte, with his overriding power and ambition. The enmity of Britain and France was a constant factor, but apart from that everything seemed to change from year to year. A major naval power like Spain might be an ally for several years, then neutral, then an enemy, neutral again and then an enemy and finally an ally. The war was not confined to Europe, as even the most casual reader of naval fiction knows. The wars are so complex that very few, apart from experts, can remember with any confidence who was fighting whom at any given moment.

The French Revolution, welcomed at first by large sections of the British public in 1789, turned to more extreme policies including the execution of the King of France in 1793. In response Britain joined a coalition of conservative European powers to oppose the Revolution. Initial military success soon turned to disaster for the continental powers, as the new French armies drove all before them. At sea the British and their allies seemed untouchable, as the French navy was disrupted by the Revolution and the main fleet base at Toulon was taken over by the allies; but this was a missed opportunity and a young artillery officer, Napoleon Bonaparte, drove the conservative powers out without great loss to the French fleet.

In 1794 Admiral Lord Howe (1726-99) scored the first great naval victory of the war at the Glorious First of June, when he defeated a French battlefleet escorting an important grain convoy. There were successes in the Mediterranean as the British, including the young Horatio Nelson, took control of Corsica as a major base. But Bonaparte was advancing through Italy and in 1796 Spain joined the war on the French side. Fearing isolation, Admiral Sir John Jervis (1735-1823) ordered the complete evacuation of the Mediterranean.

The major crisis of this naval war came in 1797, while Britain was standing almost alone against France. Jervis's fleet defeated a large Spanish force off Cape St Vincent with much initiative and daring from Commodore Nelson. Jervis became an Earl, taking his title from the battle. But there was serious discontent in the fleets at home, with large-scale mutinies in the fleets at Spithead and the Nore. The first was settled reasonably well and the seamen got their first pay rise for nearly 150 years. The second was more extreme in its demands and conduct, and eventually the mutineers gave in, to see their ringleaders hanged. But the same men, as part of the North Sea fleet, defeated the Dutch in a decisive victory at Camperdown later in the year.

In 1798 Bonaparte, realising for the moment that an invasion of Britain was impossible, planned an ambitious expedition to Egypt, where he could threaten the British Empire in India. The British could see something was happening at Toulon where the ships were massed, and Nelson re-entered the Mediterranean to find out what it was. After many vicissitudes he found the French fleet at anchor in Aboukir Bay near Alexandria and defeated them decisively at the Battle of the Nile. Bonaparte's army was isolated in Egypt, though its leader eventually made his way home to set up a new regime in Paris, with himself as First Consul and effective ruler of the country.

The British used their advantage after the Nile to build a new coalition against France, including Austria, Turkey and Russia. But the powers had little in common and their land campaigns in Switzerland and the Netherlands failed. Britain now controlled the Mediterranean again, but through lack of co-operation between its senior officers the navy failed to catch Admiral Bruey's fleet as it entered the sea in 1799. In 1801 the British and their allies invaded Egypt and defeated the remnants of Bonaparte's army. In the Baltic, the League of Armed Neutrality, including Russia, Denmark, Sweden and Prussia, threatened British supplies of timber, tar and naval stores from the area. Nelson defeated the Danish fleet at Copenhagen and at the same time Tsar Paul I of Russia, the moving spirit of the league, was assassinated. However, at home there was political crisis. The King refused to honour Prime Minister William Pitt's promise to give civil and political rights to Roman Catholics in Ireland, and Pitt's government fell. The new government under Henry Addington made peace with the French by the Treaty of Amiens, giving up conquests in Egypt, Malta, Ceylon, the Cape of Good Hope and the West Indies.

THE NAPOLEONIC WARS

Peace did not last long as the Addington government continued to fear Bonaparte's ambitions. In March 1803 the British began to mobilise the fleet again with the efficient and ruthless 'hot press' of 1803, directed by St. Vincent, now First Lord of the Admiralty. But there was no real strategy for the war that followed. The British merely prepared for an invasion of their coasts, and Napoleon obliged by setting up a camp at Boulogne and building a large fleet of barges. In an atmosphere similar to that of 1940, the country united against the threat. Volunteer units were formed and numerous far-fetched ideas for getting at the enemy were considered, including submarines, aerial bombardment, rockets and mines. More importantly, the navy blockaded the main ports of France, with Nelson off Toulon and Admiral Sir William Cornwallis (1744-1818) off Brest. Squadrons based in the English Channel harassed French coastal shipping, especially barges making their way to Boulogne under cover of coastal batteries. The attacks were so daring that Admiral Lord Keith, commander-in-chief of the North Sea Fleet, urged restraint. Meanwhile Bonaparte crowned himself Emperor Napoleon in May 1804, and Spain declared war on Britain after their homecoming treasure fleet was captured by British frigates in October.

The French slowly realised that they could not invade while the British held naval supremacy, and they implemented a plan to lure Nelson away to the West Indies. Admiral Villeneuve sailed from Toulon at the end of March, and he was followed by Nelson as planned. In the Caribbean Nelson was diverted by a false report and sailed south, missing the French; but he crossed the Atlantic not far behind them, and was able to send a frigate to warn the Admiralty that Villeneuve was coming. A force under Sir Robert Calder met them off North-west Spain and forced them to retreat, though public opinion was disappointed that he had not decisively defeated them. A huge Franco-Spanish fleet was now assembled in Cadiz, posing an immediate threat to British naval and commercial interests in the Caribbean, Atlantic and Mediterranean. Nelson was sent to blockade or destroy them. Short of supplies, underestimating Nelson's strength and goaded by Napoleon, Villeneuve came out and was decisively defeated at Cape Trafalgar on 21 October 1805. Nelson was killed, but there were no more fleet battles as British supremacy at sea was confirmed for the next century.

The beginning of the Battle of Trafalgar. The Franco-Spanish fleet is arranged in a single line in the background. The British fleet approaches in two lines, with Collingwood's squadron, in the right, just about to engage the enemy. Nelson's squadron, led by the *Victory*, is in the centre. Frigates and the schooner *Pickle* can be seen on the left, along with the ship of the line *Africa* which was late in joining the fleet. By Nicholas Pocock. (NMM PU 5708)

The Boulogne flotilla remained in existence long after the real threat of invasion of Britain had disappeared. In September 1811 the Emperor Napoleon went afloat in a barge, and the flotilla was attacked by the frigate *Naiad* under Captain Phillip Carteret. One French vessel, a prame, was captured to the embarrassment of the Emperor. (NMM PW 4788)

But seapower was only effective at one level. Great enemy fleets could no longer roam the seas and cover smaller forces raiding commerce or landing troops, but that did not automatically mean that enemy commerce raiders would be swept away. The greatness of the overall achievement after Trafalgar has been often underestimated, because the navy's success seemed less clear cut and glamorous after the death of Nelson. The next few campaigns were less than glorious, as the role of seapower was stretched to and beyond its natural limits, against fleets in harbour and enemy positions on shore. The attack on Copenhagen in 1807 was a tactical and strategic success, if morally dubious. In 1809 the Walcheren expedition was a failure, and the attack on Basque Roads was a disappointment. Moreover, by 1809, Wellington's army in the Iberian Peninsula was beginning to gain public attention. To many people the success of the British Army in the Peninsula War and at the battle of Waterloo in 1815 overshadowed the achievements of the navy during these years. After war with America broke out in 1812, the navy lost a series of high profile frigate actions. These were strategically insignificant, and were later avenged by the capture of several American ships such as the *Chesapeake* and the *President*; but, perhaps influenced by the bellicose American press, the British public began to believe that the navy had declined since the death of Nelson. In fact after the battle of Trafalgar the navy played a key role in the British war effort, contributing to the eventual success in the wars and ensuring that Britain ended the wars as the only global superpower, based on a commercially orientated global empire, control of most of the world's shipping and the premier force in global power politics, the Royal Navy.

The French and allied navies, though defeated and demoralised, could never be discounted, since they had most of the shipbuilding resources of Europe at their disposal. According to Captain Brenton, 'France, in possession of the Texel, the Scheldt, Cherbourg, Brest, L'Orient, Rochefort, Toulon, Port Espezia, Genoa, Venice and Corsica, with the extensive forests of ship timber either contiguous to or within water carriage of these places, still possessed the means of building ships....Another navy, as if by magic, sprang forth from the forests to the sea shore.'[5]

In 1806 Napoleon tried to turn Britain's sea power against itself. He ordered that European ports could no longer trade in British goods or with British ships. The British replied by blockading the ports which enforced this decree. The navy was stretched by the new policy of economic blockade. It was necessary to stop up small ports all round Europe, instead of just the major ports and fleet bases. There was a great increase in the numbers of sloops and brigs in the fleet, and greater responsibility was given to the junior officers who commanded them. A strong squadron was maintained under Sir James Saumarez (1757-1836) in the Baltic, to keep open the supply route for naval stores. As well as the enmity of Russia and Denmark for much of the period, he had to deal with the erratic affairs of Sweden, through alliance, *coup d'etat,* the election of one of Napoleon's marshals as king and a formal though ineffective declaration of war.

In the south of Europe, the Peninsular War, far from being a purely army triumph, might be seen as 'projection of seapower ashore' on a grand scale. The first British foothold in Portugal was gained fortuitously, when the blockading squadron of Lisbon landed 300 marines to support a local revolt. This served as a beachhead when Wellington arrived with 30,000 men in transport ships, having failed to land in northern Spain. The army was dependent on naval support over the next six years, and sometimes it took dramatic form. In 1812, for example, Sir Home Riggs Popham (1762-1820) harassed the French on the North coast of Spain, with the support of local guerrillas. Sea power gave him great strategic and tactical manoeuvrability over the enemy, who struggled to match his movement on the mountainous and indented coastline. Popham and his Spanish allies captured Santander in 1812, and diverted 35,000 French troops, which might have been sent to defeat Wellington at Burgos. Moreover, Wellington now drastically shortened his supply line by shifting his entire logistical base from Lisbon to Santander, allowing him to take the offensive in 1813 and 1814, driving the French from Spanish territory and facilitating the invasion of France.

After 1805 the navy was no longer struggling to gain and maintain control of the sea - it was attempting to use the advantages that control gave it to contribute to the British war effort. It aimed very high in these years, and sometimes it failed as it tried to extend the boundaries of sea power; but there is no doubt that it had a decisive effect on the victory over Napoleon. This is the age in which the great majority of naval fiction is set. The diverse heroes of Marryat mostly operated then, while only three out of eleven Hornblower novels are set before 1803 or after 1815. Patrick O'Brian's books start in 1800, but only *Master and Commander* and *Post Captain* take place before Trafalgar, and an unfeasibly large number of them are set in the years between 1812 and 1815.

INDUSTRY AND EMPIRE

Historians are divided about how far Britain had an 'Industrial Revolution' in the late eighteenth and early nineteenth centuries. The main effect of industrialisation was restricted to a few areas, mainly in northern England and central Scotland and it was confined to a few industries. Of these, the iron industry was most relevant to the navy, for it provided better quality gun-founding and the famous naval gun, the carronade, and later it supplied iron which could be used to save timber in shipbuilding. The steam engine became a major source of industrial power, though it was only just beginning to be applied to ships when the wars ended in 1815. The coal industry had no immediate relevance to the navy, but it demanded a large number of ships for its exports, and these provided men for the navy in wartime, and major shipping routes which had to be protected. The cotton industry relied on the navy to protect its imports of raw materials from America and the West Indies, and rather less on its export trade.

Bombay in 1800. Once a Portuguese colony, it was part of Charles II's dowry in 1661, but he soon leased it to the East India Company, which used it as an administrative and trading centre and naval base. It is a setting for Aubrey and Maturin's activities in *HMS Surprise*. (NMM PAH 2689)

Britain was already the centre of a great and expanding maritime empire. Though it had lost control of the future United States by 1783, in North America it maintained Canada, Newfoundland and Labrador. It ruled one medium-sized island in the West Indies, Jamaica, and several smaller ones in the Lesser Antilles. These were added to during the wars, most notably with the taking of Trinidad in 1797. The 'sugar islands' were perhaps less profitable than they had been in the past, but their plantations, worked by Negro slaves, were still seen as an essential part of the British economy. In the east the main centre of interest was India. It was ruled by the East India Company rather than by the British government, though with increasing regulation from London. The Company was far from ruling the whole of India, and only controlled the Ganges valley to the north, part of the Coromandel Coast to the east and isolated settlements at Bombay in the north-west and Madras on the east coast. Indigenous forces were still a threat to British security, for example Tipoo Sahib, ruler of Mysore, was a potential ally of Bonaparte during the Nile campaign of 1798. Arthur Wellesley, later Duke of Wellington, made his name in the Indian wars from 1799 to 1805, during which Mysore and Hyderabad were annexed and British rule in the interior was greatly expanded. During the wars with France the empire in the east was expanded, and taking the Cape of Good Hope on the route to India, and Ceylon off its southern tip, increased British security in the sub continent.

BRITISH POLITICS AND SOCIETY

British society was far from united at the start of the wars with Revolutionary France. The ideas of the French Revolution still had some appeal to the middle classes, who were largely disenfranchised, and they joined Corresponding Societies to further their aims. These were largely repressed by the government, which supported strict legislation against dissent. The repression was worst in Scotland, where the 'Scottish Martyrs' were transported, largely at the behest of Henry Dundas (1742-1811), the most powerful politician north of the border. This opposition began to decline as the war progressed and the French Revolution became ever more discredited.

In Ireland the opposition was of a different nature. The majority of the Roman Catholic population had no political rights of any kind, and had no vote for the Irish Parliament. The people were desperately poor and had no share in the industrial and trading success of mainland Britain. Much of the land was owned by absentee English magnates, who drained the wealth out of the country. Even the Protestant north was discontented and the strongest opposition movement, the United Irishmen, was founded there. In 1796-97 the French attempted to land troops in support of local rebels, but failed. In 1798 there was a rising but without material French support it was defeated at the Battle of Vinegar Hill in June. But the threat of a rising remained. Control of Ireland would have allowed the French to mount a new blockade of Britain, close to the new industrial heartlands in Scotland and the north of England and their ports of Glasgow and Liverpool. William Pitt wanted to give the Catholics the vote, but not dominance in an Irish Parliament. He forced a bill through parliament uniting the British and Irish Parliaments, but the King refused to support any measure of Catholic emancipation, so Pitt resigned in 1801; the Irish had unity without emancipation, so they were more under English domination than ever. There were many Irishmen serving on the lower deck of the navy, and they remained an unstable element, for the government feared their hand behind many mutinies.

Though the Irish issue was nowhere near a resolution, the British Isles were far more united when war re-started in 1803 than they had been for some time. In previous wars the government had feared Scottish and English Jacobites, American and Irish rebels and English and Scottish radicals. But in 1803 the last support for the French Revolution had evaporated with the rise of Napoleon Bonaparte, the Jacobite and American issues were long dead and the middle classes rallied behind the government. A new working class opposition would begin to rise in the next few years, centred on machine breaking, trade unionism and the desire for the vote, but for the moment the British were united and the Irish were quiet.

The Prime Minster, William Pitt, addresses the House of Commons on the opening of the war with France in 1793, painted by Karl Anton Hickel. (National Portrait Gallery)

The census of 1801 was the first to measure the British population in detail, and it found that there were 8,331,434 people in England, 541,546 in Wales and 1,599,068 in Scotland; the Irish were not counted, but were estimated at five million. Comparison with that of 1811 confirmed that the population of England and Scotland was becoming increasingly urban, though not overwhelmingly so. Old commercial cities like London, Edinburgh and Bristol were being overtaken by new industrial ones like Leeds and Birmingham, and new ports like Glasgow and Liverpool. The aristocracy was still rich and powerful, though it had begrudgingly accepted new blood over the last century or so, some of it naval. A small number of great lords and their families had incomes of several thousand pounds a year, mainly from land but partly from investment in trade and industry. Under them were a few hundred families with landed incomes of £4000 a year and more, followed by merchants and bankers with slightly less. There was a large group of about 47,000 minor landowners, knights and squires, traditionally the most conservative part of the nation. With their families they numbered nearly a quarter of a million.

The professional and commercial upper middle classes, who provided the bulk of naval officers, numbered about a quarter of a million. They lived in a world open to ideas through literature, science and knowledge. At the same time they were often restricted to a small social circle by geography, difficulties of transport and social stratification. It was a world well described by Jane Austen, two of whose brothers were naval officers. In such a world a social snub, a domineering parent, a failed romance or a sexual indiscretion could be magnified to great proportions.

Below this was a very different world, where most of the seamen lived, and which families on the fringe of the middle classes were terrified of descending into. The lower middle class as described by Patrick Colquhoun (1745-1820), a London Magistrate and writer, fell into two main groups. 'Lesser freeholders, Shopkeepers of the second order, Publicans and others numbered more than half a million households and nearly three million people. They were not much wealthier than the 'Working Mechanics, Artisans, Handicrafts, Agricultural Labourers who subsist by labour' and who were the largest sector of the population, with nearly nine million people and their families. There were also more than a million 'menial servants' but they were useful, and not just because of the work they did. Colquhoun believed that 'every state is supported by the poverty of the community composing the body politic. Without a large proportion of poverty, there could be no riches; since riches are the offspring of labour, while labour can only result from a state of poverty.' Below them, in Colquhoun's 'Seventh, or Lowest Class', were 'Paupers, and their families, Vagrants, Gypsies, Rogues, Vagabonds, idle and disorderly persons, supported by criminal delinquency.' They numbered 1.8 million. In an earlier work, Colquhoun claimed that 11,000 people made their living by stealing from shipping alone, and identified gangs with picturesque names like 'mudlarks', heavy horsemen and 'scuffle hunters.'

This world, with all its inequalities, complexities and coded status symbols, was one which sailors affected to despise and were sometimes glad to get out of, to the moral certainties, clear tasks and contained social life of a naval ship. When appointed to a new ship, an officer was often greatly relieved to escape from the restrictions of shore life with a demanding, snobbish or boring family. After five and a half years on the beach from 1787 to 1793, Captain Horatio Nelson was appointed to a ship and wrote, 'After clouds comes sunshine. The Admiralty so smile on me, that I really am as much surprised as when they frowned.'

BRITISH POLITICS

Industrial and social change had little impact on the political system before 1815. The monarchy was still powerful and most governments were dominated by aristocratic and landowning elements. The United Kingdom of Great Britain (and Ireland from 1801) was known colloquially as Britain, Great Britain or inaccurately as England. It was a constitutional monarchy, in which the King's powers were limited by the need to consult Parliament. The King from 1760 to 1820 was George III. He had started his reign determined to assert himself against what he saw as Parliamentary corruption, but defeat in the American War had damaged his authority, and he was subject to long bouts of an illness, diagnosed at the time to be madness, during which his estranged son took the reins as Prince Regent.

Much of the real power rested in Parliament, which was far from democratic, and indeed it did not make any such claim. The unelected House of Lords was very powerful in all but financial matters and most of the senior ministers, apart from the Prime Minister and the Chancellor of the Exchequer, were members of it. The House of Commons was elected from the towns and counties of the kingdom, using a franchise which varied from place to place, but in general the vote rested with those who were already rich and powerful, with the landowners in the counties and the wealthy merchants in the towns. The large landowners, often members of the House of Lords themselves, controlled many individual constituencies. Elections were held in the open and bribery and intimidation were common. Lord Cochrane mocked the system when he stood at Honiton in Devon in 1805. He refused to bribe the electorate, while his opponent offered his supporters £5 each. When Cochrane lost, he then gave his supporters £10 each. He stood again at Honiton where 'considerable sensation was cause by my entrance into the town in a *vis-à-vis* and six, followed by several carriages and four filled with officers and seamen of the *Pallas*, who volunteered to accompany me on the occasion.' He won the election but this time he refused to pay the £10, considering that those who had voted in the expectation of it were no longer 'disinterested'. Not surprisingly he had to find another constituency for the next election in 1807.

The City of Westminster was one of the more democratic constituencies, a 'potwalloper' borough in which everyone paying the tax of 'scot and lot' had the vote. The electorate itself consisted of about 16,000 men, mostly shopkeepers, tradesmen, artisans and craftsmen, out of a total population of 158,210, but those without the vote were almost as influential. 'The electors themselves do not fight Westminster, it is the rabble', it was said. Cochrane joined forces with Sir Frances Burdett (1770-1844), regarded as an extreme radical by the authorities, on an anti-partisan, anti-corruption ticket. After a bitter and rumbustious contest he and Burdett were elected.

Cochrane was by no means the only naval officer to take part in politics. Successful commanders, such as Nelson, St Vincent, Keith and Adam Duncan, the victor of Camperdown, were elevated to the House of Lords, and generally took an active part there. Nelson, for example, made his maiden speech in October 1801, supporting a motion that

Rear-Admiral Sir James Saumarez should be given the thanks of the house for an action with the French near Gibraltar. He sat down to cries of 'hear, hear!' It was, he wrote modestly, 'bad enough, but well meant.' Less well-known officers, rich with prize money, often had themselves elected to the Commons as part of the aura of success which crowned their careers. For example in 1780 George Elphinstone, before his elevation as Lord Keith, had won the seat of Dumbartonshire in Scotland during his absence fighting the American War. He fought against the powerful interest of the Duke of Argyll and became a member of the 'country' party in Parliament, opposed to the accretion of power by central government.

The House of Commons was supreme on all financial matters, and its direct influence on the navy was mainly through the annual Naval Estimates. These were presented in three parts. The first was for a specific number of seamen, which included officers, marines and all the other members of the fleet. This was paid at the rate of £4 per man per lunar month until 1798, when increased wages after the mutinies of the previous year, and rising prices generally caused an increase to £7 per man. It was intended to pay for the upkeep of the ships, the victuals and other services, as well as the wages of the men employed. The number of men varied from 16,000 just before the wars began to a high of 135,000 during the Revolutionary Wars, dropping to a cautious 50,000 during the Peace of Amiens, then rose to an unprecedented figure of 145,000 during the Napoleonic Wars. The second part of the Naval Estimates, was the ordinary estimate, intended to cover services such as payments to the Admiralty and Navy Board, servicing ships not at sea, and the basic functions of the Royal Dockyards. It rose from £660,000 in 1793 to more than a million pounds in 1805, largely due to inflation. But the ordinary estimate was never enough to cover new shipbuilding or other wartime needs, and every year the House voted for an extraordinary estimate in addition, partly to cover debts. The total allowed for the navy rose from £2.4 million in 1793 to £22.8 million in 1812. This was an enormous sum in that age, but in practice the money rarely appeared on time and the navy relied on a well-developed system of credit to pay its seamen, civilian employees, suppliers and contractors.

The main organ of the executive was the cabinet, whose eleven ministers included the First Lord of the Admiralty. It met irregularly during these years, on average about once every two weeks. Its relationship with the individual ministers was never quite clear. Formally it was regarded as having control of military and naval operations and Dundas, as Secretary of State for War from 1794-1801, wrote 'The operations are canvassed and adjusted in Cabinet and become the joint act of His Majesty's Confidential Servants...the Secretary of State who holds the Pen does no more than transmit their sentiments.' The same applied to the First Lord of the Admiralty, but when he was an experienced and forceful admiral, such as St Vincent or Barham, his say on naval matters was much increased.

THE LEGAL SYSTEM

The authority of the Admiralty and naval officers was enforced by the Articles of War, first passed by Parliament in 1649 and revised in 1749 and again in 1779. Apart from altering the notorious clause threatening death to those who failed to do their utmost in the presence of the enemy, under which Admiral John Byng (1704-57) was shot on the quarterdeck of his own ship, nothing was done to soften them over the years. The Articles of War did not cover all the eventualities of naval discipline, and Marryat satirises the belief that they did. When Midshipman Easy was told they 'contained all the rules and regulations of the service' he refused to be sent to the masthead as a punishment, on the grounds that no such penalty was recognised.[6]

Convicts in New South Wales. This picture, produced in 1830, shows the racial prejudice against Irish convicts who are regarded as sub-human. (NMM PAD 2131)

Life at sea was hard, but to a certain extent this reflected the hardships of life on shore. Flogging looks harsh to a modern mind, but it merely reflected a shore society in which corporal and capital punishment was common. There was no effective police force in most of the country and the law was administrated by unpaid justices of the peace and constables. Punishment was physical rather than mental, and long imprisonment was not used as a punishment in itself. Prosecution of the criminal was left in private hands except in the case of murder or offences against the state, so it was accepted that the great majority of criminals would escape punishment. Instead, the law attempted to impose dreadful punishments, mostly hanging in public by slow strangulation, for the few who were caught. The death penalty was used for more than 200 offences, mostly against property. But over time this began to lose its deterrent effect. The parade of the criminals to Tyburn was stopped because the festival atmosphere tended to undermine the message, and London criminals were hanged immediately outside Newgate Prison. In any case, the great majority of death sentences were reduced or pardoned.

Transportation to Australia began in 1787-88, as a means of disposing of the 'criminal class' in Britain. It was hoped to fulfil several functions – to develop a new colony which might provide a naval base for the Pacific, and perhaps scarce resources such as timber or tar; to get rid of the 'criminal class' of Britain by sending them overseas; to empty the overcrowded prisons and providing a workable alternative to hanging, which was clearly not working as a deterrent. The idea of being sent to Australia was a horrific one to men and women who had never even seen the sea before, and who feared, not without reason that they might never return from transportation for seven or ten years. The voyage itself was almost as terrible in reality. Eighteen convict ships made the trip between 1792 and 1800, and the death rate tended to rise as naval supervision was reduced and up to one man in six might die in the later years.

17

One convict described his experiences:

[We were] chained two and two together and confined in the hold during the whole course of our long voyage...we were scarcely allowed a sufficient quantity of victuals to keep us alive, and scarcely any water; for my part, I could have eaten three or four of our allowances, and you know well that I was never a great eater....When any of our comrades that were chained to us died, we kept it a secret as long as we could for the smell of a dead body, in order to get their allowance of provision...[7]

Naval officers were not immune to the law of the land, and in 1803 they petitioned the government when Captain Brisac was sentenced to stand in the pillory. Thomas Cochrane was also sentenced to this form of punishment, but was reprieved. The pillory was an ancient device dating from at least 1226. Charing Cross, near the site of Trafalgar Square, was in 1810:

a place very frequently chosen for this kind of punishment, probably on account of its being so public a situation, and having so extensive an area for the spectators, who never fail to be drawn together by such an exhibition. The offender thus exposed to public view, it is afterwards considered infamous. The degree of this punishment depends very much on the nature of the crime. There are certain offences which are supposed to irritate the feelings of the lower class more than others, in which case the punishment of the Pillory becomes very serious.[8]

On the other hand a popular offender, such as Daniel Defoe in 1703, might be applauded and have the pillory covered in flowers.

ADMIRALTY AND NAVY BOARD

The Board of Admiralty was the supreme authority on all naval matters, with powers which went beyond other departments of state. Technically the powers of the ancient office of Lord High Admiral's powers were held 'in commission' so that the members of the Board were jointly responsible for running the navy. It had the power of life and death over everyone in the fleet, authority to impress seamen into the navy and one of the biggest budgets of any government department.

The pillory at Charing Cross, London, by Augustus Pugin and Thomas Rowlandson, published in Ackermann's *Microcosm of London* in 1808-10. (Historical Picture Archive/Corbis)

The heroes of naval fiction saw little of the bodies which directed naval warfare, and respected them even less. Jack Aubrey's encounter with St Vincent was abrasive even by that admiral's standards. "What the fucking hell is this language to me, sir? Do you know who you are talking to, sir? Do you know where you are?"[9] Hornblower is openly scornful when his admiral hands him a complaint from the London offices; 'the Navy Board dealt with Victualling and supplies and such like matters. It could be nothing vital.'[10] Though the Board of Admiralty usually included three or four naval officers, flamboyant naval heroes such as Nelson, Cochrane and Sidney Smith were rarely considered for the posts, which usually went to safer individuals with good political connections. The main exception was St Vincent, who was in office as First Lord from February 1801 to May 1804, seconded by his friend Thomas Troubridge (1758?-1807). He believed that 'All the master shipwrights [of the dockyards] ought to be hanged, every one of them, without exception' and as a Member of Parliament he was accused of 'violence of party and scurrilous abuse of persons of the highest rank'. But most naval members of the Board of Admiralty were cautious men, such as Cochrane's rival Sir James Gambier, or nonentities such as Lord Garlies who was a junior lord at the time of Trafalgar.

The post of First Lord of the Admiralty was a very powerful one and was usually held either by a very senior and well-connected politician, or an admiral of great experience. Among politicians, the post was held from 1788 to 1794 by the Earl of Chatham, the Prime Minister's brother; from then until 1801 by Earl Spencer, a member of a powerful family; from 1804-5 by Lord Melville (formerly Henry Dundas), the Prime Minister's right-hand man. After that there seems to have been a slight decline in the office's prestige. It was held briefly in 1806 by Lord Grey, then a young man but later the architect of the Great Reform Act of 1832; from 1806 to 1807 by Thomas Grenville who is best known to history as a book collector; from then until 1811 by Lord Mulgrave, whose naval brother had once been Nelson's commanding officer on an Arctic expedition; by Charles Phillip Yorke, an experienced but unpopular politician, from 1811-12, and then by the Second Lord Melville, the son of Pitt's confidant, from 1812 until 1830.

Only two admirals held the office during this period, each outstanding in his own way. St. Vincent came in convinced that the Peace of Amiens was permanent and determined to reform the navy, at which he had little success. Charles Middleton, Lord Barham (1726-1813), who succeeded Melville in 1805, was highly effective in the crisis of the Trafalgar campaign, but an exception to the usual rules; his political connections were slight, he had a reputation for reform rather than caution, and he had little recent sea-going experience, and even less of battle. Yet his tactical dispositions were vital in saving the country from the invasion threat and winning the Battle of Trafalgar in 1805.

The junior naval lords were usually experienced captains or junior admirals who were also members of parliament. Since the post of First Lord was most often held by a non-seaman in this period, and there was no naval staff to advise him, the junior naval lords had a very important role in controlling the destiny of the navy. Barham was the first to allocate them specific duties. The 'First Sea Lord' would deputise for the First Lord and handle the routine correspondence, especially from the naval ports and secret services. The second Sea Lord would deal with the subordinate boards such as the Navy Board and the Victualling Board; and the Third Sea Lord would supervise the appointment of officers. The other members of the board, the non-naval lords, came from two sources. A few, such as Sir Phillip Stephens, who served from 1795 to 1806, had long experience as civil servants before elevation to the board. Most were junior politicians trying to establish a foothold on the ladder

Sir John Jervis, Earl of St Vincent, painted by Sir William Beechey. (NMM BHC 3001)

of power. Barham had little respect for them. They would 'keep the professional lords unin-terrupted in their duties' by signing all routine orders such as press warrants and protections.

The Board met daily in its offices in Whitehall. Grand strategy, including the movements of major fleets, was handed down from the cabinet, and the Admiralty had to provide the ships and men to fulfil these tasks. It in turn handed the detail of many of its orders down to the Navy Board, to get particular ships ready for sea for example.

Unlike today there was no naval staff as such, and the only naval officers who served at the Admiralty were the commissioners, who tended to come and go with political changes. The Admiralty had a very small office staff for the body that controlled a navy which dominated the seas of the world, in view of the fact that all orders and letters had to be copied out by hand. In January 1800 there were two secretaries and 24 clerks, a translator, a private secre-tary to the First Lord, five messengers, a porter, three watchmen, a 'necessary woman' who cleaned the toilets and a gardener. The Admiralty Court was based in the same building, but had little to do with operational matters. Other officials included the Hydrographer, the Inspector General of Naval Works and his staff, and the clerks of the Marine Department.[11]

THE NAVAL INFRASTRUCTURE

Building, supplying, feeding and preserving the health of a great navy on worldwide service required a considerable infrastructure, mostly run by subordinate boards under the Admiralty. The Navy Board was made up of administrators, naval officers and shipbuilders. It was far less political than the Admiralty, and in some senses more professional, but it had a reputation for extreme conservatism. It was based in Somerset House in the Strand, along with several of the other 'subordinate boards' under the Admiralty. It was headed by the Controller of the Navy, usually a naval captain, a post once held by the future Lord Barham and Nelson's uncle Maurice Suckling, but by no-one of such distinction in 1793 to 1815.

The most important members were the Surveyors of the Navy, former shipwrights from the Royal Dockyards who were responsible for ship design, naval stores and the running of the yards. Among the names of Sir John Henslow, Sir William Rule, Henry Peake and Joseph Tucker, that of Sir Robert Seppings (1767-1840) stands out as a great shipbuilder. He was appointed as third Joint Surveyor in 1813. The Clerk of the Acts was the secretary to the board, which also included several officials with overlapping responsibilities – the Controllers of the Treasurer's Accounts, Victualling Accounts and Storekeepers Accounts and several extra commissioners. In theory the commissioners at the Royal Dockyards were members, but rarely if ever attended. The board sat in almost continuous session every day, passing on orders to the dockyards and the other boards via a team of clerks. Despite Middleton's attempts at reorganisation in the 1780s it had little sense of priorities and like the Admiralty it often dealt with quite trivial matters.

The Victualling Board, like the Navy Board, met in the government offices in Somerset House in the Strand, London. It was responsible for the rather chaotic, but ultimately effective, supply system of the navy. From its main base at Deptford on the Thames it bought pigs and cattle to be slaughtered, cut up and salted into barrels. In its other bases in the main dockyards it operated breweries and bakeries for ships' biscuit. It operated a fleet of small coastal ships, hoys, to transport the goods out to ships. It appointed the pursers of the navy. It took much of the blame for the poor food of the navy, but Dr Thomas Trotter (1767-1823) praised it. 'This is a department where great improvements have been made of late years. The salted beef and pork are excellent; and the bread, till the high price of corn rendered a mixture necessary, was as good as could be desired.'[12]

The Sick and Hurt Board was responsible for checking the qualifications of naval surgeons and for supervising the naval hospitals at the main ports, such as Haslar near Portsmouth. It commissioned hospital ships in places where no shore hospital was available, or to follow the main fleets. It had a key role in the health of the navy, though much initiative was left to the physicians of the fleets, or to the individual surgeons. The Transport Board, with its base at Deptford, was responsible for hiring large numbers of merchant ships, not only for naval purposes but also to move and supply the armies overseas.

The Ordnance Board supplied guns to the navy. It was different from the other boards in that it was not a part of the naval administration as such, for it also supplied guns to the army and administered the technical corps, the engineers and artillery. It had its main depot at Woolwich, where new guns were received from the manufacturers and tested. There were other depots near the main dockyards, for example the gunwharf just south of Portsmouth Dockyard, with a magazine across the water at Priddy's Hard.

HOME NAVAL BASES

The Royal Navy dockyards were the centres of the major naval bases. Manned by civilians in the pay of the Navy Board, they built a large proportion of the warships in the navy, but their most essential function, as implied by the title, was the repair of ships. The dry-docks themselves were enclosed areas where water could be drained out round the hull of a ship for cleaning and repairing the underwater hull. Other work, such as rope-making, anchor construction and shipbuilding were carried out in the same yard, within a high wall to prevent theft and sabotage.

There were six home dockyards in 1800, and a new one was started at Milford Haven in Wales in 1800, and transferred across the estuary to Pembroke dock in 1813. Deptford and Woolwich were situated on the Thames near London, which gave them some advantage in

that the Admiralty and Navy Board could keep a close eye on them, when ships for special purposes were being fitted out, for example. But they were in restricted sites, where the water was too shallow and the river too narrow to handle large ships, they were slowly silting up and it was a long and often winding sail to open water in the Thames Estuary. Chatham on the River Medway was the premier east coast base, but it had declined slowly since France became the main enemy a century earlier. It had a good range of modern facilities, including a new ropery. Sheerness, at the mouth of the Medway, was a satellite of Chatham. It was an excellent site to service ships in the great anchorage at the Nore, but it was remote, with little room for development, and there was a risk of malaria from the marshy ground.

Marryat provides a description of a dockyard as seen by a newcomer to the navy:

> When we arrived there, I was quite astonished at the piles of timber, the ranges of storehouses, and the immense anchors which lay on the wharf. There was such a bustle, every body appeared to be so busy, that I wanted to look every way at once. Close to where the boat landed they were hauling a large frigate out of what they called the basin; and I was so interested in the sight, that I am sorry to say I quite forgot all about the boat's crew, and my orders to look after them. What surprised me most was, that although the men employed appeared to be sailors, their language was very different from what I had been accustomed to on board of the frigate....I asked of a bystander who these people were, and he told me that they were dockyard mateys. I certainly thought it appeared to be quite as easy to say "If you please," as "D—n your eyes," and that it sounded much more agreeable.[13]

Portsmouth was probably the most complete naval base. The dockyard alone employed 4257 men in 1814. Round the sides of the great natural harbour at Portsmouth were the other naval facilities. To the west, on the Gosport side of the Harbour, were the Weevil Victualling Yard and Haslar Naval Hospital. Just south of the dockyard was the Gunwharf, run by the Ordnance Board. There was a marine barracks in the town, which was fortified against enemy attack. The civilians and marines lived and worked on shore, but sailors were kept afloat, partly to prevent desertion. The base had a squadron of old warships reduced to har-

A model of Portsmouth Dockyard made for King George III in 1772-74. A square wet dock and several dry-docks can be seen in the centre, with building slips to the left, and piles of timber behind them. The ropery is the long building, which dominates the right-hand side, and at right angles to it is a row of storehouses, now occupied by the Royal Naval Museum.
(NMM PY 8006)

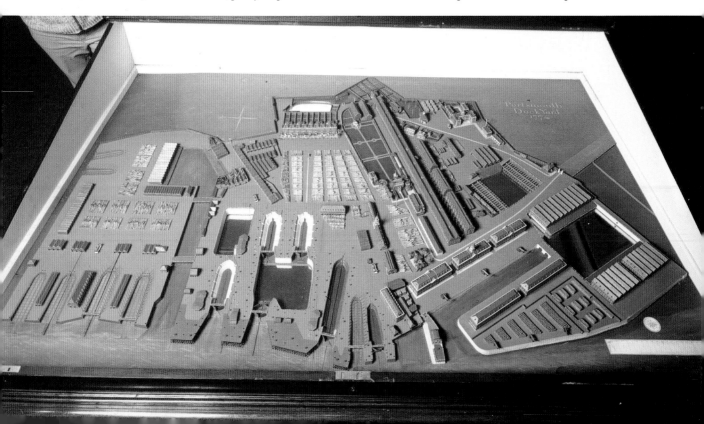

A view of Portsmouth Harbour from Portsdown Hill, showing the Medieval Portchester Castle in the centre. The dockyard is directly behind the castle, with lines of moored warships leading to the right, and a fleet anchored at Spithead on the other side of the land. Jack Aubrey had a similar view from near his home at Ashgrove Cottage.
(NMM PU 1061)

bour service as receiving ships for pressed men, store ships, sheer hulks and many others. A flotilla of smaller craft worked in the harbour, from the hoys which carried guns out to ships, to small rowing craft for every conceivable kind of purpose. Even the commander-in-chief lived afloat, in theory at least, in a flagship which gave him a great deal of dignity. Portsmouth had three great anchorages just outside the harbour, protected by the Isle of Wight. The closest was Spithead, where a fleet could assemble and perhaps wait for news of the enemy. St Helens near the end of the island was more exposed, but suitable for a fleet waiting for a favourable wind to take it down the English Channel. Between the two, close to the Isle of Wight, was Mother Bank where convoys of merchant ships could assemble.

The four Thames and Medway dockyards – Deptford, Woolwich, Sheerness and Chatham – formed part of a single naval base with many services in common. The greater part of the victualling was done from Deptford. Ordnance depots were at Woolwich and Upnor Castle on the Medway. Chatham had the only marine barracks, until a new division was founded at Woolwich in 1805. All four yards fed into the great anchorage at the Nore off the entrance to the Medway, and outer anchorages at the Downs, off the east coast of Kent for ships heading to the English Channel, and among the sandbanks of the Essex coast for ships going north and east. The anchorages were widely spaced compared with Portsmouth.

Plymouth was developing as a great naval base, with a full range of facilities, and it was an excellent site to base ships blockading Brest and controlling the entrance to the Channel, but it was rather poorly provided with natural anchorages. Plymouth Sound was too open, and Cawsand Bay on the west side of the Sound offered little shelter. The great anchorage at Torbay was some 30 miles away and it was difficult to keep contact with the dockyard. The answer was to build a great breakwater across the mouth of Plymouth Sound, but this was not started until 1812 and only completed in 1840.

OVERSEAS BASES

The navy operated in three main areas outside home waters; the Mediterranean, American waters and the East Indies. In the Mediterranean the navy began the war with only one base, at Gibraltar. Despite the threat of siege when Spain was hostile, it was never seriously attacked between 1793 and 1815. It was in a vital situation at the mouth of the inland sea, but had a poor harbour and no natural resources of its own, so forces based there had to make alliances with the semi-piratical states of North Africa. In 1793 the British took control of Corsica, which Nelson for one regarded highly as a future base for covering the French fleet base at Toulon; but when Spain entered the war on the French side, the island was evacuated. Britain was without bases inside the Mediterranean while Nelson fought the Nile campaign of 1798, but his victory allowed the British to take Minorca in 1798. This was the ideal base for watching Toulon. It had a fine harbour at Port Mahon, and unlike Corsica the island was not too large to defend against an invasion. But it was restored to Spain at the Peace of Amiens in 1802, and was not retaken during the next war. Britain also briefly held Egypt and the port of Alexandria after the invasion of 1801, but that too was given up at Amiens.

Malta was taken by Napoleon Bonaparte on the way to Egypt in 1798, after centuries of rule by the Knights of St John. The people revolted on hearing the news of the French defeat at the Nile, but despite British help it took two years to force the surrender of French regular troops in the fortified capital, Valetta. Britain held on to the island in contradiction to the Treaty of Amiens, and it became a permanent possession. It had certain advantages as a naval base. The island was small and its capital had 'wondrous fortifications' according to Lord Keith. It was easy to defend by any nation that had command of the sea. Grand Harbour at Valetta was one of the finest natural harbours in the world. The population was generally friendly and no other nation had a very strong claim on the island. However, the island was not particularly fertile and was dependent on Sicily for food supplies, necessitating British control of that island as well. Malta's main fault was in its geographical position. Unlike

Gibraltar it did nothing to control the entrance to the Mediterranean, unlike Minorca it was too far from Toulon to help in the blockade. Nelson wrote, 'As to Malta, it is a perfectly useless place for Great Britain; and as a Naval Port to refit in, I would much sooner undertake to answer for the Toulon Fleet from St Helens [Isle of Wight], than from Malta.'[14] In command of the Mediterranean Fleet from 1803-05, he preferred to base his fleet precariously in anchorages off the neutral island of Sardinia. Outside the Mediterranean, Lisbon provided a useful port for ships blockading Cadiz for example when Jervis based the Mediterranean fleet there in 1796-7, or operating in support of Wellington's armies in the Peninsula in the later stages of the war. It provided supplies and dry-docks for the fleet and served as a base for commerce protection on the vital trade routes to the West and East Indies and the Levant.

On the other side of the Atlantic, the situation was far more stable and Britain maintained some important bases throughout the wars, with a few temporary and permanent additions. Halifax in the north became important during the American War of 1812, as did Bermuda which had been held since 1609, but had its first large-scale naval facilities in 1809. In the West Indies, Port Royal in Jamaica had been used as a main base since 1735. For the outer islands the Lesser Antilles, Antigua provided a very secure harbour for the hurricane season, and a certain amount of repair facilities after 1728. Barbados was a key island because it was windward of all the others and could be used to launch raids on French possessions. It had a natural anchorage at Carlisle Bay, but repair facilities were less developed there before 1806. In the shorter term the navy also used the captured islands of Martinique from 1794 to 1802, and Curacoa from 1807.

For fleets and squadrons based in the east, the navy largely relied on the resources of the East India Company, with its dockyards at Bombay and Madras. After 1801 several ships were built in Bombay, using the fine teak timber that was available there. This process started slowly, but accelerated during the nineteenth century. Cape Town was held between 1795 and 1801 and after 1806. It was a very useful base for protecting the route to India.

Government House in Port Mahon, Minorca. This is where Jack Aubrey and Stephen Maturin met in the first scene of *Master and Commander*. Minorca was a valuable naval base with a good harbour and an excellent strategic position for blockading the French at Toulon. It changed hands several times in the course of the eighteenth century and Admiral Byng was executed for losing it in 1756. It was taken by Admiral Duckworth in 1798, but returned to Spain with the peace treaty in 1801. (NMM PAH 3657)

NAVAL INTELLIGENCE

There was no regular system of naval intelligence in the Napoleonic Wars. During the Nile campaign of 1798, the Admiralty got most of its information about enemy movements from French and neutral newspapers and from ambassadors and consuls in neutral countries. During the chase across the Mediterranean Nelson relied mainly on reports from merchant ships which he stopped and interrogated. For more general intelligence the British were able to use émigré French royalists, such as General Dumouriez who knew something of past invasion plans. There was no major single source such as a mole inside the enemy camp, or a means of intercepting and decoding enemy signals as proved very effective in the radio age. Contrary to the fiction of Patrick O'Brian, there was no head of naval intelligence. The nearest to that was Robert Maxwell, the Translator at the Admiralty, who was paid £100 per annum, less than a junior clerk.

Dr Alexander John Scott, Nelson's Chaplain at the time of his death. Scott was a part-time spy and possible model for Stephen Maturin. In 1801 he was seriously injured when his ship was struck by lightning, as shown in the painting to the top left. (NMM BHC 3016)

This did not prevent naval officers, particularly commanders-in-chief, setting up their own services. Alexander John Scott was *Victory's* Chaplain under Nelson in 1803-5, as well as the admiral's interpreter and diplomatic secretary. Born in 1768 in Rotherhithe near London, he studied at Cambridge, but his obvious brilliance did not fit in with the system there. In 1791 he was ordained in the Church of England and soon afterwards he felt the ancestral call of the sea and was appointed Chaplain of the 74-gun *Berwick*. In 1801 he served under Sir Hyde Parker (1739-1807) at Copenhagen, and showed his remarkable flair for languages. On the way to the Baltic he learned Danish and Russian from textbooks, and Nelson used him in negotiating the armistice with Denmark after the battle. Later that year he was bizarrely struck by lightning while in his hammock in Jamaica. He recovered slowly from this, but in 1803 he was still in poor health and felt that the climate of the Mediterranean might help restore him. Nelson was pleased to have a chaplain on board, and Scott's other abilities would be invaluable in the Babel of languages that was the Mediterranean. Scott, Nelson wrote, had 'abilities of a very superior cast.'[15] He was an obsessive bibliophile and collected books in many languages, but he had no administrative talents and had nothing of 'what the world calls *management*', according to his daughter and son-in-law.[16] He was described as 'pale, thin and tall in person, very romantic and enthusiastic.' His appearance was 'very remarkable' in other respects – 'his forehead was singularly fine and intellectual, and the benevolent expression of his countenance and eyes, did justice to the universal kindness of his feelings.'[17] When he described his intelligence services he was almost as coy as Patrick O'Brian would be about his. In 1803-5 he was:

> ...employed in gaining information throughout Catalonia...and in establishing every possible quick means of communication between Madrid, Barcelona and the fleet...was employed in matters of great confidentiality and not to be written in regard to Sardinia...was of service at Algiers, upon the arrangement of differences which had arisen with that Regency.

> Without naming places, it is sufficient to say generally Mr. S was often employed by the late Lord Nelson upon missions for the good of His Majesty's service.[18]

WINDS AND SEAS

An experienced officer knew his way round this world, as instinctively and fluently as a modern taxi driver knows which streets to avoid during the rush hour. He knew nothing of the theory of weather anti-cyclones or cold fronts, but he could see the signs that, in west

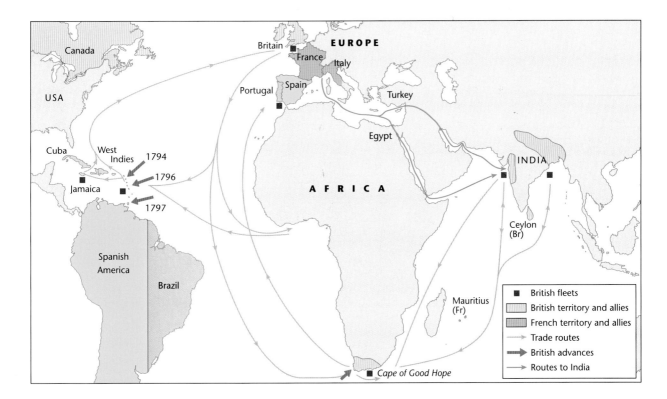

European waters, heralded the approach of a storm or a calm. He knew that the weather in British waters was highly variable, but he could often predict the direction and strength of the wind by the sea state, the cloud formation or the present wind. In the Mediterranean, the winds were weaker and less reliable, though certain local winds could be counted on – the Mistral, the Sirocco and the Gregale were available in certain regions and at certain times of the year.

The seamen was much more certain about the weather in the world at large. Marryat's *Masterman Ready* was told about the trade winds:

> The trade winds blow on the equator, and several degrees north and south of it, from the east to the west, following the course of the sun. – It is the sun which produces those winds? – Yes, the extreme heat of the sun between the tropics rarefies the air as the earth turns round, and the trade winds produced by the rushing in of the less heated air.[19]

ABOVE: A world map demonstrates the global nature of the French Revolutionary and Napoleonic Wars

BELOW: The wind patterns of the North Atlantic, showing the circular trade routes from Europe to the West Indies and North America.

This circular pattern of air made the transatlantic trade, and warfare, possible. Ships heading from Europe to America would go south as far as the Azores then begin to run west, taking advantage of the trades. Once across the Atlantic, they could steer straight for the West Indies; or if heading further north, they could use a thermometer to find the Gulf Stream, which would carry them along the coat of North America in warm and friendly waters, until they reached their destination. For the return journey they would use the westerly winds in more northerly latitudes.

For voyages to India and the far east the seaman followed the trade winds as far south as he could. He know he would eventually reach the doldrums, an area of intense heat, thun-

Commodore Dance's action against Admiral Linois in which he successfully defended his convoy of East Indiamen by pretending some of them were warships. (NMM PY 8006)

derstorms and little wind close to the equator. He tried to minimise this by passing as close as possible to the coast of Brazil, where the effect was less. Picking up the south-east trades south of the equator, he kept them on his port side until he reached the Cape of Good Hope. From there his voyage was controlled by the monsoons. Because of the great land mass to the north of the Indian Ocean these winds blew from the south-west in the summer months, and from the north-east from September to April; the whole of the East India trade, from the departure from Europe onwards, was timed to take account of this. The trade winds and their counterparts in other parts of the world caused regular trade routes, which were an essential part of naval strategy. Convoy routes, for example, were reasonably predictable while an admiral like Nelson could use his knowledge of winds to anticipate enemy movements, as he did during both the Nile and Trafalgar campaigns.

THE MERCHANT NAVY

Britain's merchant fleet was by far the largest in the world. It was seen as a great national asset, not just because of the business it created and the goods it carried. It provided the reserve of trained seamen who would man the navy in wartime, and without an ever-expanding reserve the Royal Navy would soon decline. Because of this the merchant navy was protected by the Navigation Acts, which restricted the right of foreign ships to carry British goods or trade with British colonies. The young Horatio Nelson made himself very unpopular by enforcing the acts against the new United States in the West Indies in the 1780s, and justified himself by stating, 'I felt it my duty, and certainly it was my inclination, to preserve the Carrying Trade to our country, as it encouraged British artificers, manufacturers, and seamen.'[20] Though Adam Smith's works in favour of free trade had been in print for nearly forty years, Britain in 1815 was not ready to give up this form of protectionism.

Naturally the merchant fleet was far more diverse than the Royal Navy. Far from being a unified organisation, it was owned by many thousands of small investors, each of whom bought a 32nd or a 16th share of a ship in order to spread his capital, a wise precaution when shipping was hazardous and insurance was primitive. In 1800, there were 17,885 ships registered in Britain and her colonies, of 1,885,879 tons, and needing crews of 138,721 men if all were fully employed. From this total 1,810 ships, about half a million tons, were engaged in foreign trade from London, while about half as many operated in the coasting trades for the capital. About the same number, 796 ships of 64,586 tons, operated from the next biggest port, Liverpool. At the other end of the scale, tiny ports often had a remarkable number of ships. Cowes on the Isle of Wight had 128, St Ives in Cornwall had 39 and Rothesay in Scotland had 92. Merchant ships needed far smaller crews than warships. The ships on the 1800 list had an average of 13 tons per man, and the average crew of each ship was less than eight. A typical 74-gun ship of the line had about $2^2/_3$ tons per man, or nearly five times the men per ton.[21]

Apart from the Navigation Acts the merchant fleet was largely unregulated, for there were no safety rules and no formal qualifications for officers. It included many different ships built for many different trades, but despite everything there was a certain uniformity. As with the Royal Navy, ships above about 200 tons were nearly all ship rigged with three masts, while smaller ones were rigged as brigs with two masts, and even smaller ones with single fore and aft rigged masts were known as hoys, cutters or sloops. The merchant service covered morally dubious and later illegal practices such as the slave trade, completely illegal ones such as smuggling, dirty and demanding trades such as coal, as well as the more glamorous and lucrative routes to the East and West Indies. Everyone knew that shipping was one of the keys to British success, not only because ships carried the trade which fuelled the industrial revolution, but also because it nurtured the seamen who manned the navy in wartime.

The most prestigious maritime trade was in the service of the East India Company. It had a quasi-naval rank structure and large ships which almost equalled warships, at least theoretically, in gunpower. It was the only merchant trade which could attract officers from the gentry and the upper middle classes. Besides handsome salaries, officers and crews were allowed to indulge in private trade, bringing luxury goods home on their own account. Scottish families, such as the Elphinstones and the Woods of Largo, often had sons in both the navy and the Company, as one would prosper in war, the other in peace. About sixty round trips were made per year by Company ships.

East Indiamen were the largest merchant ships and the biggest of them were measured at over 1200 tons. They were intended to look like warships, though they were not manned on a scale to make them good fighting ships. If their appearance was largely bluff, that had its uses. In February 1804 Commodore Dance of the Company was leading a convoy of 39 ships, including 16 large Indiamen, with no naval escort. He encountered a force of one French ship of the line, three frigates and a brig. Dance knew well that his ships could not fight warships for any length of time. 'No one of the crews, we believe, exceeded 140 men, and that number included Chinese, Lascars &c. Moreover, in fitting the ships, so much more attention had been paid to stowage than to the means of attack and defence, that one and sometimes two butts of water were lashed between the guns, and the decks in general greatly lumbered.'[22] Undaunted, Dance ordered three of his ships and a brig to hoist the blue ensign while the others hoisted the red, suggesting that these four ships were naval. The French admiral, Charles Linois, saw that there were more ships present than his intelligence had indicated, and suspected that the extra ones were indeed a naval escort. Both fleets waited overnight, and there was a short exchange of fire next day. The French, finally convinced that they were up against ships of the Royal Navy, withdrew without a serious fight. The East India captains had proved that they could maintain nerve and discipline in the presence of the enemy, and saved their valuable convoy.

If the East India trade was the height of respectability in merchant shipping, the slave trade with Africa was at the other end of the scale. It was already attracting the horror of the political middle classes by 1793, and William Wilberforce's campaign for its abolition was gathering momentum. William Richardson served in a slave ship and describes the precautions used to keep the slaves under control:

The next thing to do was to clear the decks of all lumber, and a barricade was built across the main deck near the mainmast about ten feet high, with wall pieces fixed on the top to fire among the slaves if necessary and a small door to let only one man through at a time. When the slaves are on deck in the day-time the males are all kept before the barricade and the females abaft it.

The 'tween-decks were entirely cleared fore and aft, and a platform fixed round against the ship's sides and hung on cranks, height about halfway between the two decks: this is for the slaves to sleep on that had not room on the lower deck, and the whole deck fore and aft was divided into four rooms or partitions, each separated by strong oak palings.[23]

The trade from Africa was abolished by the British Parliament in 1807, though the existing slaves in the West Indies did not get their freedom for another 27 years. During the remainder of the war the Royal Navy had few resources to suppress it and it continued illegally for some time.

The coal trade between north-east England and London and the south-east had little social cachet, but service among the sandbanks and varying winds produced skilled seamen. Admiral Collingwood remarked of his flag captain Edward Rotherham, 'he has very much of the stile of the Coal trade about him, except they are good seamen.' - perhaps the ultimate nautical put-down.

Apart from East India captains, merchant navy officers were regarded as much lower on the social scale than naval officers. The man in charge of a ship was a master, not strictly a captain in the naval sense, and Jack Easy is able to flatter Mr Hogg, the master of a merchant ship by calling him 'captain'. When a Miss Hicks becomes enamoured of the same captain, her father is furious. 'I shall never give my consent, Julia; one of those midshipman you turn your nose up at is worth a dozen Hoggs.'[24]

The stowage of the slaves on board the French brig *Vigilante*, taken by Lieutenant George Mildmay and the boats of the frigate *Iphigenia* and the sloop *Myrmidon* off the River Bonny in present-day Nigeria. Faster ships were used after the trade was abolished in 1807, and conditions for the slaves on board became even worse. (NMM PAH 7370)

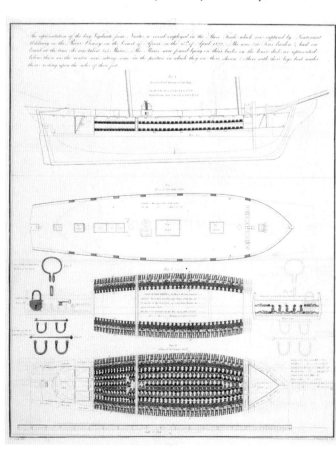

Privateers were simply private men of war licensed by a legal document known as a letter of marque, without which they were treated as pirates and subject to hanging if captured. They made a profit by capturing and selling enemy merchant ships and their cargoes. They were far less important in British naval strategy than in French. There was never any suggestion that the French might be brought down by raiding their commerce. More than 800 letters of marque were issued at the start of war in 1803, some were for very small ships of less than 200 tons but the *Marquis of Ely*, for example, carried 36 guns and was equivalent to a naval frigate. Liverpool was overtaking Bristol as the main British privateering port by the 1800s.

The seaman was separated from ordinary society for much of his life, but his world was in many ways more real than the one he left behind. He lived among winds, seas and tides that were far more permanent than the political views, social stratification or economic success and hardship that he left on shore. It is one of the great advantages of naval history that the same natural forces, despite climate changes, are still in existence to this day.

CHAPTER 2

THE SHIPS

Patriots sang about Britannia ruling the waves, and the British warship was certainly a very impressive engine of power. If one was rowed out in a small boat, the effect was overpowering. The future admiral Thomas Byam Martin passed under the highly-decorated stern of the 100-gun ship *Royal George* in 1781 at the age of eight:

> Ye gods! What a sight – what a sensation....It is impossible to forget the breathless astonishment and delight with which my eyes were fixed upon the ship. Nothing so exquisitely touching has ever occurred to me to produce the same frantic joy.

The coxswain of the boat commented, 'I see, sir you have already determined to be a sailor.' The Portsmouth correspondent of the *Naval Chronicle* waxed lyrical as he saw the fleet being fitted out for war in 1803, 'at the setting sun, to see Britannia's bulwarks, so lately commissioned, towering in all their native pride'.

Heavy loads could be moved far more easily by sea than by land, as the great engineers Thomas Telford and John Smeaton had shown. A packhorse could carry $1/8$ of a ton, a wagon pulled by a single horse could carry $5/8$ of a ton on a typically poor road of the day or two tons on a good road; while a river barge, similar in principle to a sailing warship, could carry 30 ton when pulled by a single horse.[1]

Put another way, a typical 36-gun frigate had a fire power of 558lbs. An army 12-pounder battery needed 90 horses to pull its guns, ammunition and equipment, taking up 300 yards of road. It would take the equivalent of eight batteries to match the frigate, with more than 700 horses, occupying more than a mile of road – assuming roads were available and in good condition, which was seldom true in 1800.[2] A ship of the line, with three times the gun power, would need four miles of road. Nelson's fleet at Trafalgar would have filled more than 120 miles of road; the distance from London to Derby.

The sea needed no roadmakers or maintenance, it was largely independent of national frontiers and it offered a free power source in the wind. A major warship had firepower to equal an army. Cochrane's exploits in support of Spanish guerrillas provide a good example:

> Lord Cochrane, during the month of September 1808, with his single ship, the *Imperieuse*, kept the whole coast of Languedoc in alarm – destroyed the numerous semaphoric telegraphs, which were of utmost consequence to the numerous coasting convoys of the French, and not only prevented any troops from being sent from that province into Spain, but even excited such dismay that 2000 men were withdrawn from Figueras to oppose him, when they would otherwise have been marching further into the peninsula. The coasting trade was entirely suspended during this alarm; yet with such consummate prudence were all Lord Cochrane's enterprises planned and executed, that not one of his men

The stern of the *Royal George* of
1756, from a model made for
the Prince of Wales between
1772 and 1777. The ship
capsized at Spithead in 1782
with great loss of life.
(NMM D 4082-7)

were either killed or hurt, except one, who was singed in blowing up a battery.[3]

During the same campaign the 74-gun *Excellent* and the bomb-vessel *Meteor* came close inshore to bombard and drive away French troops with their gunfire – an incident which perhaps inspired Hornblower's attack in *A Ship of the Line*.

However powerful a ship might appear against weak infantry and their mobile artillery support, the ship of the line had many disadvantages against a land fortress with its much heavier guns and a stable, fireproof base from which to fire them. The sailing warship had serious limitations. Its guns had an effective range of about 200 yards, compared with 20 miles or more for a twentieth century warship. It could not project its power ashore except by limited bombardment of targets immediately on the coast, or by landing parties of sailors and marines as infantry. It was dependent on wind for its movement – too little and it could not move at all, too much and it was in danger of being wrecked.

The warship was the most powerful weapons system of its age, by a considerable margin. Yet there were many means, not all connected with the actions of an enemy, by which it might be destroyed. Its stability always needed to be taken into consideration and the great *Royal George* herself overturned at Spithead in 1782, because of an error in loading the ship. William Cowper wrote:

> It was not in the battle;
> No tempest gave the shock;
> She sprang no fatal leak;
> She ran upon on rock.

Made almost entirely of wood, a ship could easily be consumed by fire and the *Queen Charlotte*, Lord Keith's flagship as commander-in-chief of the Mediterranean Fleet, caught fire at Leghorn in 1800 and was destroyed with the loss of more than 700 men. The admiral was destitute for provisions and had to write to his sister in Scotland for clothes – 'in short, I am as I stand.'[4] The 74-gun *Magnificent* ran onto the Black Rocks near Brest in 1804 and sank within sight of the fleet, though all hands were saved by boats from the other ships. In the spirit of the times, the correspondent of the *Naval Chronicle* assessed it as 'a trivial loss, compared with that by which we are threatened.'[5]

The loss of the 74-gun ship *Magnificent* off Brest in 1804, after striking an uncharted rock. Most of the crew were saved but 86 were taken prisoner. (NMM PAF 4778)

Britannia's wooden walls ruled the waves in the sense that they could, to a large extent, control the movement of enemies over them. Only a very foolish sailor would take the slogan literally. Wise ones knew, respected and often feared the waves, the winds and the currents among which they lived.

DESIGN

The first stage in the conception of a new ship was the order from the Admiralty, perhaps motivated by a threat of war, an increase in the size of enemy or rival fleets, or just the loss or decay of older ships. In the mid 1790s there was a perception that British ships were too small compared with the French and large ships in each class were ordered – 110 and 120 gun ships instead of 100s, long 74-gun ships and 38-gun frigates instead of 36s. There was a lull in ordering after that, partly because St Vincent, as First Lord of the Admiralty, concentrated on reforming the dockyards and equally mistrusted the private builders and timber merchants. He tended to favour slightly smaller ships and wrote, 'Frigates are grown preposterous; I never wish to see one larger than the Inconstant.'[6] There were several large orders in the mid-1800s, including the large and mediocre group of 74-gun ships which became known as the 'forty thieves.'

The Board of Admiralty would instruct the Navy Board to begin the construction of a ship of a particular type. This was usually based on previous experience, for shipbuilders were generally conservative and experiments were quite rare in those days. The Navy Board would advise the Admiralty how to implement the order – whether a building slip of a suitable size was available in one of the Royal dockyards or whether private shipbuilders of good reputation were available to tender for the job at an affordable price.

In most cases an old ship, or a captured one, was copied. Alternatively a new plan, with slight variations on previous designs, might be drawn up by the Surveyor of the Navy and his assistants for issue to the builders. There was no separate profession of naval architect, and no real professional education in Britain until the School of Naval Architecture was set up at Portsmouth in 1811. In theory all shipwrights were of the same profession, but in practice a few, who mainly started as apprentices to the master shipwrights and their assistants rather than as ordinary workmen, were trained in the art and mystery of ship design, while the others learned to cut timber, erect frames and plank hulls.

Drawing the plan was mainly an exercise in solid geometry rather than advanced hydrodynamics. Almost every shape in the hull was based on a straight line or a circle. The designer would begin with a straight line, the keel, and then add the stem, sternpost, decks, gunports, masts and some of the fittings to form the 'sheer plan' or side view. He would also mark the position of every third frame or rib of the ship, evenly spaced along the

The arcs of circles, or sweeps, used to draw out the shape of the midship section of a warship.

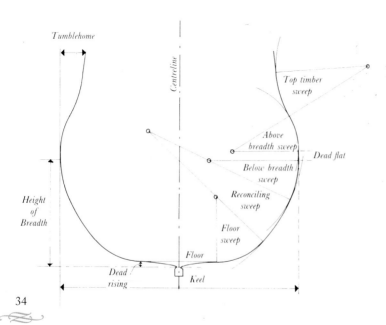

length. Then he would turn to another plane, to draw the midship frame, near the centre of the ship and its widest point. The actual width of the ship would probably be settled by the Admiralty order, but the draughtsman would decide the height of the maximum breadth and then construct the shape of the underwater hull using arcs of three circles, the floor sweep, reconciling sweep and breadth sweep. He would do the same above the maximum breadth, with perhaps an 'above breadth sweep' and a toptimber sweep which was concave rather than convex, as the hull curved inwards to form the 'tumble-home'. After that the shape became more complex towards the bow and the stern. In essence the circles of the midship frame were repeated, though sometimes reduced in radius. They were moved progressively inwards and upwards as the hull narrowed. Designers used different forms of construction lines to cope with this.

As the main curves of the hull moved progressively inwards and upwards towards the bow and stern, they left a gap at each end of the ship. This was filled by drawing a straight line or curve on each frame, and near the extremities of the ship this would form a major part of the underwater lines. This was not fully covered by the theory of naval architecture, but the designer drew waterlines in the vertical plane in the sheer draught, then drew these lines out as seen from below to show if the lines were fair or not. He also added horizontal and diagonal lines for the same purpose. There was no tank-testing of ships in those days, despite some experiments by the Royal Society for the Arts, so these lines were the main means of testing a design.

This was the main plan of the ship, and many builders could have worked from that alone, in conjunction with the contract which gave dimensions for each piece of timber and metal. But to help them more plans were produced, usually of each individual deck and its fittings, the frames and sometimes cross sections. Rigging plans were almost never produced, as that was done according to standard formulae.

The plans of the ship were taken to the Navy Board and then the Admiralty for approval, and sometimes they aroused some passions. St Vincent, never one to understate his feelings, wrote of the Surveyors of the Navy in 1800, 'I am glad Rule has plucked up spirit – Sir John Henslow appears to have none.'[7] Ship design was a matter of great public interest around 1800, inspired by the belief that French design was far superior. The Society for the Improvement of Naval Architecture was formed in 1791 by a bookseller named Sewell after he was 'so impressed with the many grave complaints which reached him as to the inferiority of our warships as compared with those of France and Spain.'

THE SHIPS

A typical ship's draft, for the 36-gun frigate *Salsette* of the *Perseverance* class, launched in 1805. The main part of the drawing is taken up by the sheer plan, or side view of the ship. The top half of this includes details such as wales, gunports, channels, stern galleries and head rails, though in this case it does not show the situation of the decks and the beams which support them. Below the main wale is a series of waterlines, each showing the level at which the ship would (theoretically) float if light enough.

On the left hand side are the body sections, forward part of the ship to the right and starboard to the left. Some of the construction lines (see illustration opposite) can be seen. At the bottom part of the plan is a view from underneath showing the waterlines from a different angle. These lines were used to test the 'fairness' or streamlining of the hull.

A plan like this, combined with a list of dimensions of the different parts, would often be enough for a builder to construct the ship.
(NMM Dr 2179/37)

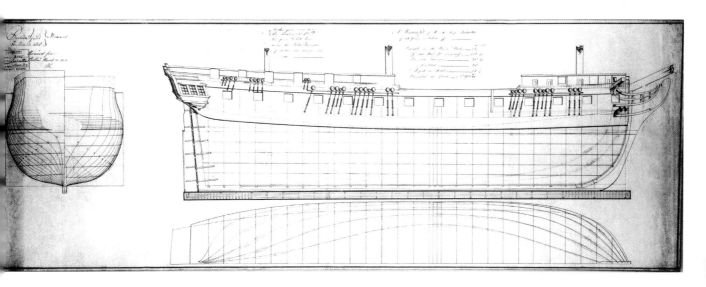

TIMBER SUPPLIES

The supply of timber was one of the main constraints of naval power. A 74-gun ship of the line needed more than 3,000 loads of timber, perhaps about 80 acres of trees. A large curved piece of timber, suitable for the frames of a ship of the line, might take up to a hundred years to grow, and the hereditary landowning system of Britain tended to encourage such a long-term investment. But despite the efforts of men like John Evelyn in the 1660s, the navy had long since outgrown the native supply of timber. In the 1790s, Admiral Collingwood planted oaks in his estate believing they would be useful for the navy of 1900. In the meantime the navy had turned to North America for supplies of straight timber for masts, though that was interrupted by the War of Independence. The most vital shipbuilding timber was oak, which formed most of the structure of the hull. Most difficult of all was curved or compass timber, used to form the frames of the hull, and the L-shaped pieces known as knees. Forest oak was little use, as it would tend to grow straight up seeking the sunlight. Compass timber tended to come from isolated trees, often deliberately constrained during their growth. A large proportion of shipbuilding timber came from the Baltic, and keeping that sea open was as important as the Persian Gulf in modern strategy – fleets fought at Copenhagen in 1801 and 1807, and a large fleet, with the *Victory* as flagship, was maintained in the Baltic for some years after that. Huge convoys of up to a thousand ships sailed from the area, largely carrying naval stores.

After 1798 the Admiralty employed officials known as Timber Masters to buy and inspect new supplies. There was a crisis in the early 1800s under the St Vincent regime at the Admiralty, for he believed that the timber suppliers were operating a ring against the public interest and attempted to destroy it. This had a serious effect on shipbuilding at the beginning of ~~the beginning of~~ the Napoleonic Wars in 1803, and was only ended when St Vincent left office the following year.

Timber was stacked in huge piles around the dockyards. Some was old wood, taken from ships that had been broken up. New timber was kept in piles according to type and function. Some was straight for keels or planks, some was curved for use in futtocks, and there were piles of Y-shaped pieces for knees. Some timber was still in its rough state, some was 'sided' with its parallel sides trimmed to size, and some was cut to shape ready for use in a ship. Mast timber was stored underwater in special ponds where it was 'pickled' to give it the right amount of springiness. Even a private shipyard was dominated by timber. Residents of the village of Bucklers Hard in Hampshire complained that the piles blocked the light from their windows.

BUILDING

The Royal Dockyards built about half of British warships in the eighteenth and early nineteenth century. They built all the largest ones, the three deckers, and in long periods of peace, such as 1714-39, they built almost all the navy's warships. They had only a limited number of building slips, which were in great demand during a wartime building programme, so in such times most new warships were built by private contractors. They were selected by competitive tender from a list of approved firms, which had experience of such work, or were trusted by the Navy Board. Each firm offered a fixed price per ton of the new ship, and the lowest tenders were accepted. When Mr Edward Graves contracted to build a new 74-gun ship at Limehouse on the River Thames in 1782, he agreed to a price of £36 per ton and to complete it within $2^1/_2$ years; if he failed he would lose 5 shillings (25p) per ton.

The Navy Board had no intention of losing control of the process after signing the contract. A naval overseer, usually a dockyard foreman, was appointed to each contract-built ship, but there was always the risk that he would be bribed or persuaded into accepting inferior materials or poor workmanship. To remove this possibility the Navy Board preferred to build ships within range of the Royal Dockyards, so the great majority of naval ships were built in the Rivers Thames and Medway, or in the Portsmouth and Plymouth areas.

Shipbuilding required large quantities of timber and skilled labour, but not a vast amount of capital, for there was no heavy machinery, while shipwrights and other workers supplied their own tools. A private shipbuilder needed some money to pay his men while awaiting payment from the Navy Board on his contract, and to purchase timber for the ship, but he was helped by the advances he received at various stages. Graves of Limehouse, in his contract for a 74-gun ship, was to receive six instalments of £3136, one of £3672 and one of £3600 at different stages in the process, for example 'when the frames are raised, set to rights, levelled, and shored, the lower futtocks and all cross chocks fayed, and the keelson bolted' and 'when the upper deck, quarterdeck, forecastle and roundhouse beams are in, the knees fayed and bolted, flat of the deck laid, and the ship planked up to the top of the side.'

Apart from capital the main requirement was a suitable site, on the banks of a river or sheltered waterway, with enough firm ground to erect the ship, and water which was deep and wide enough to launch it. The building slip itself was a piece of ground slightly bigger than the ship to be built, with its surface angled towards the water. Blocks were laid along its centre to support the ship. As with design, the building of the ship began with the keel, a straight line made up of several pieces of elm joined together. The stempost was a curved timber which continued the keel forward and upwards in the bows. The deadwood was raised above the keel towards the bow and stern, to support the ends of the frames in those areas. The sternpost was a straight piece angled upwards for the after end of the keel, and it was fitted as part of a complete assembly, including the transom pieces which formed a main part of the structure of the stern.

The frames or ribs were now fitted and began to create the three-dimensional shape of the hull. Since it was impossible to find a suitable piece of timber to make a single frame, each consisted of several parts, beginning with a floor timber laid across the keel, and a number of futtocks (or foot-hooks). Frames were fitted in pairs, with joins staggered between them to avoid a single source of weakness. The 'full' frames which went all the way up the side were fitted first, and the sills of the gunports placed between them. Then the shorter or filling frames were fitted, between the keel and the lower edge of a port, or the upper edge and the top of the side. At the bows the structure was rather different. After a certain point each successive frame angled increasingly towards the bows, so that they approximately formed the radius of a circle. The very forward part of the main structure consisted of hawse pieces, run-

The framing plan of the *Amazon,* 36 guns, of 1795. It shows how some of the frames are interrupted by the gunports, and how the frames towards the bow and the stern are progressively angled forward. (NMM Dr 1999/35)

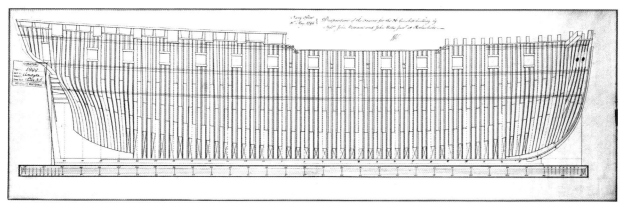

A model of the stern of a ship
of the line, probably the
64-gun *Intrepid* of 1770. It was
made to demonstrate the
framing to King George III, and
the names of the different
timbers are marked on it.
(NMM D 7361)

ning parallel to the line of the keel as seen from above. The structure forward of this was known as the knee of the head and supported the figurehead and its rails. The stern had yet another variation. After the angled, or cant frames, the main structure consisted of transoms, which were set horizontally. Above them was a very light structure pierced with doors and windows and often fitted with galleries on a ship of the line.

The planking of the lower hull was of uniform thickness (four inches on a 74-gun ship of the line) to give a smooth surface. Above the waterline there were much thicker areas of planking, the wales. These were under the line of gunports to give extra strength, and might be 8½ inches thick on a ship of the line. Internally, the planking was thickest over the line of joins in the futtocks, and under the deck beams, for it performed a vital role in support-ing them. The deck beams themselves were usually made in several pieces scarfed together and those on the lower deck of a ship of the line were 14 inches square. Besides the beams there was a lighter structure of carlines and ledges, for the guns might weight up to 3 tons and could be moved anywhere on the deck. The centre line of each deck had spaces for hatches, capstans and the partners, which supported the masts. Some of the beams were curved to join another one before reaching the centre line, in order to leave room for these fittings. The deck beams were held against the sides by means of L-shaped pieces of timber known as knees; their peculiar shape made them expensive and difficult to procure.

When complete the whole structure was caulked – workmen drove pieces of oakum, or fragments of rope, into the spaces between the planks and covered them with tar to make the structure as watertight as possible. Two wooden rails were built under the hull and four cradles were built to support the ship on the rails. The blocks were removed and the ship was ready to launch at the next high tide. It was not yet common for a woman to launch a ship, but there was a good deal of ceremony involving wine and large flags. It was a tense moment for the shipbuilder as the last props were knocked away and the restraining ropes were cut to allow the ship to slide slowly down into the water, to the cheers of workmen, guests and bystanders.

EXPERIMENTS AND IMPROVEMENTS

In 1805, as the French prepared for their most serious invasion threat for many years, the British fleet was desperately short of serviceable ships. There had been no large building programme during the last war (1793-1802) and during the Peace of Amiens St Vincent had been in dispute with the shipbuilders in both the royal and merchant yards. When he came to office in 1804, Lord Barham found many ships 'in a very dilapidated state' and resolved to get them into service. He turned to Gabriel Snodgrass, surveyor to the East India Company and a long-standing critic of naval practices. Snodgrass suggested a programme of 'doubling and bracing.' Selected ships would have the planking of their bottom doubled for greater strength, and braces would be placed diagonally across the hold. This was applied to 22 ships of the line (including the 74-gun *Bellona*) and eleven frigates. Though intended as an emergency measure, some ships saw distinguished service in this condition – the 80-gun *Caesar* was Sir Richard Strachan's flagship when he defeated a French squadron just after Trafalgar. Some lasted very well and the *Bellona* was still on active service in 1814.

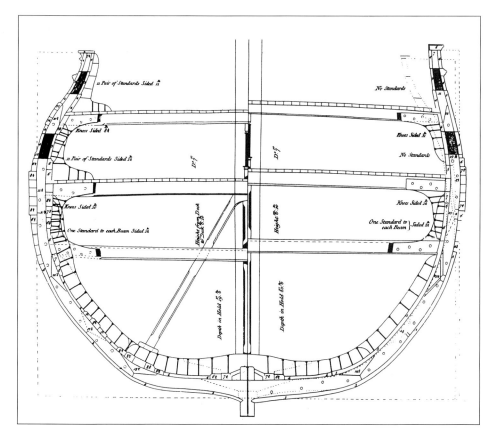

The cross section of the hull of a ship of the line near midships. On the left, the hull is the conventional shape though fitted with Snodgrass's diagonal braces. To the right is the shape recommended by Snodgrass for new construction with less narrowing of the hull, or tumble-home, above the waterline. It shows the futtocks and how they are joined together by wedges; the internal and external planking, including wales; the riders inside the main structure with the numerous metal bolts, which hold them in place; the deck beams and the L-shaped knees and standards which brace them.

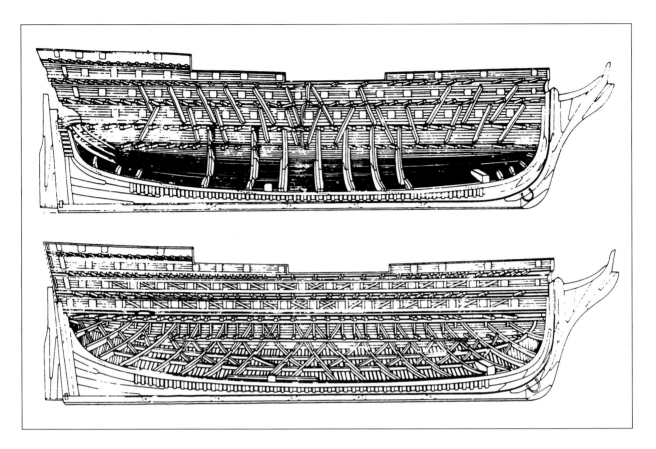

Robert Seppings, who became Master Shipwright at Chatham Dockyard in 1804, was far
better educated and more inquiring than the great majority of shipwrights. He produced
many inventions to improve building techniques, and saw at least three major faults in the
way ships were designed. One of the greatest flaws was that all the pieces of the ship – keel,
frames, planks, deck beams, knees etc, were placed at right angles to one another with very
little diagonal support. As Seppings came to realise, this was contrary to the principle, 'well
known to the meanest mechanic', that a triangle was much stronger than a rectangle. He
invented a system of 'diagonal bracing' on rather a different principle from Snodgrass. The
braces replaced the old riders inside the main hull of the ship, and ran fore and aft attached
to the main structure to create a great deal of rigidity. This was combined with other measures – the spaces between the lower frames were filled with concrete, diagonals were fitted
in the spaces between the gunports where they would have the greatest effect, and even diagonal deck planking was fitted. First fully tested on the 74-gun *Tremendous* in 1810, the
Seppings system soon confounded its critics and transformed ship design. It was now possible to build much longer ships without hogging (or sagging at the ends), and ultimately to
fit them with steam engines.

The next reform was obvious enough after Nelson's fleet sailed into the Battle of Trafalgar
almost at right angles to the enemy. The upper part of the bows of a ship of the line, formed
of only a fragile bulkhead instead of the usual structure of frames and planks, were very weak.
The remedy was simple and uncontroversial – starting in 1811, Seppings built up the structure of the frames to a higher level to create the 'round bow', greatly improving the strength
of the ships at little cost in aesthetics. But later, after the war had ended, Seppings turned to
a much greater weakness, in the stern. He tried to minimise the doors, windows and stern
galleries and again built up the main structure to form the 'round stern.' This proved very
unpopular with peacetime captains, and was eventually superseded.

At this time shipbuilders had no conception that any material other than wood could be used as the main structure of a ship, but over the years they began to use iron more and more for subsidiary purposes. As curved knees became more difficult to obtain, a triangular knee was substituted under the beam and reinforced with an iron frame to hold the beam and knee together.

FITTING

After launch, a privately-built ship was towed to the nearest Royal Dockyard for fitting; if built in the dockyard, she was simply towed into a dry-dock for the final 'graving' of her hull. By 1793 it was common to cover the hull in sheets of copper to protect it from the twin dangers of worm, which might eat its way long the planks, and weed which would create friction and slow the ship down. This had given the British a great tactical advantage when it had been introduced more than a decade earlier, but now it was common to all the naval powers. After coppering the ship was moved out into the river alongside a sheer hulk. This was an old warship fitted with a gantry or 'sheers' to hoist the lower masts into place. If not needed immediately in peacetime, the ship might be left in that state, with no guns, few stores and little rigging. If she was to go to sea, a crew was recruited by one means or another and they would do most of the rest of the work in preparing the ship for sea.

A ship was steered by means of a rudder, which was hinged on the stern post of the vessel. The smallest ships had a simple tiller arrangement, but in the large ships the tiller was connected by blocks and tackles to a steering wheel on the quarterdeck, from which position the officer of the watch could control the steering and keep an eye on the sails. Anchors were vital for ships in those days, for they had to be able to use them when there was no wind. Warships rarely came alongside piers or jetties, and in harbour they were mostly at anchor some distance offshore. The universal pattern of anchor had two arms with spade-like flukes. A wooden stock was fitted at the other end of a long shank, in a plane at right angles to the arms so that one or other of the flukes would bury itself in the sea bottom. A warship carried four main anchors, two hung from the cathead at the bows, two more, including the sheet anchor, which was the last reserve in a crisis, stowed behind them. There were also two smaller ones, the kedge and the stream, which might be slung under boats and rowed out to be dropped in the water ahead of the ship. The cable was then hauled in, pulling the ship forward.

Anchor cables consisted of very thick ropes which were stowed in the hold when not in use. The anchors were raised, and heavy weights were lifted, by means of the capstans. Each of these had a barrel set vertically and usually passing through two decks of the ship. Pieces of timber known as whelps were used to extend the diameter of the barrel, and to prevent a rope from riding up it. Most capstans had two heads, one on each deck, with holes for the capstan bars where the men would push. The anchor cable itself was too large to wrap round the capstan and an endless rope known as a messenger was used to link the cable to the capstan. Most warships had two capstans, one between the foremast and the

An anchor, with a pointed crown forming its lowest part. It has a typical wooden stock, square in cross section and held together by metal hoops. It is hung from a cathead projecting from the side of the bow of a ship and attached to an anchor buoy, which will mark its position when in the water. Behind it is a kedge anchor, much smaller and with an iron stock.
(*The English Encyclopaedia*, 1802)

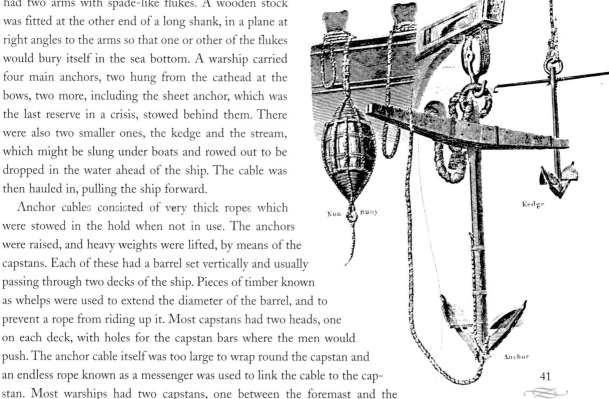

Nun Buoy   Kedge

Anchor

41

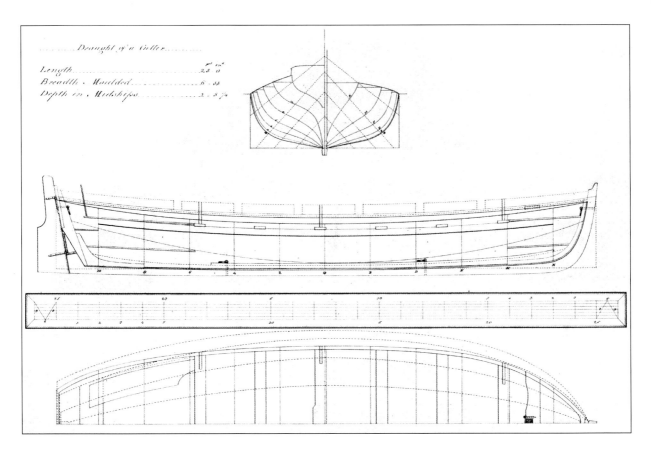

The plan of a cutter, a common and favourite type of ship's boat. Like all ship's boats it could be rowed, but it was best known for its good sailing qualities. This plan was used as the basic design for two cutters made for HMS *Victory* in 1993, one of which is used at sea and can be seen at many events in north European waters. It was also used in the opening scene of the BBC Television production of Jane Austen's *Persuasion* in 1995. (NMM Bu(h)7)

mainmast and one just forward of the mizzen. For heavy work they could be used in tandem and the effort of several hundred men might be employed in a large ship.

Seamen of the Napoleonic Wars used ships' boats for purposes that were undreamed of by a modern sailor. Today they are most often seen as lifeboats, but that function was barely developed in 1800. Instead boats were used to carry stores to the ship, to lay out anchors and even to tow the ship in a calm; to ferry officers to conferences in other ships, to launch press gangs on shore or to raid other ships; to attach mooring lines to stakes or to the ship in narrow waters; to take men ashore for leave; to board enemy ships in battle, usually after they had surrendered; and to raid enemy ships in port and at anchor in 'cutting out' expeditions.

Boats were designed to be sailed and rowed. Each ship had a launch, designed for heavy work such as carrying stores and laying out anchors. The cutter was the best boat for sailing and was often used at sea. Pinnaces and barges were best for rowing and were intended to ferry officers about in port. A 38-gun frigate of 1805 carried a 32ft 10-oared barge, a 26ft launch, two 25ft cutters and an 18ft jolly boat, a small cutter. Sometimes captains added their own favourite design of boat, such as gigs and wherries.

No wooden ship is ever completely dry, and a system of drainage and extraction of water was needed. The deck beams were curved upwards, or cambered, to allow water to drain to the sides, while low walls or comings round the hatchways prevented water from taking that route. Once near the sides of the ship the water drained out through lead pipes known as scuppers. Much water would find itself into the hold of the ship, whether by drainage or leaks in the hull. It was led towards the main pumps close to midships. There were operated by means of an endless chain fitted with saucers and placed inside a vertical pipe. Men on the lower deck turned the chain, with some difficulty; it was a very fatiguing operation, sometimes used as a punishment. The chain pump delivered a good deal of water per hour, but not under pressure. For fire-fighting and washing the decks, suction pumps were installed.

RIGGING

Each full-rigged ship had three masts. The largest, the mainmast, was near to the centre of the ship. The second largest, the foremast, was well forward leaving a large gap between it and the main, for both would be swung in opposite directions when the ship was tacking. The mizzen mast was rather smaller and it was intended to provide balance to the rig, rather than a large amount of drive through its sails. Each mast was made in three sections, starting from the bottom. A lower mast might be up to three feet in diameter on a large ship and was made of several pieces joined together by rope and alter iron hoops. The fore and the main started just above the keel of the ship and passed through several decks, where they were braced in position by timber known as partners. Each reached the appropriate height above the deck to carry the lower sail. It supported a top, a wide, flat platform which was useful for spreading the rigging of the upper mast, and as a base for the men working the rigging. It also formed part of the join with the next mast up, the topmast. The lowest part of the topmast was held by the structure in the top, and the highest part of the lower mast was joined to the topmast some way up by means of the cap. The topmast was joined to the highest part of the mast, the topgallant, by a similar but less elaborate structure. There was no top as such, only a light framework known as the cross-trees. The very highest point of the ship was the truck of the mainmast, with a button-shaped top.

The masts were supported by the standing rigging, which remained in place except during maintenance and was tarred to protect it from the weather. The shrouds supported the masts against pressures from the sides and stern. There were about a dozen of them on each side, fixed to the channels which projected from either side of the ship. The top end was looped round the head of the mast. The lower end of each shroud could be tightened by means of the lanyards, which passed between skull-shaped blocks known as dead-eyes on the channels and shrouds. The topmasts and topgallants were supported in similar fashion by shrouds fixed to the tops and cross–trees.

A rope stay ran diagonally forward from each mast to support against pressure from ahead, for example when tacking. The forestay, mainstay and mizzen stay ran forward from the tops to the deck, the fore topmast and topgallant stays to the bowsprit and the top and topgallant stays of the main and mizzen masts to the tops and crosstrees of the masts ahead. All stays had elaborate means of tightening them using blocks and lanyards.

The running rigging served two separate functions – to support and control the yards, and to control the sails which were fitted to them. A full-rigged ship of the period had three yards across each of its masts, known as the course, the topsail yard and the topgallant yard. Later a fourth yard, the royal, was added above them. Each yard was smaller than the one below it, and it tapered towards its ends, the yardarms. The yards were raised at their centres by jeers in the case of courses, or halyards for the upper yards. The yardarms were kept level by ropes known as lifts. Their movement in the horizontal plane, essential in trimming the sails, was controlled by means of braces, ropes leading aft from each yardarm.

A sail was hung from each yard, except the lower mizzen yard, which served only to spread the foot of the mizzen topsail. They were known as square sails, though none was precisely square and only the courses were near to being rectangular. The topsails, topgallants and royals all tapered towards the head, because the upper yardarms were smaller. Sails were made of strips of canvas 2 feet wide sewed together, with ropes, the bolt-ropes, sewn round the edges. Most had at least one line of reef points, sort ropes which projected on each side

The sails of a ship of the line. The top drawing shows the fore and aft sails, though they were seldom, if ever, set on their own. At the stern is the mizzen sail, known as the spanker or driver, supported by a wooden gaff above and a boom below. Between the masts are the quadrilateral staysails, hung from the stays as their name implies. Between the foremast and the bowsprit are the triangular jib-sails.

The lower drawing shows the fore and aft sails, including studding sails set to extend the sails of the fore and main masts. The highest sails, the royals, have no studding sails. The spritsails, under the bowsprit, were seldom used in this period. (From Rees's *Cyclopaedia,* 1819)

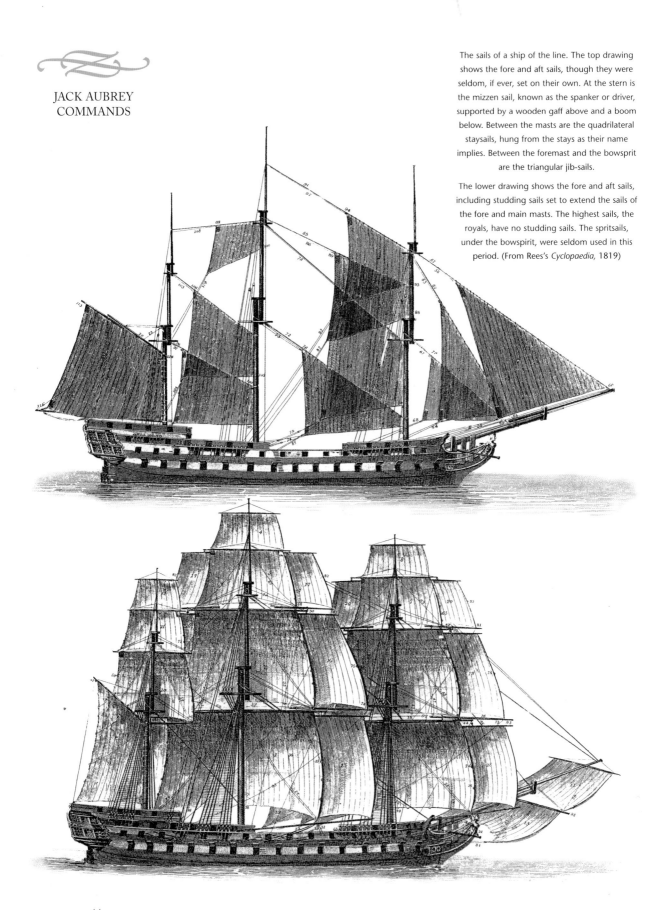

of the sail and could be tied together over the yard to reduce the amount of sail exposed to the wind. They had loops known as cringles at the corners and close to the ends of the lines of reef points. Each sail was tied to the yard by means of small ropes known as rope-bands or 'robbands'.

The lower corners of the sails were controlled by ropes called sheets. In the case of the upper sail these merely attached the lower corners, the clews to the yardarms. In the case of the courses the sheets ran aft from the clews, through blocks on deck. The clews of the lower sails also had to be held forward when the ship was sailing close to the wind. This was done by ropes called tacks. The edges of the sails could be held forward by bowlines. The sail was furled by means of buntlines and slab lines which ran from the lower edge of the sail through blocks in the yards and down to the deck to the yards, and by clewlines which ran from the corners to the centre part of the yard. Once raised, the sail was furled by tying ropes known as gaskets round it.

The mizzen course was fore and aft rigged, in that it ran fore and aft rather than across the ship in its neutral position. Its upper edge was supported by a diagonal gaff and its lower by a horizontal boom projecting over the stern. The other fore and aft sails were hung from the stays which supported the masts. Those attached to the forestays were set over the bowsprit and known as jibs. It was still possible to set square sails under the bowsprit on their own yards, though they were largely superseded by the jibs and were seldom used. A triangular staysail needed far fewer ropes to control it than a square sail – a halyard to raise it, a tack to control its lower corner, and a sheet one each side to set it to the correct angle to the wind.

A ship of the line needed about a thousand pulley blocks to lead ropes down to the deck, or to be used in combination to create a block and tackle effect. It needed perhaps 40 miles of rope of different sizes for its rigging, gun tackles and anchors. The sails of a first rate took up an area of more than two acres. With a thousand ships in the navy in 1812, this required an enormous effort to make, maintain, service and operate.

Some of the ropes attached to square sails.

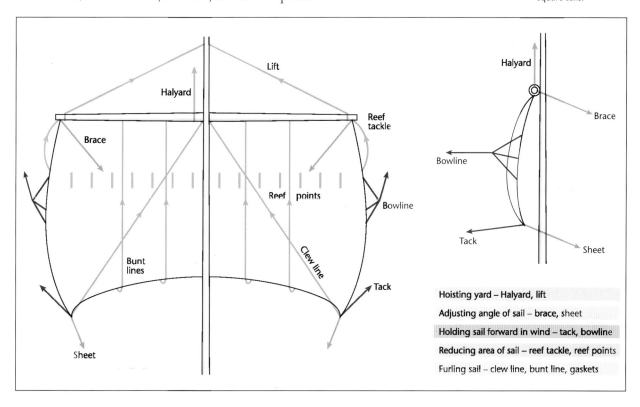

Hoisting yard – Halyard, lift

Adjusting angle of sail – brace, sheet

Holding sail forward in wind – tack, bowline

Reducing area of sail – reef tackle, reef points

Furling sail – clew line, bunt line, gaskets

ARMAMENT

The gun armament was the essential feature of almost any warship of the age. Merchant ships carried guns, but their primary aim was to carry cargo or passengers, and the guns had to be fitted in where convenient. A good warship design, on the other hand, would carry the maximum gun armament consistent with suitable sailing qualities for the intended task. After long years of experience ships, especially the larger ones, were mostly designed round particular weapons; the 74-gun ship, for example, was the smallest that could carry an effective battery of 32-pounder guns.

Guns were classified by the weight of the standard round ball and ranged from 42-pounders to 3-pounders. Research by Benjamin Robbins in the middle of the eighteenth century had shown that larger guns were more effective for their weight. The 42-pounder had been carried by the largest three-deckers, but it was found that the ball was too heavy for a man to carry in action, so it was obsolete by 1793. The next size down, the 32-pounder, was regarded as the ideal, with good penetrating power and range. It was the standard weapon on the lower decks of ships of the line, except for the obsolescent 64s, which carried 24-pounders. The main armament of frigates was still evolving during this period. There were still plenty of 32-gun ships left over from previous wars, with a main armament of 12-pounders on the main deck, but more recent ships had 18-pounders. During the war of 1812 the Americans used 24-pounders on their larger frigates, with devastating effect. In response, the British began to build large frigates of their own, and cut down some two-deckers as *razees*, with 24-pounders on the lower deck.

British guns were much improved in the 1780s and early 1790s by Thomas Blomefield the Inspector of Ordnance. He simplified the design of the gun, added a ring to retrain the breech rope and improved casting techniques with the aid of the ironfounders of Scotland

An older pattern gun (top) and a 32-pounder Blomefield pattern gun (bottom), as issued to the navy after 1790. The breech is more rounded to withstand the effect of the powder, and a ring has been incorporated in the rear of the gun.

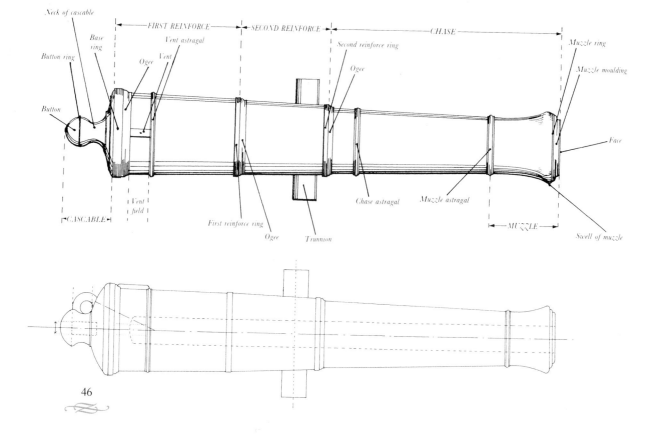

and the north of England. More revolutionary was the Carronade, produced at the Carron iron works in Scotland. It was a short, fat gun which fired a very large ball in proportion to the weight of the gun, though only over short ranges. It proved very useful in the close-range fighting of the wars with France, though it was dangerous to arm a ship entirely with carronades – the enemy would simply keep out of range and bombard it with more conventional artillery. Carronades were almost universal on the forecastles and quarterdecks of ships by the early 1800s, though in 1805 the *Victory* carried only two, very large 68-pounders in her bow.

The laws of physics demanded that a ship's centre of gravity and therefore her heavy guns be kept as low as possible. It was always a difficult compromise between this and raising them out of the water so that they could be used in rough weather. It was easier in a frigate which had relatively light guns and an unarmed lower deck; her lower gunport sills were usually about eight feet above the waterline and this allowed her to heel some way in the wind, to the advantage of her sailing qualities.

ABOVE: an early form of carronade, a short, fat gun with a large ball.
BELOW: the more developed form. It has a ring below it instead of trunnions on each side and a nozzle in its muzzle to help contain the blast.

Builders aspired to raise the sills of ships of the line 6ft above the waterline in the 1800s, though they did not always succeed. To reduce weight in the higher parts of the ship, it was normal to mount lighter weapons on the upper decks. This was obviously more important with multi-decked ships; a standard three-decker would carry 32-pounders on the lower deck, 24-pounders on the middle deck, 12-pounders on the upper deck and 12-pounders and carronades on the quarterdeck and forecastle.

The smooth-bore gun was essentially a very simple weapon, a tube closed at one end with a small hole near there to light the powder. It had a trunnion on each side to form a pivot for elevating and depressing it. It was fitted on a wooden carriage with four wooden wheels or trucks. When fired it was allowed to recoil, but restrained by large ropes, and hauled back into place when loaded by thinner ropes which ran through blocks.

SHIPS OF THE LINE

Warships were divided into rates, reflecting the size of a ship rather than its quality. The rate of a ship determined the pay of the captain and of certain officers. First rates carried 100 guns or more; there were ten of these in the fleet in 1803, including those building or under repair. Second rates had 90-98 guns and there were 20 of them. Third rates, the most numerous class of ship of the line, ranged from 64 to 84 guns; there were 147 of them in 1803. Fourth rates, of 50 to 60 guns, were not particularly popular and there were only 21 of them. The fifth rate, of 32 to 44 guns, included the bulk of the frigates and comprised 157 ships. The sixth rate included ships of 20 to 28 guns and had only 43 ships. Below, them were numerous unrated ships, too small to have a full captain in charge, they had a commander as the senior officer.

Warships of many different types were built, but these could be divided into three main groups. At the head, the largest vessels of the age, were the ships of the line. They had evolved

in the 1650s, during the First Anglo-Dutch war, when it was discovered that a fleet could fight best if it stayed in a single line, instead of a melee battle as used in the past. The discipline of the line became very rigid before the century was out, and this meant that only relatively large ships could be selected for the line of battle, as each had to stand and fight against its opponent in the enemy line. Thus the 'ship of the line' or the 'line of battleship' evolved. The minimum size tended to increase over the years. Fifty-gun ships were accepted until the 1750s, but 64s, though still used in practice, were regarded as too small in the 1790s. Ships of the line invariably had at least two decks of guns, and the larger ones had three. The rigid line of battle had been in decline since the 1740s, and especially under Nelson, but it was not obsolete, and the ship of the line remained the most powerful arbiter of naval power. Seafaring nations measured their strength by the number of ships of the line they could put to sea.

Some of the main types of warships, 1793-1815

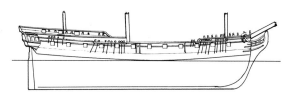

The *Royal George* of 1788, successor to the ship lost in 1782 and one of the last 100-gun ships before they were superseded by 110s and 120s.

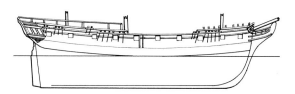

A 28-gun sixth rate of 1775. Some of this type survived to fight from 1793 to 1815, though no new ones were built.

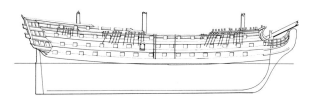

A standard 74-gun ship, typical of many built between 1757 and 1780, 168ft long on the gundeck. Many survived to fight in the wars of 1793 to 1815.

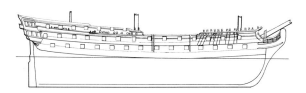

The *Buffalo*, a ship-sloop of 1797, mainly used as a storeship

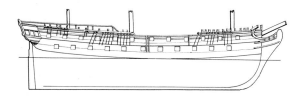

The *Grampus*, an old 50-gun ship of 1780. She was broken up in 1794, but many of the class survived much longer.

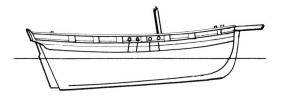

The cutters *Cheerful* and *Surly* of 1806, single-masted and designed for speed.

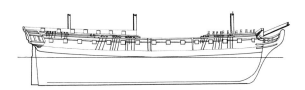

The *Active*, a 38-gun frigate of 1799, similar in layout to most frigates of the period.

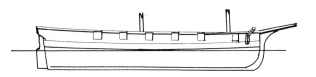

A gunboat of the *Active* class, powered mainly by oars and designed for inshore operations.

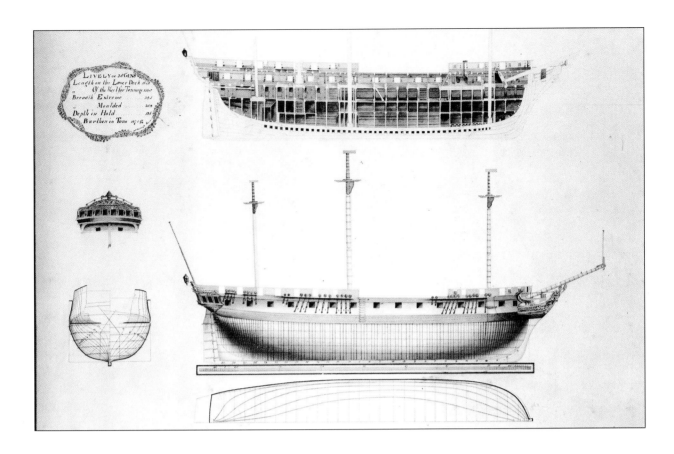

CRUISING SHIPS

The next great group consisted of the cruising ships, too small for the line of battle but with good sailing qualities and an adequate armament. There was an intermediate class of small two-deckers of 40 or 50 guns, but these were little regarded by 1800. The best known and largest of the effective cruising ships were the frigates. This type had been evolved by the French in the middle of the eighteenth century. Characteristically, a frigate had a single main deck of guns, with some on the quarterdeck and forecastle, as in most warships. The lower deck, which in a ship of the line would have carried the heaviest armament, was unarmed and was not pierced for gun ports. The frigate was designed for a myriad of tasks. A modern naval historian identifies nine main roles with the fleet. In strategic reconnaissance they sought out the enemy fleet; in tactical reconnaissance they informed the fleet commander about enemy strengths and movements on the approach to battle; during the engagement they stayed aloof from the fighting but helped with communication and towed damaged ships; they fought in squadron actions, carried out much of the work of blockade, served as tenders to larger warships, took part in coastal operations and amphibious warfare and exercised sea control by means of patrols and hunting groups. Away from the main fleets they could escort convoys and raid and 'annoy' the enemy.[8] In 1803 there were 39 frigates of 38-guns in the fleet, with 43 of 36 guns and 50 of 32 guns.

Below the frigates were the sixth rates, with 20 to 28 guns. They could carry out most of the functions of a frigate, but not fleet reconnaissance, for in that role they would be expected to match the enemy's frigate screen. Smaller unrated ships, such as sloops and brig sloops, carried out essentially the same functions. They were smaller and could be spread more thinly as convoy escorts or commerce raiders. They were often faster in light winds, and could go closer inshore than most frigates.

A fine drawing of the 38-gun frigate *Lively* of 1804, the first of a class of 16 ships. It is unusually well drawn, showing the internal detail above, the framing below and the stern decorations to the left. The ship took part in the operations against the Spanish treasure ships in 1804, in reality under the command of Captain Graham Eden Hamond, in fiction (*Post Captain*) under Jack Aubrey. She was lost off Malta in 1810. (NMM X1976)

49

A naval cutter, single-masted and mainly fore and aft rigged, with sharp bows and a wide hull to prevent the ship heeling too much in a wind. (NMM PAD 6080)

SPECIALISED SHIPS

The third major grouping was made up of ships which were specialised in either function or rig. There were two main types with specialised functions in action. The fireship was designed to be set alight and aimed at an enemy fleet. It had combustible materials on its decks, gun-ports which opened downwards so that they would fall open when their ropes were consumed, and a special exit for the last of the crew on the final stage of the voyage. There were 13 of them on the Navy List in 1799, but only four in 1803. In practice they were little used, and often served as sloops on general duties with the fleet. Bomb vessels were rather more useful. In the past they had been rigged as ketches, with only two masts, the forward one being the largest. This was no longer the case, and now they had a conventional three-masted rig as ships. Each carried a pair of mortars, firing diagonally upwards rather than horizontally like all other ship's guns. They fired explosive shell rather than solid shot and were used to bombard shore targets such as towns and forts. There were a dozen in the fleet in 1803.

Other ships were distinguished by their rig. Every ship above about 200 tons carried the conventional ship rig, with three masts, all carrying square sails. They were so called, not because they were square in shape, but because in their neutral position they were fitted square to the line of the ship; other sails ran 'fore and aft' in the neutral position and took that as their name. Square sails were best when the wind was on the beam or behind the ship, for they could not be hauled round as far as fore and aft sails to sail into the wind. Smaller vessels, such brigs, had two masts, both square rigged; in function they were similar to small sloops. Schooners also had two masts, both fore and aft rigged, which meant that they could sail much closer to the wind. They had evolved in America during the last few decades and were only just being accepted in Britain. There were only eight of them in the navy in 1803, though many more would be added during the war. The cutter, on the other hand, was a native British design. It was single masted, with a very large rig including both fore and aft and square sails. It had been developed by smugglers on the south coast of England during the eighteenth century, and taken up by the revenue services then the navy in an attempt to counteract them, but it found many roles in reconnaissance and message carrying. The smallest class of warship, the gunboat, was beginning to emerge for certain functions. Some had been designed for protection against invasion in 1798 and 1803. Others were used in local defence at Gibraltar and in the Baltic. There were several designs, but most mounted one or two large guns and were propelled mainly by oars.

Finally there were the numerous non-combatant or semi-combatant vessels. Some sailed the high seas or worked around the naval ports as storeships and transports of various kinds. Yachts were used for the transport of important personages, including royalty, diplomats and naval officials. Others, often old warships, were hulks which no longer sailed. The sheer hulk was used to put masts into other ships, receiving ships held pressed men, while others served as store ships, prison ships and hospital ships.

THREE DECKERS

The three-decker, the largest type of sailing warship, does not figure strongly in naval fiction, mainly because the heroes are usually in command of small ships on detached missions. Hornblower endures a court martial on board the *Victory* in *Flying Colours*, and Jack Aubrey is sometimes called on board a flagship to receive his orders, but by the time Hornblower reaches the rank of admiral the peacetime navy employs few large ships on active service. The *Victory* as she can be seen at Portsmouth today is in many ways a typical example of a three-decker. She was called a three-decker because she had three complete decks of guns, though she also had guns at one other level, the quarterdeck and forecastle, and many ships had yet more above that on the poop. She also had a complete deck, the orlop, without any guns. The extra deck of guns created considerable fighting power, and some believed that a three-decker was worth two two-deckers in battle. According to one French tactician:

> When it comes to boarding they dominate vessels of lower rate. The small-arms fire of large ships commands that of small ones; all the shot plunge and get home over the bulwarks…the crew can get down to board a small ship more easily than they can climb onto a big one. In heavy seas big vessels can use their lower batteries more easily….Large ships, too, have greater solidity and better resistance to attack.'

Against this, she tended to cost rather more; the *Victory* cost £63,176 to build in the 1760s, while her contemporary the *Bellona* cost £43,391. The undoubted advantage of the three-decker was that she gave state and majesty to a flagship, and extra accommodation for an admiral and his staff.

The *Victory* at sea in light airs with her studding sails set, showing the ship as she was in 1803-5, before the Battle of Trafalgar. (Artist: Geoff Hunt RSMA)

By the 1800s the *Victory* had been overtaken in size. She had been built between 1759 and 1765 and was measured at 2142 tons. The next 100-gun ship, the *Royal Sovereign* of 1786, which was Collingwood's flagship at Trafalgar, was not substantially bigger. The real expansion began in the 1790s, in response to French building policies. The *Ville de Paris*, launched in 1795, was measured at 2351 tons and carried 110 guns; the *Hibernia* had a similar gun armament and a slightly larger hull, but was not launched until 1804. In the meantime an even larger ship, the *Caledonia* of 120 guns and 2626 tons, had been laid down in 1797, but she was not completed until 1808. After that five 120-gun ships were laid down before the end of the wars, though only three were completed before Waterloo.

The second rate ship of 90 or 98 guns was essentially a cut-price first rate. The difference between 98 and 100 guns does not seem very large, but in fact the 98 had 18-pounders instead of 24-pounders on the middle deck, so her gun power was considerably less.

TWO DECKER SHIPS OF THE LINE

To many people the two-decker was the most important type of warship. Ship design involves many compromises, between gun power, strength, speed, seakeeping, long range, crew accommodation and many other factors. There is no perfect warship, but over a period

A model of the *Bellona,* the classic 74-gun ship. This model is one of the earliest known with copper sheathing, and its case has carrying handles. It is known that Charles Middleton (later Lord Barham) used a model to demonstrate the principle of coppering to King George III, and this may well be the one he used.
(NMM C 1099)

52

a type might evolve to the best possible state for a particular type of war. After a century and a half in which broadside gunpower had dominated naval warfare, and the fight for empire had played a large part in naval strategy, the two-decker ship of the line was coming close to this stage. It could carry a good battery of 32-pounder guns, keep the seas in all seasons, employ its men economically and still sail well in most conditions of weather. Within the two-deckers, the 74 had evolved as the best. It was better-proportioned and more effective than smaller two-deckers as used in the past, such as the 70s, 64s and 44s. It was more long-lasting than larger two-decked ships with 80 guns, which were prone to 'hogging' after long periods afloat. The naval architect Marmaduke Stalkaart wrote in 1781:

> Of those ships that carry [their guns] on two decks, the 74-gun ship is the most approved. The reason is evident. The ship whose topside is the shallowest in proportion to their capacity under water is the most stiff, and will hold the least wind. The guns of a sloop should be so much above the water as those of a large frigate, and if possible more so, if her dimensions are similar. For the same reason, the 74-gun ship will require but little more topside than 44-gun ships in commission with the difference in their dimensions, and therefore it must be expected that the 74-gun ship will work as easy as the 44-gun ship, and must sail faster, because she will bear the greater pressure of canvas…The 74-gun ship…contains the properties of the First Rate and the frigate. She will not shrink from an encounter with a First Rate ship on account of superior weight, nor abandon the chase of a frigate on account of swiftness.[9]

The Royal Navy had eighty-seven 74-gun ships in 1803, the largest class in the fleet and more than half the line of battle.

The 74 was originally developed in the French navy in the 1740s, and much admired by the British until they captured the *Invincible* in 1747. They then made some copies of that ship, but in general they preferred to evolve their own version, slightly shorter and with a slightly different gun arrangement. The *Bellona* was one of the first of the new 74-gun ships, as they evolved in the Royal Navy during the Seven Years War. The 74 was in effect the ideal compromise between gun power and sailing qualities. In the previous generation, ships of 80 guns with three decks had proved dangerously unstable, two deckers with 70 guns had only 24-pounders on the power deck and were too weak. The 74 was the smallest ship which could carry an effective battery of 32-pounder guns, the most effective in action. She was a two-decker, long enough to keep a good proportion between length and height above the waterline; any longer and she would have tended to hog, as some later ships often did.

The *Bellona* and her sisters the *Dragon* and *Superb*, were the first to have a gundeck length of 168ft, which was standard for at least the next twenty years. The *Bellona* herself was hurriedly built at Chatham Dockyard between May 1758 and February 1760 and first saw action in August 1761 when, in a very important single-ship action, she captured the large French 74 *Courageux* off the River Tagus. After that her career in action was disappointing; she went aground in the entry to the Battle of Copenhagen and in 1805 she got separated from Sir William Strachan's squadron just before it captured four French survivors of Trafalgar. Then she took part in two unsuccessful expeditions to the Basque Roads in 1807 and Walcheren in 1808. But she had a very long career, aided by the fact that she was fitted with Gabriel Snodgrass's diagonal braces in 1805. The 74-gun ship lasted for about sixty years as the mainstay of the British line of battle, and the *Bellona* saw almost all of them, before being broken up for scrap timber at Chatham in 1814.

Bellona had the same layout as almost every other 74, and indeed almost every two-decker of the epoch. Most of the guns, as the name implies, were carried on two decks above the

JACK AUBREY
COMMANDS

A model of the 50-gun *Leopard*, similar in style to the *Bellona* model. When the model was opened a piece of paper was found bearing the name of the maker, George Stockwell, providing a very rare glimpse into the world of the eighteenth century model maker. (Private collection, photograph courtesy Simon Stephens)

waterline, twenty-eight 32-pounders on the lower deck and the same number of 18 pounders on the upper deck ('large class' 74s, closer to French design, had thirty 24-pounders there). The lower deck was covered in and served as the sleeping and dining area for the crew, as well as a fighting and working space.

50-GUN SHIPS

The 50-gun ship was an old type, which had been much in favour at the beginning of the eighteenth century, in the belief that it was large enough to serve in the line of battle when needed, but small and cheap enough to spread round coasts and convoys for commerce protection. In fact it was an unhappy compromise, successful in neither task. In the 1750s it was dropped from the official lists of ships of the line, and it was superseded by the new frigates in the commerce-protection role. It was revived in the 1770s in a lighter form, partly as a peacetime flagship on distant stations, where its two decks would look impressive. It found some use in the limited war against the American colonists after 1775, but none in the great fleet battles after France, Spain and the Netherlands joined the war. The *Leopard* was one of a batch ordered in 1775-8, but her construction was delayed. Her partly completed frames were removed from Portsmouth Dockyard to Sheerness in 1785, and she was finally completed five years later, a relic of a previous age. There were 13 such ships on the *Navy List* in 1805, some of them captured from the smaller naval powers like the Dutch, some taken over from the East India Company in an emergency. They found work as transports, troopships and static harbour vessels. Jack Aubrey was not alone in regarding them as 'a poor and declining class.'[10]

FRIGATES

The 38-gun frigate *Lively* was the first ship of a class designed by Sir William Rule, the Surveyor of the Navy, in 1799. Her construction at Woolwich Dockyard was delayed during the Peace of Amiens; she was not begun until late 1801, and was launched in July 1804. Her design was a success and seven more ships were ordered to the same draught in 1803-5, and eight more from 1808-12. Perhaps this was why the *Lively* was chosen as a sample ship for a series of very high quality drawings of different classes of ship, showing the interior in more detail than usual. She was 154ft 1in long on the gundeck, 39ft 6in broad and measured at 1076 tons. She carried twenty-eight 18-pounder guns on her upper deck with two

9-pounder long guns and twelve 32-pounder carronades on the quarterdeck, and two 9 pounders and two 32-pound carronades on the forecastle.

The *Lively* was commissioned by Captain C E Hammond in July 1804 and sent to cruise against enemy shipping. In October she took part in the famous attack on the homecoming Spanish treasure fleet, an event which is recorded in more than one of the sagas of naval fiction. In May 1805 she was in an inconclusive action with the Spanish ship of the line *Glorioso* off Cadiz. She continued cruising under Captain G McKinley until 1810, when she was sent to the Mediterranean. On 26 August she was wrecked on Salina Point, Malta.

SLOOPS

The sloop was the largest type of unrated vessel, with a 'master and commander' or simply 'commander' in charge, rather than a captain. The term sloop was deeply ambiguous, but in naval terms it meant a vessel of ten to eighteen guns. The largest were built like miniature frigates, complete with forecastle and quarterdeck, and with three masts. A slightly smaller version was flush-decked, with no quarterdeck and forecastle; another type, a brig, had only two masts.

The most famous of the last class was Cochrane's *Speedy*, built by King of Dover in 1781. According to her captain she was:

> …little more than a burlesque on a vessel of war. She was about the size of an average coasting brig, her burden being 158 tons. She was crowded, rather than manned, with a crew of eighty-four men and six officers, myself included. Her armament consisted of fourteen *4-pounders*! a species of gun little larger than a blunderbuss, and formerly known in the service under the name of "minion," an appellation which it certainly merited.

Cochrane applied for 12-pounders to mount on the bow and stern, but there was not room on deck to work them. He managed to deceive the dockyard into fitting an unconventional but effective rig. His own accommodation was poor even by naval standards. The cabin:

> …had not so much as room for a chair, the floor being entirely occupied by the small table surrounded by lockers, answering the double purpose of storerooms and seats. The difficulty was to get seated, the ceiling being only five feet high, so that the object could only be accomplished by rolling on a locker…the only practicable mode of shaving consisted in removing the skylight and putting my head through to make a toilet table of the quarter-deck.

But Cochrane went on to capture a mass of enemy shipping in the Mediterranean and defeat the Spanish frigate *Gamo* in the most celebrated single-ship action of all time, as well as providing the inspiration for the exploits, if not the politics, of O'Brian's Jack Aubrey.

EXPERIMENTAL CRAFT

Though ship design was essentially conservative around 1800, there were many experiments on the fringes of the naval architect's profession, many lone inventors who believed they possessed a secret which would change the face of seafaring, and a few who were allowed to try their ideas in practice. There was no precise equivalent of Jack Aubrey's command 'the *Carpenter's mistake*', 'a theorising landsman's vessel…built by a gang of rogues and jobbers', but there were several ships which looked very strange to the seaman. Captain Schank of the navy was one of the more successful inventors. He knew that a deep hull was essential for a warship if it was to avoid being driven sideways by the wind, but at the same time it created resistance, and it necessitated a deep draught of water which restricted inshore operations. Schank's

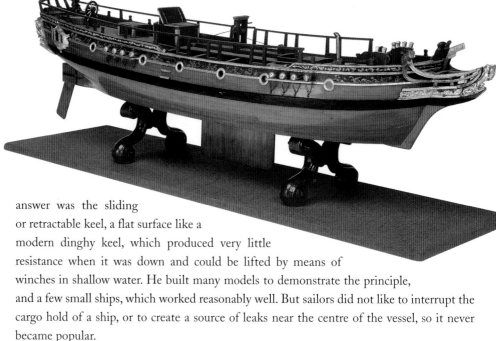

A model of a sloop with Captain Schank's sliding keel. The ship is shallow drafted and flat-bottomed. The square retractable keel can be seen under the centre of the hull, with the winch to raise it directly above on deck. Aft, the rudder has a retractable extension. (NMM D 7801)

answer was the sliding or retractable keel, a flat surface like a modern dinghy keel, which produced very little resistance when it was down and could be lifted by means of winches in shallow water. He built many models to demonstrate the principle, and a few small ships, which worked reasonably well. But sailors did not like to interrupt the cargo hold of a ship, or to create a source of leaks near the centre of the vessel, so it never became popular.

PRIZES

The Royal Navy, like any other predator, was dependent on its prey. There was no doubt that it hungered for prize money from the capture of enemy ships to reward and satisfy its officers and men. Many also believed that the navy needed a constant supply of foreign prizes to give it the fast ships that it needed, or at least to update its ideas on ship design. French ships tended to have finer lines. Ships of the line were larger for a given gunpower, and sailed better. Frigates were larger and had more guns than their British equivalents. In the 1790s several incidents appeared to confirm the French superiority, for example the escape of the French from the Channel Fleet in 1793. One captain wrote 'the ships of France and Spain were generally superior to those of England, both in size, weight of metal and number of men, outsailing them in fleets, and often in single ships, carrying their guns higher out of the water, and in all other respects better found for the material of war.'[11] These views had reached the Admiralty, which ordered ships of the line and frigates based on captured ships. By the turn of the century this was changing. In 1798 Lord Bridport (1727-1814) the Commander-in-Chief of the Channel Fleet wrote:

> …it is supposed that French frigates sail faster than English-built ones. But they are confessedly weaker, are oftener in port and not able to keep the sea on long cruises as they stow little and, having no orlop deck, they must move their cables whenever they want to get at the water that is towed under them, which is sometimes difficult at seas.[12]

Shipbuilders had always known that French ships were more difficult to maintain after long service at sea, and Gabriel Snodgrass of the East India Company wrote that they were 'ridiculous ships.' The new ships ordered in the 1790s entered service and their captains found nothing superior about them. The dockyards found that they tended to 'hog' more than other ships. St Vincent was opposed to the further enlargement of ships and wrote that the 110-gun *Ville de Paris* was the *ne plus ultra* of first rates. Little more was heard of the superiority of French design in the early nineteenth century. The evidence suggests that

French ships were indeed faster in light winds and good conditions, but the advantage was not enough to override their defects.

Perhaps the ideal ship was one built to French design in British yards. Such vessels included the 74-gun *Valiant* and *Triumph,* based on the *Invincible;* the large number of 74s based on the French *Courageaux,* and the numerous frigates built to the design of the captured *Hebe.* Two of them, the *Trincomalee* (at Hartlepool) and the *Unicorn* (at Dundee), survive to this day. Interestingly enough the idea has been revived in a different form. The Royal Navy's new aircraft carriers are being designed in France and built in Britain.

Nevertheless some individual prizes were highly valued. The *Unite* had originally been built at Le Havre in 1794, as a 'corvette' in the French navy. She was captured by the 38-gun British frigate *Inconstant* in the Mediterranean in 1796, and incorporated in the British navy. As there was already a French prize named *Unite* in the Royal Navy, she was renamed *Surprise.* She was quite a small ship at 579 tons, compared with 950 for a typical 36-gun frigate of the period, but she had the mainmast of a 36. 'Thus rigged', according to the leading naval historian of the period, 'the *Surprise* appears not to have been complained of as a sailer.' She was rated as a sixth rate 28-gun ship, based on the number of long guns she theoretically carried, but in fact she had a remarkably heavy armament of short-range carronades – twenty-four 32-pounders on the main deck, and eight of the same guns on the quarterdeck and forecastle, with two or four long 6-pounders in the same areas. She was upgraded to a fifth rate from 1797, but dropped again to the lower rate in the following year. She sailed to Jamaica in July 1796 under Captain Edward Hamilton and captured several French privateers. Her most famous exploit took place in 1799. Two years earlier the crew of the frigate *Hermione* had revolted and took the ship into a Spanish port. The *Surprise,* in a famous cutting-out expedition, recaptured the *Hermione* and several of the mutineers, much to the joy of all naval officers. She returned home and in February 1802, during the short-lived Peace of Amiens, she was sold out of the service and presumably broken up. Though the ship was real enough, her later career was entirely the invention of Patrick O'Brian.

The layout of the *Surprise* was not very different from that of a frigate such as the *Lively.* The 'gundeck' was 126ft long and actually free of guns, for it was just below the level of the waterline. It accommodated everyone in the ship except the captain, with the gunroom aft for the officers and the crew in the open spaces for the forward two-thirds of the ship. The deck under the gunroom was lowered slightly, to give greater headroom.

Jack Aubrey's favourite ship, the *Surprise.* (Redrawn from the plans in the National Maritime Museum by Brian Lavery/British Library)

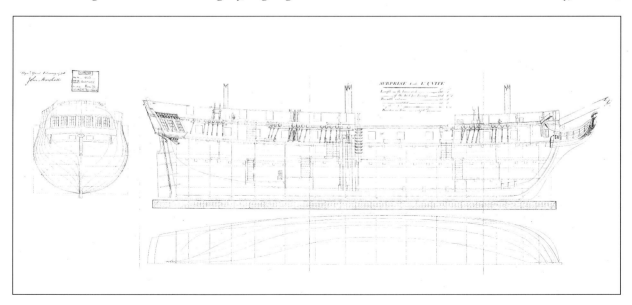

The naval powers of Europe tended to concentrate their efforts on strong, seaworthy ships of considerable gun power. Even French frigates, though considered fast, were constrained by the needs of all warships to fight at least as well as they could sail. Merchant ships had deep, square hulls to carry large cargoes, and monopolies like the East India Company had no need for ships to race home to catch the market. Only local craft – the English cutters and the French luggers, were designed mainly for speed, at the expense of range, fighting power and cargo carrying. They tended to use fore and aft sails to take them closer to the wind.

Across the Atlantic this tendency was taken rather further. Shipbuilders were less constrained by traditional practices and had good supplies of timber. Businesses were not protected by monopoly. They needed fast short-range vessels as pilot cutters, for getting a pilot on board an arriving ship was a fiercely competitive business. They needed longer range vessels for the slave trade, for they were intended to carry a perishable cargo. The Bermudans evolved their own small vessels, with a characteristic fore and aft rig, which eventually became very influential. The citizens of Baltimore in the United States evolved a design which they called a 'clipper'.

A classic example of this type was the *Lynx*, captured by the Royal Navy in 1813 and renamed *Mosquidobit*. She was 94ft 7ins long on the gundeck and 24ft broad. She had exceptionally sharp waterlines and a V-shaped bottom, with two sharply raked masts which were rigged as a schooner, with fore and aft rigs on both masts, though probably with square topsails to aid in running before the wind. The Royal Navy paid her the complement of measuring her and taking off her lines to produce a detailed plan. The Baltimore clipper ultimately had some influence on the classic clipper ship of the late nineteenth century, and possibly in the shorter term on Royal Navy ship design after 1815.

The Royal Navy peaked in 1813 with 1017 ships, of which 723 were in commission, 220 laid up in reserve or 'ordinary' and 74 more were building. There were 15 ships of 100 guns or more, 178 two-decked 74s, 80 frigates of 38 guns and 70 of 36, 161 sloops and 191 brigs. The navy was on the verge of several revolutions in ship design and construction. The full benefits of the Seppings system were just being felt, and soon this would allow much longer ships to be built in each rate. The idea of fast ships with v-shaped bottoms appealed to Sir William Symonds, a naval officer who became Surveyor of the Navy in 1832 and produced fast ships, which provided very poor gun platforms. Steam power was only just visible in 1815 – Henry Bell's *Comet* entered commercial service on the Clyde in 1812 and the navy hired its first steam tug, the *Monkey*, in 1821. The idea of shipbuilding in iron was some way in the future, though wooden warships of 1815 used more iron in their construction than ever before. The real revolution in shipbuilding, which would eventually produce steel, steam-powered ships with huge long-range guns, was only just beginning.

The *Musquidobit,* formerly the *Lynx,* one of several Baltimore clippers that were taken by the Royal Navy in the War of 1812. She served as an American privateer before being taken in the Chesapeake in 1813. In the Royal Navy she served on the Irish station and was sold in 1820. (NMM Dr 4564)

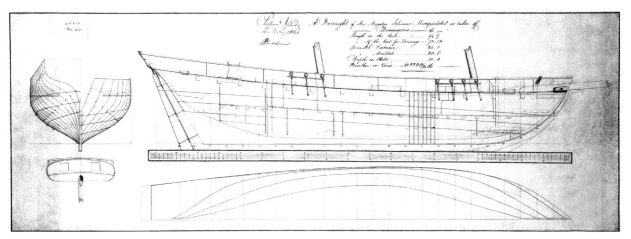

CHAPTER 3

OFFICERS

COMMISSIONED SEA OFFICERS

The Royal Navy never had any problem in recruiting its officers, in contrast to the situation with seamen. In the early seventeenth century there were two main sources. Some were experienced merchant ship captains, or 'tarpaulins', and others were courtiers raised to high office - the 'gentlemen'. It became accepted that all sea officers should have real sea experience before they were granted a commission as a lieutenant, and several years' prior service as a midshipman was insisted upon. Samuel Pepys established the first examination for naval lieutenants in 1677, and slowly the 'class' problem began to disappear. Naval officers were given a regular uniform in 1748, more than a century before the seamen, and this fostered their professional cohesion.

The naval profession offered a unique way to serve king and country with the highest honour, while still giving the chance to make great sums of money. It was particularly attractive to members of the aristocracy and landed gentry, especially younger sons who had to make their own way in the world, or those from impoverished branches of the nobility who hoped to restore family fortunes without descending into commerce. It was equally attractive to rising commercial and professional families from the middle class, who could gain honour by service to the king, without losing sight of the need to make money. Nelson came from precisely this background. It was also possible for an ordinary sailor, with a reasonable amount of education, to rise to commissioned rank.

It was not the salary alone which attracted young men. Officers often had to pay their own expenses, including travel to and from their ships, uniforms and food consumed in excess of the normal ships' provisions as issued to the seamen. Edward Rotherham, as a lieutenant in the 1790s, complained that he spent more than £90 to travel to his ship, replace his uniforms and pay various fees and his share of the wardroom expenses during the first year of a commission. This was more than a year's pay of £72. 'This good officer hath served one whole year in defence of his King and country, his clothes worn out and stock exhausted, finds himself in debt £18/17/10?'.

THE ETHOS OF THE NAVAL OFFICER

The commissioned sea officers were the only people who had all their training within the Royal Navy. Specialist officers, such as surgeons, pursers and carpenters, learned their trade ashore. Seaman ratings mostly learned their craft in the merchant service, as did many seaman warrant officers such as masters and boatswains. A minority of commissioned sea officers (like

59

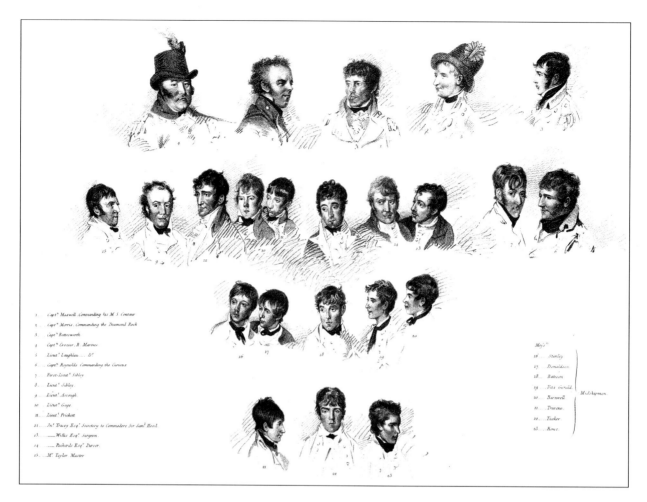

1   Capt.ⁿ Maxwell Commanding his M S Centaur

2   Capt.ⁿ Morris Commanding the Diamond Rock

3   Capt.ⁿ Bettesworth

4   Capt.ⁿ Crozier R Marines

5   Lieut.ᵗ Laughlan .... Dᵒ

6   Capt.ⁿ Reynolds Commanding the Curieux

7   First-Lieut.ᵗ Sibley

8   Lieut.ᵗ Sibley

9   Lieut.ᵗ Aceough

10   Lieut.ᵗ Gage

11   Lieut.ᵗ Prickett

12   Jnᵒ Tracey Esq.ʳ Secretary to Commodore Sir Sam.ˡ Hood

13   —— Willes Esq.ʳ Surgeon

14   —— Richards Esq.ʳ Purser

15   M.ʳ Taylor Master

Mey'ʳ

16 .... Stanley

17 .... Donaldson

18 .... Bateson

19 .... Fitz Gerald

20 .... Barnwell

21 .... Truscow

22 .... Tucker

23 .... Rowe.

Midshipmen

Some of the officers involved in the capture of Diamond Rock, off Martinique, in 1804. (NMM 2066)

James Cook) started as mates in the merchant service and entered the Royal Navy to become masters' mates and then commissioned officers. Others, including Nelson and Admiral Keith, served part of their time in merchant ships at times when naval postings were rare, and up to three years in the merchant service counted towards seniority in the Royal Navy. The rest of the commissioned sea officers – the future lieutenants, commanders, captains and admirals - served at least six years in the Royal Navy before being commissioned.

Adam Smith was sceptical about the status of a naval officer in 1776, when he wrote, 'The great admiral is less the object of publick admiration than the great general, and the highest success in the sea service promises a less brilliant fortune and reputation than equal success on land....By the rules of precedency a captain in the navy ranks with a colonel in the army; but he does not rank with him in the common estimation.'[1] Jane Austen records a change in attitude by 1814. She was close to the navy, having two brothers at sea, and her observation of the social life of the era is extremely acute. It has much in common with the picture painted by Patrick O'Brian, especially in *Post Captain*. True, she never shows the horrors experienced by Jack Aubrey – pursuit by bailiffs, debtor's prison, and even the pillory – but the fear of this is at the root of Mrs Bennett's constant refrain in *Pride and Prejudice* – 'What is to become of us all?'

Austen writes about the status of the army and militia officer in *Pride and Prejudice*, and the naval officer in *Persuasion* and *Mansfield Park*. Unfortunately she never compares the two, but no-one could read *Persuasion* without feeling that there had been significant changes over the last forty years or so. At the beginning of the book, Sir Walter Elliot is firmly against the navy. 'Yes, it is on two points offensive to me; I have two strong grounds

of objection to it. First, as being a means of bringing persons of obscure birth into undue distinction, and raising men to honours which their fathers and grandfathers never dreamt of; and secondly, as it cuts up a man's youth and vigour most horribly; a sailor grows old sooner than any other man.'[2] But Sir Walter has already been revealed as a snob and a fool. We are soon introduced to Admiral Croft and his brother-in-law Captain Wentworth, both admirable characters, and Wentworth is all the more acceptable because of his £20,000 in prize money. He soon finds suitors, including eventually Anne Elliot who had been forced to reject him some years earlier because he 'had no fortune'.[3]

In the 1930s, as C S Forrester began his Hornblower series and started modern naval fiction, the training of naval officers was rigid and centralised:

> For the most part what emerged was a definite breed of fit, tough, highly trained but sketchily educated professionals, ready for instant duty, for parades or tea parties, for catastrophes, for peace or war; confident leaders, alert seamen, fair administrators, poor delegators; officers of wide interests and narrow vision, strong on tactics, weak on strategy; an able, active, cheerful, monosyllabic elite.[4]

This world is perhaps reflected in the Hornblower novels, which portray a navy of rigid discipline and officers of limited resources – even the hero himself has severe restrictions in the social field. Patrick O'Brian's heroes have their share of flaws too, but the navy is very different – mutiny and disorder are never far from the surface, danger always threatens and sometimes only the charisma of the individual officers prevents collapse and defeat.

Most important of all, Patrick O'Brian's navy reflects the great variety among naval officers. In the first half of the twentieth century, nearly all regular officers trained at Dartmouth to a common syllabus. They began at about thirteen, as did Jack Aubrey's contemporaries, but spent several years in classrooms before they went to sea. In the navy of Nelson's day, the Naval Academy at Portsmouth trained an insignificant proportion of officers, for example Frances and Charles Austen, but it contributed little to a career and merely delayed the entry to the real navy and the beginning of seniority. The rest learned the trade by a kind of apprenticeship to an individual captain. The Admiralty had virtually no control over entry, and very little over the actual training given. Today we would expect naval officers to be socially conservative with a small and often a large C. In an earlier age Thomas Cochrane, Earl of Dundonald, who was the model for Jack Aubrey's exploits in *Master and Commander*, became a Radical MP. Yet his protégé, Frederick Marryat, was essentially a conservative.

ENTRY

A young man's family would often debate the advantages in a naval career, as George Elphinstone's did in 1769. After he returned from a voyage in his brother's East Indiaman, they considered whether he should return to the Navy or stay in the service of the East India Company. Earl Marischal, his great-uncle, had no doubt that the Royal service offered more honour, if the Company seemed more lucrative; but there would be family debates about it:

> …my lady will be of opinion to continue in the service of the Company as least dangerous; your father will say that in time of peace there is less danger in the navy as well as more honour - that you will mostly be at home; and that in time of war you will be exposed to fight in the service of the Company, and the ship not fitted for fighting.[5]

A cousin, Charles Gascoigne of the Carron Iron Company, pointed out that in the navy his education was free, a great advantage to an impoverished aristocratic family.

The son's inclinations towards the sea life were also important, at a time when the Royal Navy was far more successful than the army, when it offered an unrivalled chance to travel and was the country's main defence. Thomas Cochrane entered against the wishes of his father, who had once served as a naval lieutenant but wanted his son to enter the army. Basil Hall wrote, 'The holidays, also, which released me from the irksome confinement of the High School of Edinburgh, were passed in the country, on a part of the rugged sea-coast of Scotland, peculiarly calculated to foster nautical propensities. During the weary months which preceded and followed these six delicious weeks of liberty, my thoughts, instead of being devoted to the comprehension of the abstract rules of grammar...invariably strayed back to the picturesque and iron-bound shore...'[6]

The boy's temperament had to be daring and active. Like Nelson, Frances Austen had begun life as a spirited youth, as described by his admiring sister:

Fearless of danger and braving pain,
And threaten'd very oft in vain[7]

A boy's entry to the navy cost a certain amount of money. Thomas Cochrane needed £100 for his whole outfit in 1793, furnished by the Earl of Hopetoun who also had relatives in the navy. Jeffrey de Raigersfield was provided with a 'large chest of clothes, which including the ten pounds that was in it, in halfpence and silver, cost my parents one hundred pounds, besides bed and blankets that were bought for me before I left...'[8]

While the navy gave the prospect of wealth and independence to the younger sons of the country gentry, it also offered respectability and military glory to families which were rising from the middle class. Nelson and the Austens were sons of clergymen with limited financial resources and large families, but with connections in the naval administration.

A young man packs his chest to go to sea for the first time, showing the varied reactions from family and servants. Though exaggerated, the kit laid out in front of the chest gives some idea of what a well-equipped midshipman might take. From a series on the career of 'Ben Blockhead', produced by Captain Marryat and George Cruikshanks. (NMM PAD 4721)

Of rival careers, the law demanded expensive training and was not directly in the service of the King. The church demanded a university degree and a good deal of patronage to get on, and natural ability was rather less likely to shine through than in the navy. Medicine also demanded a long training, and had low social prestige. The army needed some expenditure to buy a commission in the first place, and more for each step in rank up to colonel. It had the greatest social prestige of any profession, but little chance of making a large amount of money. It was often the chosen career for the eldest son of a landed family, for it could be taken up or set down more easily than a naval career, as estate and family demanded.

There were geographical influences in the choice of profession. Most naval officers came from the counties of Kent, Hampshire, Devon and Cornwall or the City of London, in the vicinity of the great naval ports. About 20% came from Scotland, where the combination of possible wealth and royal service was particularly attractive to a declining aristocracy with many younger sons, like Lords Cochrane and Keith. Inland counties of England like Worcestershire and Shropshire produced very few officers per head of population, as did northern English ones such as Yorkshire and Westmoreland. About ten per cent of naval officers came from Ireland, mostly from the Protestant landed gentry.[9]

Naturally the navy was something of a family business, as practically all professions were in those days, but it was not always a simple case of father following son. If the father did well in prize money he might enter the ranks of the landed gentry, in which case he would have other ambitions for his eldest son. Furthermore the officer corps was expanding during the wars, and many boys from other backgrounds were able to enter. Thus Nelson's captains during the Nile campaign of 1798 included one cousin of a Viscount, six sons of the landed gentry, five from the professional middle classes and two from the 'lower orders'.[10] Only about a quarter of naval officers were the sons of naval officers in those days, though they tended to reach higher rank than the sons of other professions.[11]

For a young man needed a patron of some kind, at least a captain to give him a start in his first ship. Others had higher-placed patrons, perhaps a relative in the naval administration. Nelson's uncle Maurice Suckling was Controller of the Navy and manipulated young Horatio's career from afar, to give him a very thorough and varied training, as well as opportunities for quick promotion. Frances and Charles Austen were supported by Lord Gambier, married to their mother's cousin, and a Lord of the Admiralty from 1795 to 1801. In 1798, while Charles was a midshipman, their sister Jane wrote:

> I am sorry that our dear Charles begins to feel the Dignity of ill usage. – My father will write to Admiral Gambier. – He must already have received so much satisfaction from his acquaintance with & Patronage of Frank, that he will be delighted I dare say to have another of the family introduced to him.[12]

CAPTAINS' SERVANTS AND VOLUNTEERS

The first stage in a naval officer's career was to be taken on in a particular ship as a trainee officer, at the age of around thirteen. Until 1794 these boys were known as 'captain's servants' and a captain was allowed four for every hundred men in his ship – 24 in a 74-gun ship, eight in a small frigate. Only a few of these were domestic servants. For the rest, the term was used to mean something like an apprentice rather than a servant as known today – they were trainee officers, doing the three years necessary before being rated as a midshipman. The boys were Volunteers First Class after 1794, but the system changed little. Popularly they were known as 'younkers.'

It was common, especially for those with relatives in the sea service, to have one's name borne fictitiously on the books of a ship for several years before actually joining. Thomas Cochrane's name appeared in the muster book of several of his uncle's ships for some years before he actually joined at the advanced age of 17. This allowed him a quick promotion to midshipman.

Often the arrival at the midshipman's or volunteer's berth of a ship was a shock. Jeffery de Raigersfeld describes the accommodation in the *Mediator*:

> The place where I messed was upon the orlop deck, in a space left between the sheet and small bower cable tiers; a piece of old canvas was nailed up to the beams, and served as a screen to the berth, and my hammock was slung or hung up alongside the sail room over the spare oars, close to the forepart of the main hatchway on the larboard side. My messmates consisted of one mate, four grown-up midshipmen, a younker who had been at sea, myself, and a blackguard boy, that served the mess as cook and all else besides.[13]

On a well-run ship he would spend his days learning navigation and mathematics under the master and schoolmaster, being trained in ropework and elementary seamanship by an experienced man, and climbing the rigging to take in sails and act as a lookout. Even at this stage he had a certain amount of authority, which not all could cope with. Seaman William Robinson of the 74-gun *Revenge* describes a young tyrant in 1805: 'He was a youth of not more than twelve or thirteen years of age: but I have often seen him get on the carriage of a gun, call a man to him, and kick him about the thighs and body, and with his fist would beat him about the head; and these, though prime seamen, at the same time dared not murmur.' He was Edward F Brook, registered in the muster book as 13 years old. During the rapid expansion of the navy there must have been many appointments of unsuitable officers.

MIDSHIPMEN

In theory a young man should serve at least three years at sea, in either the Royal or the merchant navy, before being rated midshipman. After his promotion he was allowed a place in the midshipman's berth and would take some responsibility as a junior officer in the ship, though not yet commissioned. He would serve as an assistant to the officer of the watch, would command one of the ship's boats and supervise a group of seamen for health and welfare purposes as part of the divisional system. In action he would command a group of the ship's guns, or take charge of signals, or act as a messenger for the captain.

A midshipmen's berth in 1821. Dress is probably rather more formal than it had been during the wars, but it gives a good impression of the overcrowding, and the pranks which the young men played on one another. As usual, there is a black servant. From a print by G Humphrey. (NMM PW 3730)

Ben Blockhead sent to the masthead as a punishment, and feeling the effects of exhaustion and perhaps seasickness. (NMM PU 4833)

The quality of a midshipman's training varied greatly from ship to ship. Captain Edward Codrington of the 74-gun *Orion* allowed the youngsters:

...to take charge of the deck in the day time, taking care of course, that he or the Commander or First Lieutenant or Master were in sight, in case of anything going wrong. Nothing so habituates a young boy to consider the nature and casualties of his profession or his practice. A squall to windward, what shall I do? Are the men at their stations to shorten sail? A vessel is crossing us, will she weather? Are we on tack to bear up or hold the wind? Are the yards properly braced up, and the bowlines hauled? Are the topgallant sheets home and the jib taut up? What shall I do if the captain tells me to shorten, or make sail? And a thousand such like cogitations exercise a boy's mind in a way which walking to leeward and repeating orders could never affect.[14]

Frederick Marryat's services under Lord Cochrane between 1806 and 1809 were as active as any hero of naval fiction. In the Mediterranean he was 'Employed in more than fifty engagements with the enemy in which 16 batteries and signal posts were destroyed and many armed vessels and merchantmen cut out. Was twice wounded in these services. In the defence of the Castle of Rosas by Lord Cochrane.' Off the coast of France, 'In one of the explosion vessels which was laid against the boom previous to the fire ships being sent to the attack of the French fleet at Basque Roads. Also in the action of the following day.' Later, 'In the expedition to Walcheren I was attacked by fever and sent home.'[15] Life in a crack ship could be expensive and Marryat wrote to his father, 'the midshipmen keep up a most extravagant mess in my opinion and I must either pay or quit it since I have been on the ship I have paid £25 for mess.'[16]

Marryat's most famous fictional character, Midshipman Easy, is not precisely modelled on Cochrane, for Marryat did not know Cochrane until he was already an experienced captain. But Easy is perhaps a caricature of what Marryat imagined Cochranes's youth must

have been like – a well-connected young man with an inventor father and outrageously rad-ical politics, who entered the navy rather late in life and had little understanding of naval dis-cipline, but who mastered the trade very quickly. The essential difference was that Cochrane's family was impoverished, Easy's was rich. Marryat was probably reflecting a gen-eral view when one of his characters says of Easy, 'A young man possessing such ample means will never be fitted for the duties of a naval officer.'[17]

A senior midshipman might take slightly more responsibility, and earn higher pay, by being rated Master Mate. Though some holders of this rating were on the way to the war-rant rank of Master, a large proportion were preparing for commissioned rank as Lieutenants.

Thomas Cochrane, Earl of Dundonald, one of the great-est, and most ambiguous, naval heroes of the wars.
(NMM PAD 4567)

THE EXAMINATION

The oral examination for lieutenant was one of the great ordeals of an officer's career. Some officers found they could get by with the help of family or naval friends on the examining board, but Captain Charles Middleton, later First Sea Lord, would ask among other questions:

> You are sent in a ship ordered to be fitted out, the Captain not having appeared; the lower masts and bowsprit are in but not rigged: What part of the rigging goes first over the mast heads?
> Upon receiving orders to sail from Spithead with a south-east wind, at what time of tide will you begin to unmoor that you may have the advantage of it in plying down to St Helens?
> Your sails are still all set; the wind begins to freshen: what sails will you take in first?[18]

William Badcock was examined in May 1805 by three captains including Sir Andrew Snape Hammond, 'whose character for turning mids back frightened me not a little.' He met a failed midshipmen on his way out, and entered nervously. The questioning began:

> I was ordered to find the time of high water at Plymouth, work an azimuth amplitude, double altitude, bearings and distances, &c., which being performed, I was desired to stand up, and consider myself on the quarter-deck of a man-of-war at Spithead - "unmoor" - "get underway" - "stand out to sea" - "make and shorten sail" - "reef" - "return into port" - "unrig the foremast and bowsprit, and rig them again." I got into a scrape after reefing for not overhauling the reef tack-les when hoisting the sails. However, they passed me, and desired me to come again the next day to receive my passing certificate. I made the captains the best bow I could, and, without staying to look behind me, bolted out of

the room, and was surrounded in a moment by the other poor fellows, who were anxiously waiting their turn to be called in for examination, who asked what questions had been put to me, and the answers I made, &c.

But there was no suitable vacancy and Badcock remained in his ship as a 'passed midshipman', as many did.

LIEUTENANTS

The first lieutenant was the second in command of each ship, ready to take command if the captain was unable to do his duty. Unless that happened, his main duties were administrative. According to Captain John Davie in 1804, 'As he is the executive officer who regulates the ship's company, he should endeavour to ascertain each man's ability, to acquire the number of effective men, and then dispose of them accordingly.'[19] He drew up the watch, quarter and station bills which allotted tasks to every man during every possible evolution, and kept a record of the men's messes. In return he was free from watchkeeping duties and could sleep most nights in relative comfort.

The most important duty of a lieutenant, apart from the first lieutenant, was to serve as officer of the watch, taking charge of the ship for a four-hour spell. His main concern was the efficient sailing of the ship. According to Captain Capel's orders for the frigate *Phoebe*, 'The officers of the watch are to pay the strictest attention that the sails are well set, topsail sheets close home, jib and staysails taut up, and whenever a jib or staysail is hauled down, it is to be immediately neatly stowed.' He was to muster the men twice during each watch and to keep them on deck, except in bad weather when they were allowed to shelter under the half-deck.[20]

Watch duty was an exacting test of an officer's competence, for mistakes could not be concealed in front of nearly half the ship's company. An officer who made mistakes or was excessively fussy would soon attract the criticism of the crew. In the *Royal George* in 1782, for example, Lieutenant Monins Hollingberry was known as 'Jib and foresail Jack' because, according to one of the men, 'he would be always bothering the men to alter the sails, and it was 'up jib' and 'down jib' and 'up foresail' and 'down foresail' every minute'.[21]

Outside watchkeeping hours, a lieutenant was in charge of a division of the ship's company, of perhaps a hundred men. Divisions were assembled at least once a week on most ships, and the officers inspected the clothing and the cleanliness of the men.

OFFICERS' LIVING CONDITIONS

A lieutenant lived in the wardroom of a ship of the line, or the gunroom of a frigate, along with the marine officers and higher-grade warrant officers such as masters, surgeons and pursers. Chaplain Edward Mangin describes the wardroom of the 74-gun *Gloucester* in 1812:

It is usually in a line-of-battle ship, about 35 feet in length, and 16 or 18 feet wide. Within the walls, which are of painted canvas, are the cabins of six officers; the centre of the room is occupied by the mess-table; and the extremity, under the stern windows, by a projection called the rudder-head. The opposite end is so arranged as to do office as a side-board; with the door of entrance on one side of it; and a space to sling a quarter-cask of wine, on the other.[22]

A Lieutenant in full dress uniform, with white lapels. He is carrying a quadrant, the predecessor of the sextant, made mostly of wood and covering a smaller arc than the sextant. (NMM A5596)

The gunroom of a frigate was rather smaller, and a deck lower so that it had no stern windows, and very little natural light. In either a ship of the line or a frigate, however, each officer had his own tiny cabin. In a ship of the line most of those allocated to the senior officers were along the side of the wardroom, and most had to be shared with a gun.

In contrast to the seaman who could change his mess almost at will, the junior officer's social life was confined to a dozen or so men of roughly equal rank – the naval lieutenants, marine officers, master, surgeon, purser and later the chaplain. With such a small groups serving together perhaps for years, tiny conflicts were often magnified into real quarrels, and almost every account of wardroom life suggests conflict between the inhabitants. On board one ship, a dispute over whether women of the West End of London were superior to those of the East End led eventually to a court martial. Captain Griffiths warned, 'It is a notorious and melancholy fact, that in several instances of mutiny, it has been traced, if not to have positively originated in the conversations of the wardroom mess.' Surgeon Robert Gillespie, who later served under Nelson in the Mediterranean Fleet, said goodbye to his ship in 1787. 'Thus after three years and four months spent on board the *Racehorse* I left her without regret, rather rejoicing that my military bondage and narrow confinement within a sloop's wretched gunroom had expired, and sincerely wishing that I might never more be necessitated to serve on board a man of war.' Chaplain Edward Mangin wrote of his mess, 'I have as yet designedly omitted to mention our second lieutenant of the ship; we greatly disliked each other, I believe mutually'. Lieutenant James Anthony Gardner served with dozens of officers over the years, including some he described as 'crabbed as the devil', 'waspish, snappish and disagreeable' or 'a snapish cur.' He knew one purser who insisted on taking his meals by himself, and showed fear when anyone approached him. Pictures of wardrooms suggest formality and indifference at best, or open conflict at worst.

PROMOTION

There was no regular system of assessing officers for promotion beyond the rank of lieutenant – no annual appraisals, no examinations, nothing formal to distinguish one officer from another. This was good enough in the much smaller navy of Samuel Pepys's time, but not for a force

of over 140,000 men and more than 4500 commissioned officers, many of them serving well away from home. Yet the Admiralty remained the source of all promotion of commissioned officers, a power delegated to a certain extent to the commanders-in-chief on overseas stations.

It was necessary for a lieutenant to attract the attention of the authorities with power of promotion, and essentially there were two ways of doing this. Those with influence could arrange to be posted to the flagship of an overseas commander-in-chief, where they would rise to become first lieutenant and then be promoted to the first vacancy for a commander, as Nelson did in 1771, to become the youngest commander in the navy. Others with slightly less influence, or on home stations, could use contacts within the Admiralty. Again the Austen family used the services of Admiral Gambier to get their sons promoted, and Jane wrote in 1798:

> Frank is made. – He was yesterday raised to the Rank of Commander, & appointed to the Peterel Sloop, now at Gibraltar. A letter from Mr. Daysh [a clerk in the naval administration] has just announced this, and it is confirmed by a very friendly one from Mr Mathew to the same effect transcribing one from Admiral Gambier to the General.[23]

Many officers had very little influence outside their own ship, and had to follow a very slow and uncertain route by becoming first lieutenant of a ship through seniority, and then being promoted when the ship distinguished herself in battle. This was a policy which had been introduced by Lord Anson in the 1750s. It had both advantages and disadvantages; in particular, there was no guarantee that a ship would find an opportunity for such distinction.

There seems to have been a group of highly competent and experienced senior lieutenants who were much sought after as first lieutenants, but had little immediate hope of promotion. One such was William Pryce Cumby, from a family which was struggling hard to climb the naval ladder. His grandfather had been a master, his father a captain and two of his mother's brothers were lieutenants. Born in Dover, he entered the service at the age of 13. In the Mediterranean Fleet he was known as a 'Merry, clever little fellow' and an 'excellent officer'. He produced a Biblical satire on St Vincent's style of leadership. Copies were circulated until it came to his lordship's notice. He forced Cumby to read it out to the assembled captains, much to his horror and their amusement. Then St Vincent, who was not lacking in a rather cruel humour, gravely pronounced a verdict:

> Lieutenant Cumby, you are unanimously found guilty, *and without a court martial, Sir,* of parodying the Holy Writ, and that too for the purpose of bringing your commander-in-chief into ridicule …The sentence, therefore, upon you, *without a trial,* I do adjudge, - that for this your offence you have my permission of three months leave of absence in England, to, I hope, amuse yourself there, as you have amused me here; and that, on the day in which you report yourself returned, you do me the honour of dining with me.[24]

Cumby resumed his service but for the next five years his career was patchy until he became first lieutenant of the *Bellerophon*. At 33 he must have felt that promotion was passing him by, unless he could distinguish himself in action. This he did at Trafalgar, taking command when his captain was killed and earning an instant promotion to captain.[25]

Another was John Quillam, a Manxman who had entered the navy through the lower deck and served with Peter Heywood of *Bounty* fame. He was in the frigate *Amazon* at the Battle of Copenhagen and soon attracted the notice of Nelson, who had him appointed first lieutenant of the *Victory* in 1803. At 32 he was older than the run of lieutenants and could bring experience and maturity to the job. Being without influence, he was not likely to be whisked away to take command of a sloop and he provided the stability which Nelson needed. Like Cumby his reward came after Trafalgar, when he was promoted commander and then captain in rapid succession.

COMMANDERS

A commander was the officer in charge of a ship which was able to carry at least ten guns, but was too small to be rated. In its original form the rank was titled 'master and commander', implying command of a small ship which was too small to carry a master in addition to a captain, and therefore needed a captain who had risen from the ranks of the masters. By the 1740s it was a regular rank, a step on the way to full, or 'post' captain. It is significant that there were only 586 commanders in the navy in 1812, compared with 777 captains, reversing the usual pyramid structure of an armed force. It implies that most commanders quickly moved on to higher rank. However further promotion was not a foregone conclusion. Many commanders had been promoted for service in battle, rather than to fill any actual vacancies, so there was something of a promotion block and some found it difficult to get back to sea. Even then, unless the original service was distinguished enough, or influence was powerful enough to warrant a further promotion soon afterwards, a commander had to distinguish himself yet again. Even then there could be difficulties. After the capture of the *Gama*, Lord Cochrane was denied the promotion due to him for some time, almost certainly on the orders of St Vincent who was now First Lord of the Admiralty. When told 'We must make Lord Cochrane "post"' he replied 'The First Lord of the Admiralty knows *no must*.'[26]

CAPTAINS

In the fiction of the age of sail, the main heroes are invariably commissioned sea officers – lieutenants, captains and admirals. The major exception is Stephen Maturin the doctor, who shares the main role in the Patrick O'Brian novels. Nearly always, except when the author is describing the early career of a future hero, the central characters are captains or at least commanders. Most often they are officers on detached service, who have a great deal of freedom to make decisions on their own. C S Forester, the founder of modern naval fiction, was obsessed with the idea of 'the man alone' and made Horatio Hornblower a very introverted character who shunned the company of even his own officers. 'This voyage he had started with the firm resolve (like a drinker who cannot trust himself to drink only in moderation) to say nothing whatever to his officers except what was necessitated by routine…'[27] Patrick O'Brian's Jack Aubrey is very different in character. He has no taste for introspection, he is surrounded by an entourage of junior officers, proteges and servants, and he takes an intimate friend, Stephen Maturin, to sea with him on most voyages. But what the two heroes share is a need and an ability to make daring and ingenious decisions in the face of great danger, without any opportunity to refer to higher authority, and in that sense they both have to work alone.

In fact most captains worked with fleets for most of the time, and often their tactical initiative was very tightly controlled. But each captain was a supreme authority in his own ship, and his character was thrown into sharp relief. Captain Hugh Pigot of the *Hermione* flogged the last two men off the yardarm and provoked a vicious mutiny in which he and most of his officers were murdered – the *Surprise* gained real-life fame by recapturing the ship from the Spaniards. Captain Corbett took part in the Mauritius campaign of 1809 in the frigate *Neriede* but had very bad relations with his crew because of excessive punishment, which led to a court martial. He was eventually killed in action in command of the *Africaine*, and it was never established which side fired the fatal shot. For a while Frank Marryat was commanded by John Taylor of the 18-gun *Espeigle*, a flogging tyrant.

If such men attracted much publicity, they were more than balanced by the good leadership and humanity of others. Captain Anselm Griffiths wrote in 1811:

> Seamen are nowadays a thinking set of people and a large portion of them possess no inconsiderable share of common sense, the most useful sense after all. They are certainly capable of judging when they are well treated, whether those in authority over them exercise it with mildness and a due attention to their comforts, and it is natural to suppose they sit lighter under the yoke of a man who they see knows and does his duty.[28]

ADMIRALS

Whereas promotion up to the rank of captain depended on a peculiar and complex combination of interest and ability, after that it was perfectly simple and depended entirely on length of service, dated from the crucial moment when an officer was promoted captain. The

An admiral's full dress uniform of the 1795-1812 pattern, worn by Sir William Cornwallis, and a captain's full dress of 1812-1830, with white facings. (NMM C 9550)

only possible interruption to this, apart from death or court martial, was to be pushed aside as a 'yellow admiral' – promoted to rear admiral of no specific squadron, with half-pay to match but no hope of ever being employed at sea in the rank.

Apart from that there were four ranks of admiral – Admiral of the Fleet, Admiral, Vice-Admiral and Rear-Admiral, and three 'squadrons' – red, white and blue – within each rank. Thus an officer would be appointed Rear-Admiral of the Blue, entitled to fly as blue flag at the mizzen mast, and through time to Rear-Admiral of the White and Rear Admiral of the Red, until at last becoming Vice-Admiral of the Blue, and going through the whole process again. There was no Admiral of the Red until 1810, for the role was taken by the most senior rank of all, Admiral of the Fleet. It was a system which, like many other naval ranks, had originated during the Dutch Wars of the mid seventeenth century, when the whole fleet fought as a single unit. It was modified in the 1740s, when more than one officer was appointed to each grade. By 1812 there was only one Admiral of the Fleet, but 21 Admirals of the Red, 24 Vice Admirals of the Blue and 17 Rear-Admirals of the White among a total of 187 flag officers on the active list.

WARRANT OFFICERS

Apart from marines, the sea officers were the only ones in the navy who bore the King's commission. All the specialist officers, from physicians and surgeons to caulkers and cooks, were technically warrant officers, appointed by the Navy Board on the advice of bodies like the College of Surgeons and Trinity House which regulated the individual professions and trades. There were essentially three categories of warrant officer. At the top were the professional men, the master, surgeon and purser of each ship, who had done most of their training outside the navy and lived in the wardroom with the commissioned officers. Below them were the standing officers, the boatswain, gunner and carpenter, who had almost invariably served on the lower deck. They stayed with the ship when it was out of commission for maintenance purposes, hence the name. They tended to mess together, forming a separate group from both their superiors and juniors. Below them were various craftsmen and officials – caulkers, coopers, sailmakers, cooks and masters-at-arms for example, who had warrants from the Navy Board to protect them from disrating by the captain, but were essentially members of the lower deck.

MASTERS

The master of each ship was an experienced seaman who had probably learned his trade in the merchant service. He was responsible for the navigation of the ship in the broadest sense, which included handling it in confined waters and in difficult situations. He was responsible for the trim of the ship, and therefore the stowage of the hold. The master of Marryat's *Aspasia* was:

> In external appearances, a rough, hard-headed north-countryman; but, with an unpromising exterior, he was a man of sense and feeling. He had every requisite for his situation; his nerves were like a chain-cable; he was correct and zealous in his duty; and a great favourite of the captain's who was his countryman. He was about fifty years of age, a married man with a large family.[29]

The master's status was as high as any officer in the ship, except the captain and the first lieutenant. In a ship of the line he usually had one of the aftermost cabins in the wardroom. Marryat writes:

The rank of master in the service is above that of a midshipman, but still the midshipman is a gentleman by birth, and the master, generally speaking, is not. Even at this moment, in the service, if the master were to d—n the eyes of a midshipman, and tell him that he was a liar, would there be any redress, or if so, would it be commensurate to the insult? If a midshipman were to request a court-martial, would it be granted? Certainly not.[30]

PURSERS

Pursers were the supply officers of ships. Unlike other officers they were not paid straightforward salaries; a purser was paid less than half that of a master, for example. He was expected to make up the difference by making a profit on certain transactions, for example on unconsumed portions of food. Not surprisingly, pursers as a group had a reputation among the crew for meanness and fraud. The purser issued food, beer and spirits to the crew, and sold them clothes (slops) and tobacco. At home the job was relatively simple as provisions were issued from the Victualling yards near the naval bases, and the purser had no difficulty in finding supplies of candles, coal, bedding and wooden bowls for the crew. In foreign waters, for example the Mediterranean, their work could be quite complex, as he negotiated for supplies with lukewarm allies or precarious neutrals, in transactions involving exotic weights and measures and various foreign currencies. As purser of the *Victory* from 1795-98, Richard Thomas's accounts included:

Mr Marsh, the Purser of the 100-gun *Queen Charlotte* when she was destroyed by fire in 1800. (NMM PAH 4888)

To firewood at San Fiorenzo, 37 crowns, 12 Spanish dollars, 2 livres and 1 sol, see receipt.
To Mr Warner's expense in carrying hides from the landing to Mr Heatly's at San Fiorenzo
To greens etc at San Fiorenzo
To a chest at Leghorn for keeping books and papers free from mice and cockroaches.[31]

SURGEONS

Surgeons were the medical officers of the navy – each ship with more than about 60 men in its crew had one, with a mate (also a fully-qualified surgeon) for every 200 men or so. A surgeon was far inferior to a physician in status, skilled at amputation, bleeding and not much else. Most entered the trade by means of apprenticeship rather than university degree, and many naval surgeons came from Scotland, where the education system tended to be better than in other parts of the United Kingdom.

Surgeons often had little to do in a healthy ship which was not involved in battle, and it is not surprising that they developed their own interests. Marryat's Mr Macallan was overqualified by normal standards, with a university degree. He was 'deservedly a great favourite' with a particular captain and sailed regularly with him. He was a devotee of natural history, and sometimes fell into the water while pursuing his subject. He was also a sincere Christian. Lest one should go too far in seeing him as a model for Stephen Maturin, it should be noted that he was a Scotsman, like many other naval surgeons.[32]

Above the surgeon was the physician, normally university-trained. There were only four fully trained physicians in the navy in the early 1790s, all acting as Physician of the Fleet, the senior medical officer. Leonard Gillespie was an Irishman who had served as surgeon of the sloop *Racehorse* from 1787-91. Like many surgeons he pursued his own course of study,

A surgeon's medicine chest. Like all officers and craftsmen, a surgeon was expected to provide most of his tools and equipment. (NMM D 7562 B)

though in his case he believed it was highly relevant to his profession. He believed that changes in weather had a profound effect on health, and made copious notes on how this affected his patients:

> For three days we have had a horizon free of clouds, a bright sun, a frosty, dry air, wind in the east and SE quarters. The consequence of this change in air on the state of man's health is remarkable enough. Several are affected with hoarseness of three days, some with coughs, some with rheumatism. The melancholic seem affected with excurbations. Constipation of the belly is frequent. My venereals are getting better.[33]

He left the *Racehorse* with 'a large medicine chest. A black trunk, leather, containing linen clothes and some books, a hair trunk, containing a case of instruments, a writing box, books, two cases of books, a cot with feather bed and two pillows…' He was not sorry to go. 'I left her without regret, rather rejoicing that my military bondage and my narrow confinement within a sloop's wretched gunroom had expired, and sincerely wishing that I might never more be necessitated to serve on board a ship of war where, alas, indolence, intemperance, spleen, envy etc too often infect the crew and spread unhappiness and discord.'

Despite this, Gillespie quickly returned to naval service in larger ships. He had already studied medicine at St Andrews and Edinburgh, so he was well qualified when he was appointed physician to Nelson's Mediterranean Fleet in 1803. This seemed to change his outlook on life and he wrote to his sister:

> Breakfast is announced in the Admiral's cabin, where Lord Nelson, Rear-Admiral Murray, the Captain of the Fleet, Captain Hardy, Commander of the *Victory*, the

Chaplain, the secretary, one or two officers of the ship, and your humble servant assemble and breakfast on tea, hot rolls, cold tongue etc., after which, when finished, we repair upon deck to enjoy the majestic sight of the rising sun (scarcely ever obscured by clouds in this fine climate) surmounting the smooth and placid waves of the Mediterranean which supports the lofty and tremendous bulwarks of Britain, following in regular train their Admiral in the *Victory*.

CHAPLAINS

Chaplains were quite rare in the fleet before 1812, for their pay was poor and they did not even have the automatic right to live in the wardroom. Nevertheless Nelson, himself a deeply religious man, tended to ensure that he had a chaplain in his flagship and this seems to have filtered down to his captains for about half his ships at Trafalgar had chaplains. Like surgeons, chaplains were educated men who entered the navy late in life, and were often deeply touched by what they saw, so they provide excellent witnesses to the age of sail. The Reverend Cooper Willyams took part in the Nile campaign in the 74-gun *Swiftsure* and wrote a detailed account of the Battle of the Nile and the events leading up to it. Edward Mangin joined the *Gloucester* in 1812 after the chaplain's conditions had been much improved, but he did not like life in the wardroom, and left after three months. Chaplains were exclusively from the Church of England; the many Scottish seamen had no outlet for their Presbyterian beliefs, while the Roman Catholic religion of the great majority of Irish seamen was considered anti-British and almost subversive in some parts of the fleet.

STANDING OFFICERS

The boatswain was responsible for the rigging of the ship, its care and maintenance, and the supplies of rope and blocks which were used to keep it in good order. He was often better known for his second role, in mustering, disciplining and punishing the crew. Boatswains had almost invariably risen from the ranks, and the tended to make a strong impression on those who served under them. The boatswain of the *Harpy* in *Mr Midshipman Easy* was 'a slight, dapper little man, who, as captain of the foretop, had shown an uncommon degree of courage in a hurricane, so much so, as to recommend him to the admiral for promotion.'[34]

In most ships the boatswain was a 'character' and this is reflected in fiction as well as fact. Marryat's Boatswain Chucks, apparently based on a real individual, had pretensions to gentility, which soon evaporated under pressure:

> "Allow me to observe, my dear man, in the most delicate way in the world, that you are spilling that tar upon the deck – a deck, sir, if I may venture to make the observation, I had the duty of seeing holystoned this morning. You understand me sir, you have defiled His Majesty's forecastle. I must do my duty, sir, if you neglect yours; so take that – and that – and that – (thrashing the man with his rattan) – you d—-d haymaking son of a sea-cook. Do it again, d—-d your eyes, and I'll cut your liver out."[35]

When asked why he swore so much, Chucks pointed out one of the facts of naval hierarchy. The captain and first lieutenant, it was agreed, only swore in an emergency. Chucks answered, "Exactly so; but, sir, their 'mergency is my daily and hourly duty. In the continual working of the ship I am answerable for all that goes amiss. The life of a boatswain is a life of 'mergency, and therefore I swear."[36]

Another of Marryat's boatswains had a 'character of a very peculiar nature.' He had deeply-held Methodist beliefs, 'notwithstanding which he contrived that his duty towards his Maker should not interfere with that of the boatswain of the ship.' He 'had long been considered one of the best boatswains in the service.'[37] Boatswains as a class were notoriously bad at resisting the temptations of drink and corruption. Fifty-five of them were convicted by court martial between 1807 and 1814, compared with 37 carpenters, 24 gunners, 14 pursers and one surgeon.

The carpenter, in turn, was a craftsman who had served an apprenticeship, probably in one of the Royal Dockyards. Nicholas Rodgers of the frigate *Aurora* gave a sample of the duties of his department to his court martial in 1788:

> I went directly to Robert Maynell and asked him what he was going about. He said he was going to make some cleats to hang the cabin ports to, by the captain's order. I told him to get the piece for a stern first and desired Alexander Pain to go and get the bottom boards and stern sheets out of the cutter, as I was going to give her a coat of tar. When I had given them all jobs, I went down to my cabin and fell asleep.

Despite this fine example of delegation, Rodgers was dismissed the service for neglect, disobedience and frequent drunkenness.[38]

If the boatswain was a disciplinarian and the carpenter a craftsman, the gunner often had higher pretensions. According to Marryat's Gunner Tallboys:

> The boatswain and carpenter are merely practical men; but the gunner, sir, is, or ought to be, scientific. Gunnery, sir, is a science – we have our own disparts and our lines of sight – our windage and our parabolas, and projectile forces – and our point blank, and our reduction of powder upon a graduated scale.[39]

William Rivers joined the Royal Navy in 1778, at the age of 23. He had almost certainly spent some time in the merchant service and he was quickly rated master's mate in the 74-gun *Triumph*, with good prospects of promotion to lieutenant after three years in the navy. But early in 1781 he moved sideways to become the gunner of the ship, in charge of the maintenance of the guns, their carriages, tackle, gunpowder and shot. Rivers was promoted to the first rate *Victory* in 1790, as high as a gunner was likely to go. Better educated than the average gunner, his writing was good when he was not in a hurry and he kept meticulous tables on such matters as the composition of fuses, gun carriages, powder allowed for service and salutes, and the making of rockets.

William Richardson was promoted to acting-gunner of the *Prompte* after two years service, though he had 'never been so much as in a gunner's crew.' He could not go forward for the examination until he had completed four years, much to his relief. He studied 'the art of gunnery' from books supplied by his brother, while other officers taught him how to keep accounts. He passed the examination, apparently with ease, a year and a half later.[40]

The warrant officers had to keep detailed accounts of their expenditure of stores, and on the face of it they did so. For example in the week before Trafalgar the carpenter of the 64-gun *Africa* records that he and his mates made a main topgallant studding sail boom after one was carried away, two vanes from wainscot, two thwarts for the jollyboat and a false deck in the head. He used eight staples to repair the rudder, made hammock cleats for the ship's company and repaired the glass in the quarter gallery. Much material was thrown overboard before the battle, including hen coops and some of the crew's tables. In the action the ship lost its foremast and mainmast with all their rigging and many other stores.[41]

There is no way of knowing how much negligence or corruption is concealed in these documents. According to one of Marryat's characters, '…after every action there is more canvas, rope, and paint expended in the warrant-officers's accounts than were destroyed by the enemy.…How are we to have white hammock-cloths, skysail masts, and all other finery, besides a coat of paint for the ship's sides every six weeks, if we don't expend all these things in action and pretend they were lost overboard or destroyed?'[42] This implies a kind of 'noble cause' corruption which was put to the use of the ship as a whole, but it would have been just as easy for officers to line their own pockets, with the connivance or ignorance of the captain.

UNIFORMS

In the modern age uniform tends to be worn by the lower ranks of any civil organisation. The management wears none, unless grey suits can be considered a uniform. Even servicemen and women get out of uniform as soon as they finish duty, and this is encouraged by the authorities for fear of terrorism. Attitudes were very different in 1800. People were used to the idea of devoting the whole of their life to a single organisation and the Royal Navy attracted more loyalty than most, at least from its officers. They would not regard it as unusual to wear uniform on leave and when attending social events, and often felt elevated by the status which it gave them. But naval uniform was the prerogative of the officers in those days, and there was none for seamen. They had petitioned for one in 1748 and patterns were soon approved, and changed occasionally to follow civilian or military fashion. At first it applied only to commissioned officers and midshipmen. Warrant officers were granted uniforms by stages – a general blue coat from 1787, then specialised uniforms for sur-

A ship's carpenter, from a well-known series of prints by Rowlandson. (NMM PW 4968)

geons in 1805, and masters and pursers from 1807. This at least ensured that they were treated as officers if taken as prisoners of war.

The status of the officer was marked by a complex system. The midshipman wore a white patch on his collar, perhaps the most enduring of all rank badges. White was also the theme for lieutenants. They wore white lapels in full dress, and white trim in less formal or 'undress' uniform. Commanders wore a single epaulette on the left shoulder from 1795, a captain of less than three years seniority had one on the right shoulder, and a senior captain had one on each shoulder. Admirals had a system of stars on the epaulettes to distinguish grade (though nothing in the uniform told the difference between an admiral of the red, white or blue, or for that matter of the yellow). The admiral also had gold stripes on his lower sleeves – one ring in undress for a rear-admiral, two for a vice-admiral and three for a full admiral. In full dress these were supplemented by a thick ring above and vertical gold stripes leading up to buttons.

Status was important to a naval officer, though uniform was only one way of marking it. The respect of the seamen, the esteem of his fellows in the wardroom, the acclaim of the public and the material rewards of promotion and prize money were all powerful factors in causing him to make almost superhuman efforts in blockade and battle.

Rank distinctions of commissioned officers, 1795-1812.

	Epaulettes	Full Dress			Undress		
		Lapels	Cuffs	Collars	Lapels	Cuffs	Collars
Admiral							
Vice Admiral							
Rear Admiral							
Captain (over three years)							
Captain (under three years)							
Commander							
Lieutenant							
Midshipman	No full dress						

CHAPTER 4

THE LOWER
DECK

The seaman of the age of sail was an exotic creature, commonly regarded as a different race, almost a different species, from the rest of mankind. According to Dr Thomas Trotter:

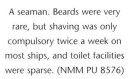

> It is only men of such description, that could undergo the fatigues and perils of a sea life; and there seems a necessity for being inured to it from an early age. The mind, by custom and example, is thus trained to brave the fury of the elements in their different forms, with a degree of contempt at danger and death that is to be met nowhere else. Excluded by the employment which they have chosen from all society but people of similar dispositions, the deficiencies of education are not felt, and information on general affairs is seldom courted. Their pride consists in being reputed a thorough bred seaman; and they look upon all landmen, as beings of inferior order. This is marked, in a singular manner by applying the language of seamanship to every transaction of life, and sometimes with pedantic ostentation. Having little intercourse with the world, they are easily defrauded, and dupes to the deceitful, whenever they go; their money is lavished with the most thoughtless profusion; fine clothes for his girl, a silver watch, and silver buckles for himself, are often the sole return for years of labour and hardship. When his officer refuses him leave to go on shore, his purse is sometimes with the coldest indifference consigned to the deep, that it may no longer remind him of pleasures he cannot command.[1]

A seaman. Beards were very rare, but shaving was only compulsory twice a week on most ships, and toilet facilities were sparse. (NMM PU 8576)

The ordinary sailor of the lower deck is underrepresented in naval fiction, in both the age of Marryat and Chamier and of Forester and O'Brian. It is not that the writers despise the common seamen. Chamier, temporarily reduced to the lower deck in his *Life of a Sailor*, comments, 'Sailors have hearts, and feelings too. I soon found my new acquaintances possessing a good proportion of Christian feeling.'[2] Jack Aubrey also served 'before the mast' for a time as punishment for smuggling a woman on board. That did much to form his attitudes, but it is described in retrospect, not in any detail in the fiction. Captain Hornblower could only imagine such a fate in his most morbid fantasies. Brooding on the possibility of being dismissed his ship by court martial, he concludes, 'He might perhaps ship before the mast, and with his clumsiness and abstraction he would be the victim of the cat, of the boatswain's rattan. Death would be better. He shuddered with cold.'[3] But this never happened. Modern naval fiction deals with officers rather than the lower deck. A recent exception is the work of Julian Stockwin, but it seems not unlikely that his hero Thomas Kydd will be commissioned in due course.

The nineteenth century wave of naval writing was clearly led by officers, including Captains Marryat, Hall and Chamier. It is unfortunate that none of the lower-deck seamen of the age were willing or able to write fiction. But many of them, realising that they had led exciting, dangerous and interesting lives compared with the average landsman, used their pens to produce autobiographies, which collectively form an invaluable historical source and give a uniquely detailed picture of the age.

The officer-novelists of the nineteenth century did not see an insurmountable barrier between the lower deck and the quarterdeck, and sometimes their heroes, such as the young man eventually known as William Seymour in *The King's Own*, move between the two with relative ease. It is perhaps dangerous to read too much into a work of fiction in which the author specifically denies contact with reality; but it does warn us against seeing the early nineteenth century navy through a Victorian historical filter, in which the gulf between the two parts becomes almost unbridgeable.

All good officers knew how much they depended on good crews to achieve their aims, and the sailors themselves shared in the naval triumphs. Samuel Leech called his memoirs *A Voice from the Main Deck*, rather than the more common 'lower deck', perhaps emphasising that seaman were at least as important as officers. Nelson always recognised the value of the lower deck. After his experiences in a merchant ship in his youth he was apt to say, 'Aft the more honour, forward the better man.' As he sailed into the Battle of the Nile in 1798 he was confident of victory because, as he put it, 'I knew what stuff I had under me'. Four years later he acknowledged that his victories were due in part to 'the undaunted courage of the British sailors…I had only to show them the Enemy, and Victory crowned the standard.'[4] Fictional captains were no less aware of the importance of a good crew. In command of the *Hotspur*, Horatio Hornblower delighted that his men were the pick of the press. In the *Sutherland* he despaired of ever running the ship successfully without experienced topmen, until a windfall from some East Indiaman remedied the situation.

BECOMING A SEAMAN

Most sailors started their career in the merchant service and only reluctantly entered the Royal Navy. Many of them came from seafaring families, in an age when it was naturally assumed that a son would follow his father's profession – but unfortunately these were not the sort of men who wrote their memoirs, so we see little of their point of view. Nor was that the whole story. With the great expansion of the merchant service in the decades before 1793, many men from other backgrounds were likely to be recruited. As with officers, it was not the wages which attracted young men. As Adam Smith put it in 1776:

> The lottery of the sea is not altogether so disadvantageous as that of the army. The son of a creditable labourer or artificer may frequently go to sea with his father's consent; but if he enlists as a soldier, it is always without it.…Common sailors, therefore, more frequently get some fortune and preferment than common soldiers; and the hope of these prizes is what principally recommends the trade. Though their skill and dexterity are much superior to that of almost any artificers, and though their whole life is one continual scene of danger and hardship, yet for all the skill, for all the hardships and dangers, while they remain in the condition of common sailors, they receive scarce any other recompense than the pleasure of exercising the one and of surmounting the other. Their wages are not greater than those of common labourers at the port which regulates the rate of seaman's wages.[5]

Often it was the sense of adventure which attracted young boys, and the sight of sailors telling yarns in a local inn was decisive. Samuel Leech was impressed with his cousin George Turner, a seaman of eleven years standing, who turned up at his aunt's house. He was 'A smart, active sailor, over six feet in height and well proportioned', who was 'so jolly, so liberal, and so full of pleasant stories, that I began to feel quite sure that sailors were pleasant fellows.[6]

Most started at the age of twelve or thirteen and thus were 'bred to the sea' and became 'inured to the hardships of a sea life', as common expressions of the time puts it. As Admiral Collingwood found, boys of 14 to 16 years were at an ideal age, strong enough to begin to work hard, but young enough to learn. 'Such boys soon become good seamen: landsmen very rarely do, for they are confirmed in other habits.'[7] Seamanship was like a language. Learning it at the right age is not considered particularly clever, but to become fluent in later life is very difficult.

Marryat's Poor Jack was advised against the navy when he expressed a desire to go to sea:

On board a man of war? You'd soon be sick enough of that. Why, who would be at the beck and nod of others, ordered here, called there, by boy midshipmen; bullied by lieutenants; flogged by captains; have all the work and little of the pay, all of the fighting and less of the prize money.'[8]

Not everyone agreed and Jack's father commented 'Let a man do his duty, and the service is a good one.'[9]

Nevertheless, naval service was generally unpopular with seamen. There is no reason to believe that discipline, food and other conditions were significantly worse than in the merchant navy, but two factors caused problems. One was pay. In peacetime, there was no great difference between naval and merchant pay. In war, however, merchant service pay rose sharply because of the great demand for seamen, while the naval seaman did not have a pay

An allegory on the role of the Marine Society in recruiting orphans or boys from poor families (on the right), equipping them with sailor's clothes (left) and sending them into the navy, in the background. From Marine Society, *A Letter From a Member...* London, 1757. (NMM D 1790)

FOR THE SERVICE OF OUR COUNTRY.

MARINE SOCIETY'S WAREHOUSE

S. Wale delin.t et donavit.   C. Major sculp.t et donavit.

rise for nearly 140 years, from 1658 to 1797. Secondly, the merchant seaman could leave his ship at the end of a voyage, whereas the naval man would probably be transferred from one ship to another until the end of the war, which might be years away. David Hay records an encounter with a recruiting officer in 1811:

"Are you willing to join the King's service?"

"No, sir."

Why?"

Because I can get much better wages in the merchant service and should I be unable to agree with the Captain I am at Liberty to leave him at the end of the voyage."

Hay was eventually persuaded by the officer.

Take my advice, my lad, and enter the service cheerfully, you will then have a bounty, and be in a fair way for promotion. If you continue to refuse, remember you are aboard (cogent reasoning), you will be kept as a pressed man and treated accordingly.[10]

PRESS GANGS

The growth of the Royal Navy in the eighteenth century was constrained by two main factors - the supply of timber for shipbuilding and the supply of skilled and experienced seamen. Both were important enough to cause wars for their own sake - Britain sent fleets to the Baltic several times in order to keep the supply route for naval timber and stores open, and the claim to impress seamen from American ships led directly to the war with America in 1812. Impressment of seamen was founded on the medieval right of the king to call on all his subjects to defend the realm. This still applied to men on land, who could be conscripted by lot to serve in the militia. However, such service was much less onerous than that demanded of the seamen. For the Navy was increasingly important in defence but recruited its key men from a much smaller sector of the population, and often forced them to serve for years away from home against their will.

The majority of naval seamen were either pressed into the navy, or volunteered to avoid the uncertainty and indignity of impressment, or were lured by huge bounties paid on entry. Captain Basil Hall recognised that some believed pressing was a deterrent to becoming a seaman in any capacity:

From the hour they go to sea as boys in a merchant vessel, they become familiarises with the probability, I may almost say certainty, of being impressed into His Majesty's service; and all their measures are taken in that expectation, and the risk I speak of enters into the calculation of their parents as well as their own throughout their whole career. It is indeed alleged that many lads are prevented from becoming sailors by the fear of impressment.[11]

The press gang was the basis of naval recruitment in wartime but two important facts must be remembered about it. Contrary to popular myth it was only allowed to take experienced seamen and in general it followed this rule, as captains had no wish to have large numbers of unskilled landsmen aboard their ships. Secondly, it operated afloat as much as on land, often stopping merchantmen at sea and taking men off them. The nature of impressment was at first misunderstood by the founder of twentieth century naval fiction. In the first of the Hornblower his novels C S Forester wrote of the crew of the *Lydia*, 'three quarters of them had never been sailors until this commission, and had no desire to be sailors either, but had been swept up by the all-embracing press three months ago.'[12] Forester was perhaps crit-

A classically melodramatic (and inaccurate) view of the press gang, in which a man is dragged off from his family. (NMM PAD 4772)

icised by one of the naval historians of the day, for the next novel, *A Ship of the Line*, begins with a detailed and well-researched account of the manning of a ship.

One of Marryat's characters expresses the typical view of a naval officer about impressment as an unfortunate necessity. 'Men must be had for his Majesty's service somehow. It's not their fault, Mr Easy – the navy must be manned, and as things are so, so things must be. It's the King's prerogative, Mr Easy, and we cannot fight the battles of the country without it.'[13] William Burney was prepared to justify impressment in his *Universal Dictionary of the Marine* of 1815:

> Humanity has often raised a plaintive tone against the practice of impressing seamen....He who voluntarily goes to sea, is fully aware beforehand, that the line of life he has chosen subjects him to the impress, and at the same time frees him from the chance of being balloted for the militia: having made his election, he must take his chance of being compelled to serve his country, should his Majesty at any time deem it necessary.[14]

Against this, it was often argued that impressment caused a vicious circle. According to an anonymous pamphleteer in 1810 'the repugnance created and constantly kept up by the Impress, added to its inseparable consequence, confinement on board the ship he is sent to serve in; the man so obtained cannot be trusted on shore for a long time after he comes on board; his imprisonment is thus the inseparable concomitant of the Impress.'[15]

At the beginning of the eighteenth century press gangs were mostly members of the crews of individual ships, operating on behalf of their captain. These gangs were still common in the 1800s. According to Marryat, Seamen that have been pressed themselves into the navy, are invariably the most active in pressing others'.[16] In addition to the ships press gangs were the permanent members of the impress service. This was greatly expanded in 1755, and permanent press gangs were set up the major ports of the United Kingdom under officers appointed by the Admiralty in London. Seamen could be pressed both afloat and ashore. The Impress service operated tenders at most major ports, sending them to the naval anchorages at Portsmouth, Plymouth and the Nore when they were filled with men.

No-one was really happy with the system of impressment, and numerous bills came before Parliament to modify it, but none had any real success. Though impressment was a huge gap in British claims to support liberty of the subject, the average backbencher felt that it was better than the state bureaucracy which would be needed to replace it. The sailor and his employer the merchant tended to prefer a ramshackle system to one which might be rather more difficult to evade.

RESISTANCE TO THE PRESS GANG

Seamen might resist the power of the press gang by hiding or by disguises. According to Marryat, seamen wore 'long togs' when they wanted to look like landsmen to avoid the gang.[17] If it came to the worst, the seaman was already making his plans to desert as soon as he was pressed. According to Marryat, 'it was not the custom for seamen to give their real names when entered or pressed into the service.'[18]

The press gang was not immune to the law of the land, and that might be enforced by magistrates and juries influenced by local merchants, who had no wish to see their seamen taken away. During the hot press of 1803, for example, gangs from the frigate *L'Aigle* landed in the village of Crediton, Devon. The villagers fled in terror and during a scuffle Captain Wolfe fired his pistol. The ship's marines then opened fire and killed three men. An inquest returned a verdict of wilful murder against Captain Wolfe and the gang. The captain and seven men were eventually tried and acquitted.[19]

The seamen might resist the gangs collectively, often with the aid of the local population. On Clydeside in the 1790s, pressing was very difficult for Captain Jahleel Brenton and his gangs. The area had no major naval or military presence and Brenton had a force of two press gangs and two tenders afloat, perhaps forty or fifty men under his command. Without at least some co-operation from local magistrates, his tiny force would soon be overwhelmed by the local population, who were not slow to resist what they regarded as oppression. The magistrates of Greenock did indeed offer some support, in the form of a subscription of £500 to be paid in bounties to men who might volunteer. But they also warned that 'it would be detrimental to his majesty's service to attempt the impressing of seamen on shore and that on the first alarm it would drive all the seamen from the town and prevent them from entering as volunteers.' Brenton informed his superiors that he could not carry out a general impress in the area without much more support, perhaps from the crew of a warship.

Meanwhile, the local population gave notice of their intention to resist. The riggers, caulkers, carpenters and seamen of Greenock had a meeting and 'it was resolved by the whole body to stand by and support each other in case an impress should take place.' In June 'the lower class of people in Greenock became very riotous and proceeded to burn everything that came in their way and about 12 o'clock they hauled one of the boats belonging to the rendezvous on the square and put her into the fire.' It was recovered, much damaged, as the authorities began to restore order, while one of the press gang lieutenants wounded a rioter with his sword.

However, Brenton sent his tenders and gangs out on a 'press from projections', in which, by Admiralty order, the exemptions which were issued to seamen in certain trades, were revoked. At two in the morning of 16 June his boats set out to raid ships in the River between Dumbarton and Largs. They found plenty seamen, but most turned out to be too old for the navy, or to be young apprentices who were still exempt.[20] This was typical of the frustrations felt by many officers, especially those on the fringes of the press gang's power.

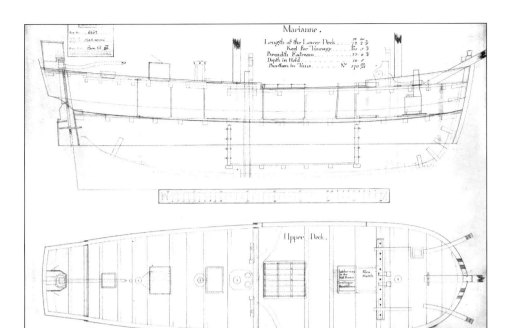

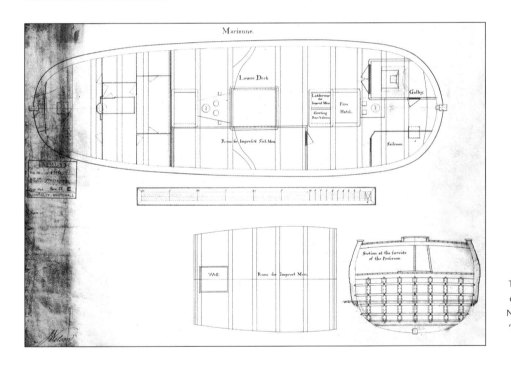

The plans of a pressing tender, date unknown but circa 1800. Note the stout bulkheads in the 'Room for Imprest Men' below decks. (NMM Dr 6650)

THE PRESSING TENDER

Impress service officers tried to get their victims afloat as fast as possible, partly because the power of local magistrates and mobs was much diminished at sea. They employed small vessels known as pressing tenders at all the major ports. William Robinson, aged 20 from Fareham in Surrey had volunteered in London in May, but repented when he was sent down to the hold of the receiving ship off the Tower of London to spend the night 'with my companions in wretchedness, and the rats running over us in numbers.' Things did not improve next morning when he and nearly 200 companions were ordered into a tender to take them down river to the fleet:

Upon getting on board this vessel, we were ordered down in the hold, and the gratings put over us; as well as a guard of marines placed round the hatchway, with their muskets loaded and fixed bayonets, as though we had been culprits of the first degree, or capital convicts. In this place we spent the day and the following night huddled together, for there was not room to sit or stand separate; indeed, we were in a pitiable plight, for numbers of them were sea-sick, some retching, others were smoking, whilst many were so overcome by the stench, that they fainted for want of air.

The tender finally arrived at the Nore, where two men tried to desert by swimming ashore with their clothes tied round their necks. One got away, the other stuck in the mud had had to be rescued by a boat. The rest, including Robinson, were drafted on board the *Zealand* at anchor there, and Robinson went with a draft to the *Revenge* on 5 June.

Cochrane's famous recruiting poster for the frigate *Pallas* in 1805. A captain who was as successful with prize money as Cochrane (or Jack Aubrey) could largely rely on voluntary recruiting. (NMM A 765)

OTHER MEANS OF RECRUITMENT

No-one was entirely happy with the system of impressment, and Parliament often considered bills which might mend or eliminate it, with no success. Either they were talked out, or they failed to make any impact on the problem. Other acts tried to supplement the supply of skilled man and the most important of these were the Quota Acts of 1795. Each local authority was ordered to find a specific number of men for the navy, with a skilled seaman being worth two landsmen. Seaports and counties were obliged to offer quite large sums of money, perhaps equal to several years of a seaman's wages, to induce men to enter. The act was adjudged a success in that the navy was rapidly built up to strength in a time of crisis; but a failure in that it was followed by the mutinies of 1797. Some officers suggested that it was the new landsmen, often failed artisans or businessman with something of an education, who inspired the mutinies. The evidence suggests that in fact the ringleaders were mostly experienced seamen, though the Quota men by their very existence, and their huge bounties, produced an atmosphere of instability on the lower deck. One of Marryat's characters was 'a man of talent and education. He had entered on board the ——— in a fit of desperation, to obtain the bounty for a present support, and his pay as a future provision, for his wife, and an only child, the fruit of a hasty and unfortunate marriage.'[21]

Despite everything there were some true volunteers for the Royal Navy – not starry-eyed boys in search of adventure, not hardened seamen who only volunteered after being trapped by the press gang, not men who had failed in other walks of life and desperately needed a means to live. The captain was largely responsible for recruiting men for his own ship and issued posters in the hope of attracting such men, often describing the prospects of prize money in the most glowing terms. Cochrane's poster for the *Pallas* is one of the most appealing, though in view of that captain's record it was not wholly overstated. It promised treasure from Spanish galleons and claimed, 'None need apply, but SEAMEN, or stout hands, able to rouse about the Field Pieces, and carry a hundred weight of PEWTER without stopping, at least three miles.'[22]

A captain would set up a rendezvous ashore where he could attract men, or pressed men could be kept until they were sent afloat. Captain Hall described the procedure:

> A rendezvous should be opened at a public-house in some street frequented by the seamen; and a flag, with the ship's name on it, exposed before the door; while bills, containing the ship and captain's name, should be stuck up and distributed in the proper quarters. If her destination be India, South America, the Mediterranean, or any other favourite station, that circumstance will be sufficiently noticed in these cards of invitation. The master-at-arms, the captain's coxswain or some other old and steady hand who has an interest in getting the ship manned, will be usefully employed at the rendezvous, to talk to the sailors as they drop in to consider the *pros* and *cons* of the new enterprise in which they are invited to engage.[23]

THE CULTURE OF THE SEAMAN

No-one disagreed that the life of the eighteenth century seaman was filled with danger and discomfort. Trotter wrote of 'the unparalleled hardships to which seamen are exposed from the nature of their employment. Toil and danger are their constant attendants. They suffer privations to which all other men are strangers.' They had 'unfailing fortitude' and 'matchless patience'. Perhaps the actual amount of work was not as much as some believe; another naval surgeon wrote:

> While employed in the ports of those regions [ie the coasts of Great Britain], more particularly those termed their own, or even in those of the European allies of Great Britain, they are liberally supplied with diet at once nutritive and invigorating, consisting of a due admixture of well-chose articles from the animal and vegetable kingdoms....It will also be admitted that during even their longest cruises on these stations, unless some unforeseen exigency has occurred requiring a great share of exertion and some degree of sacrifice on the part of the sailor, his duty is not only light but his allowance as above is profuse in quantity and of an excellent quality.

But separation from family, very limited shore leave, crowding below decks and many other hardships made the seaman's life very hard nevertheless. To the outsider, it seems surprising that the seamen did not have a general mutiny much earlier than 1797.

There were contradictory views about the seaman's attitude to religion. John Martingale Powell of the *Revenge* wrote to his mother in 1805, 'blasphemy reigns' and he was unable to read his Bible as recommended. 'I once attempted to pass part of the day in such manner as I ought well convinced that nothing will prosper without it but I was interrupted so many times that I thought it better to do no good myself rather than make others do worse so I

THE LOWER DECK

imploy this time in writing to you.' Chaplain Mangin of the *Gloucester* wrote in 1812 that, 'nothing can possibly be more unsuitably or more awkwardly situated than a clergyman in a ship of war; every object around him is at variance with the sensibilities of a rational and enlightened mind.' Marryat thought differently:

> How wrong are those on shore, who assert that sailors are not religious! On shore…you can you can rise in the morning in peace, and lay down your head at night in security – God may be neglected and forgotten for a long time; but at sea, where each gale is a warning, each disaster acts as a check, each escape is a homily upon the forbearance of Providence, that man must be indeed brutalized who does not feel that God is there.[24]

It is always dangerous to generalise about service in the navy at this time. Officers and seamen went through no common training course, so ideas about how a ship should be run were very varied. A ship might spend years away from the supervision of an admiral, so that the captain had complete control. Service in a small ship was very different from that in a large one, and the type of protest available to the men varied - small ships were much more prone to the 'revolutionary' type of mutiny in which the officers were overthrown, as in the *Bounty* and *Hermione*. Sailors were not uniformed or drilled in the modern sense and under the cover of naval discipline, still retained some vestiges of personal liberty.

MESSDECK LIFE

Seamen lived, ate and took their recreation in small groups called messes, each associated to some extent with a particular table on the lower deck. Samuel Leech describes it: 'The crew of a man of war is divided into little communities of about eight, called 'messes'. These eat and drink together, and are, as it were, so many families.' Often the messes were quite well equipped at the men's own expense:

> As Jack is mighty fond of a bit of show in his way, many of the berths or mess-places exhibit goodly ranges of tea-cups and regiments of plates worthy of the celebrated Blue Posts Tavern, occasionally flanked by a huge tea-pot, famously emblazoned with yellow dragons and imitation Chinese. The intervals between the shelves are generally ornamented with a set of pictures of rural innocence….On the topmost shelf stands, or is tied to the side, a triangular piece of mirror, three inches perhaps by three, extremely useful in adjusting the curls of our nautical coxcombs, of whom one at least is found in every berth.[25]

The Royal Navy seaman had very few liberties. He could not decide whether to be in the Navy or not, which ship to be on, how long his service was to last or his duties on board. His greatest privilege, jealously guarded, was the right to choose his own companions for the hours of day, especially mealtimes, when he was off duty and able to relax. Seamen could change their messes on request, and indeed Leech soon found himself confronted with 'a real gruff old 'bull-dog', named Hudson, who took it into his head to hate me at first sight.' The rest of his messmates advised him to change his mess, 'a privilege which is wisely allowed, and which tends very much to the good fellowship of a ship's crew.'[26] Yet there are signs that even this moderate right was under attack during the years of mutiny. As Captain Griffiths wrote:

> 'Till within these few years [before 1811], the privilege the seamen and marines had of changing their messes the first of the month if they thought fit was their Magna Carta and I confess I am inclined to attach much benefit to it. The original interference there-

with I trace to the complaints of the pursers and the little squabbles about double days and single days where there was an odd man. To obviate this it became common to order all messes to be even numbers, and afterwards they were in many ships obliged to be not less than four or more than eight. In some others the number was decided by the size of the berths, each being one mess. Some little probable advantage might be gained by these arrangements, but as the pursuit of man is to obtain the largest possible portion of happiness his situation is capable of affording and as there are infinite varieties of opinion wherein it consists, mine is that few things are more annoying than an unpleasant or quarrelsome messmate. Few but have experienced this in their passage through a midshipmen's berth, or a wardroom mess.

There is very little data on the messes aboard a ship, but certainly there were more than one would expect. It is often assumed that each mess was allotted a single table, but this was not the case on a ship of the line. According to Captain Griffiths, 'While in command, my crew ever messed as they liked. The berth was allotted to the number it was calculated to hold and if one, two or three messes were in it, that rested with themselves'. This was confirmed by Captain Basil Hall who wrote 'In a line of battleship the tables are larger [than those of a frigate] and two messes sit at the same table, one on each side.' This explains how very small messes of a few as four, or variable numbers such as those allowed in some ships, might be viable. In the *Victory* in 1797 there were 165 messes for a crew of about 800 – approximately five men in the average mess.

Even so, it must have been difficult to accommodate all the men on a ship of the line. According to 'Jack Nastyface', 'each mess…generally consists of eight persons who berth in between two of the guns on the lower deck and where there is a board placed which swings with the rolling of the ship and answers for a table.' If there were at most 28 such places on board the ship, then only 224 men could have been accommodated, whereas at least 500

would have been needed on a 74 gun ship. If we accept Hall's premise of two messes per table, then 408 men can be accommodated. If we then accept that further berths were placed along the centre line and perhaps yet more could be sited on the orlop on a ship of the line, as is suggested in a book by Daniel Ross, then we might be close to a figure of 500. Even so, 16 men round a mess table between the guns might be considered as gross overcrowding, extreme even by the standards of a sailing warship.

The problem was not solved by having the crew eat by watches, in either a frigate or a ship of the line, for in general both watches ate together. This is made clear by the recurring phrase in many captain's order books, 'The ship's company are never to be interrupted at their meals but on the most pressing occasions.' Captain Riou elaborates on this; 'the commanding officer should be very punctual as to their hours of dinner and breakfast….But with this time allowed it is expected they will, when the hands or watch is turned up, be ready to run up immediately'. This is confirmed by Seaman Robert Wilson, 'If the duty of the ship is required to be executed at meal times, so that the hands, or the watch is disturbed, the time they may want of their allowed times is made up to them when the duty is done.' It is quite clear that the crew ate as a whole, apart from a few helmsmen, sentries and lookouts.

After about 1805 there seems to have been an era of slightly greater liberalism towards the ship's company, after the immediate effects of the mutinies had died down. It was part of a general humanisation of the Navy, with many small reforms such as the abolition of running the gauntlet and starting and the regularisation of the position of the chaplain on board ship. Admiral Patton believed:

> Although seamen may have been regarded (by certain characters who have unfortunately had power and who were ignorant of their real dispositions) as a species of mankind deficient in the nicer feelings of humanity, whose attachments might be sacrificed, their friendships disregarded and even their healths ruined or destroyed upon the most frivolous occasions; yet they are very far from being inferior to other men, either in generous or in elevated sentiments. They are, like landmen, fully sensible of the eternal obligations and immutable effects of justice; they are open to the dictates of common sense and uncommonly alive to every generous and to every noble feeling. Nor will they ever fail to return the full measure of gratitude and affection that commander who treats them as rational beings, endued with the same faculties and perceptions which he himself possesses. The author of these pages, from a long course of experience in the management of seamen, can affirm that if they are governed with justice and candour they will not only show an affectionate attachment to superiors, but they will enter with pleasure into the views and second the intentions of the person who hath evidently pursued a line of conduct most favourable to the happiness of the whole, without deviating from a zealous discharge of his public duty.

CLOTHING

There was no uniform for seaman, except what was imposed by fashion, supply problems and necessity on hard service. According to Marryat the typical seaman's dress consisted of 'loose trousers tightened at the hips, to preclude the necessity of suspenders – a white duck frock, with long sleeves and blue collar – while a knife, attached to a lanyard, was suspended round his neck. A light and narrow-brimmed straw hat on his head completed his attire.'[27]

Some seamen, according to Captain Hall, had so little clothing that it could be transported in a pocket handkerchief. Another might be 'not a little of a dandy in his way.' Captains attempted to control the amount:

THE LOWER DECK

> In a well regulated ship, the sailor's kit consists generally of at least two blue jackets, and one pea jacket, which is a sort of lumbering shaggy surcoat, or curtailed great-coat, capable of being wrapped round the body to cover the thighs....A seaman must also have two pairs of blue trousers, two pairs of shoes, six shirts, four pairs of stockings, two Guernsey frocks, made of a sort of worsted stocking work, without any opening in front; two hats, two black handkerchiefs and a comforter to wrap round the throat; together with several pairs of flannel drawers and waistcoats...[28]

Captain Edward Riou deplored the vanity of some seamen, 'Flimsy white linen trousers, cloth waistcoats of variegated colours and other trash are only brought on board to catch the eye of and cheat the inexperienced boys.'[29] The tastes of individual seamen varied, as did the extent of their outfits. In the *Conquestador* in 1813, William Seymour had nine jackets and William Smith had none.[30]

Sailors also embellished themselves in other ways. According to Captain Marryat, 'The practice of tattooing is very common in the navy; and you will see a sailor's arm covered with emblems from the shoulder to the wrist; his own initials, that of his sweetheart, the crucifix, Neptune and mermaids being huddled together, as if mythology and scripture were one and the same thing.'[31] This is borne out by the description book of the *Bellerophon* just after Trafalgar, to take the example of a single gun crew, Peter Johnson from Sweden tattooed with a flowerpot on his right arm; Richard Schofield was tattooed with signal flags on his right arm and a pierced heart on his left, John White of London had the letters SBMM on the back of his left hand. One suspects that the practice was encouraged by the officers as a means of identifying deserters.

Another anonymous drawing of a seaman, showing the short jacket and loose trousers.
(NMM PU 8577)

RATINGS

On arriving at his ship, a man or boy was called before the first lieutenant who questioned him, assessed his character, build and experience and rated him accordingly. At the bottom of the heap were two classes of boy – second and third class, for first class volunteers were potential officers. Boys third class were under the age of fifteen and were generally employed as servants to the officers. Boys second class might begin some training on decks and in the rigging. Parents who wanted a seafaring career for their sons generally chose the merchant service, so most naval boys came via the Marine Society, a charity which found places for orphaned, abandoned and destitute children.

A landsman was an adult who entered the navy without any previous experience. A few, mostly those who started under the age of 25, might eventually learn the skills of the seaman and rise though the rates, while a very small number of educated men might find more congenial work on board as clerks. But a large number of landsmen were hopeless cases, men who were too old to learn anything new and could never really adjust to sea life. Bartholomew Hughes of Dublin served on the *Bellerophon* from 1803 to 1815 and was 40 at the end of the period, but he never rose above landsman.

The ordinary seaman had at least two years at sea, and was able to do

most of the tasks on board ship. The able seaman had served somewhat longer. According to Captain Basil Hall, such men:

> …can not only 'hand, reef and steer' but are likewise capable of heaving the lead in the darkest night, as well as the daytime; who can use the palm and needle of a sailmaker; and who are versed in every part of a ship's rigging, in the stowage of the hold, and in the exercise of the great guns. Of course, an A.B must be able to pull an oar, as well as use it in sculling, understand the management of a boat under sail, and know how to cross a surf. He must also learn the art of placing an anchor in a boat, in order to its being laid out; and how to get it in again when weighed. In these, and twenty other things which might be pointed out, he ought to be examined by the boatswain and other officers before the rating of A.B. is fully established on the books.[32]

PETTY OFFICERS

A bosun's mate with his rope's end and the crest of his ship painted in gold on his hat, by Chaplain Edward Mangin, 1812. (NMM D 7689 C)

Above the able seamen was a hierarchy of petty officers who formed the link between the men and the officers. Promotion to petty officer was entirely at the behest of the captain of the ship, usually advised by the first lieutenant and the warrant officers. It was a question of character, according to Captain Hall:

> The higher ratings of quarter-master, gunner's mate, captain of the forecastle and of the tops, and so on, are given chiefly to men who may not, in fact, know more than every Able Seaman is supposed to be acquainted with, but who have recommended themselves by their superior activity and vigilance, and have not only shown themselves fit to command others by their decision of character, but evinced a sincere anxiety to see the work of their department well performed.[33]

The boatswain's mates were perhaps the best known petty officers. As well as their work in helping with the maintenance of the rigging, they mustered the crew on watch, bellowed orders during sailing evolutions and in action, and wielded the cat during floggings. The quartermasters were slightly more intellectual. They supervised the steering of the ship and helped with basic navigation such as casting the lead and running out the log line. The quarter gunners were appointed at the rate of one for every four guns in the ship. They were intended to assist the gunner with maintenance, but often there was not enough for them to do, so they tended to work as an elite division of seamen. All these groups were paid extra for their rate, and had a higher share of the prize money after a capture.

For ordinary working purposes the main body of the crew was divided into six groups. There were three teams of topmen, one for each mast, and they were the most skilled and agile men in the ship, with a combination of experience and fitness. The mizzen mast team included a proportion of boys under training, for it had the smallest sails and was less vital than the other masts for most purposes. The forecastle men were stationed well forward and had to work with the anchors

and cables, so they included a number of skilled men who were perhaps too aged to go aloft in the rigging. The afterguard worked on the quarterdeck under the eye of the officers, hauling on ropes and cleaning the decks. They were not particularly skilled, but smart men were useful in the circumstances. The lowest group of all was the waisters, who worked in the decks in the centre of the ship and often had no talent or experience.

Each of these groups had a man in charge for each watch, known as the captain of the foretop, the captain of the waist and so on. These were the true leaders of the ship's company, for they relied on their skill and personality to encourage their men. They did not dominate by force like the boatswains mates, and they were not distant like the quartermasters and quarter gunners; they had to work day to day with the men under them. Yet in the early days they had no extra pay or prize money and were not fully recognised as petty officers until 1806.

ARTISANS AND SERVANTS

The navy also included a large number of craftsmen who were essential in running and maintaining the ship. Most had served apprenticeships ashore or in merchant ships, and they had skills which were easily transferable. The senior one of each trade was usually a warrant officer, protected from disrating by his warrant from the Navy Board. The carpenter headed quite a large team in a big ship and his status was high. The other warrant officers, such as the armourer, sailmaker, caulker and gunsmith, had no more privileges than ordinary petty officers, while their mates were unprotected by warrants and were equivalent to able seamen. The ship's cook was a special case. He had no great culinary skills and was usually a disabled seamen given a job in lieu of a pension.

The officers also had real servants, besides the boys training to be officers and the younger boy seamen. Captain and admiral often had their own men who followed them from command to command. Perhaps the most famous was Nelson's Tom Allen, who had a very ambiguous relationship with his master. A native of Norfolk like Nelson, he had been a waiter in the *Agamemnon*, Nelson's first command after the start of the great wars. He retained his broad accent even when serving the King of Naples. He took many liberties with his master and had a 'feeling heart under a very rough exterior.' He was clumsy, ill-formed, illiterate and vulgar, his very appearance created laughter at the situation he held; but his affectionate, bold heart made up for all these deficiencies; and…Tom Allen possessed the greatest influence with his heroic master.'

MARINES

The marines were the only men of the lower deck who wore regular uniform, with red coats similar to those of the army. They were recruited like soldiers, though under the control of the Admiralty since 1755. They formed up to about a fifth of the crew on most ships and had a hierarchy similar to that of the army, with corporals and sergeants under the officers. They were trained at three marine divisions at Chatham, Portsmouth and Plymouth, and a fourth was later added at Woolwich. Their training was entirely military, and they knew virtually nothing of ships when they arrived on board. There was a serious shortage of recruits during the 1790s and several army regiments were drafted on board ship.

Marines had several roles on board ship. They could obviously be useful in amphibious operations and Marryat felt that marines were more useful than army troops in landings, because they were more experienced in them and could be brought firmly under naval command. 'Unless the military force required is very large, marines should invariably be

The Royal Marine Barracks at Portsmouth, showing a squad of recruits drilling under an NCO in the centre of the square, with officers meeting in the foreground and a sentry to the left. (Royal Marines Museum)

employed, and placed under the direction of the naval commander.'[34] They acted as sentries in key parts of the ship, such as the captain's cabin and spirit room, though most of them were employed in general shipboard duties about the decks, wearing seamen's slop clothes rather than marine uniform. In action some of them formed a small-arms party which plied the enemy with musket shot in close-range battle, though again the majority of them were employed with the seamen among the gun crews.

Marine discipline seemed strange to a seaman, including Marryat:

> Having been well drilled at barracks, he never answered any question put to him by an officer without recovering himself from his usual "stand at ease" position – throwing shoulders back, his nose up in the air, his arms down his sides, and the palms of his hands flattened on his thighs. His replies were given with all the brevity that the question would admit…[35]

During the crisis surrounding the great mutinies of 1797, St Vincent planned to use the marines as an armed guard to intimidate the seamen. He ordered that in port they should be constantly drilled on the quarterdeck as a deterrent. But in practice marines were as likely to mutiny as seamen. Furthermore some, like Admiral Patton, believed that to interpose marines between officers and seaman was subversive of real discipline. The skilled seamen were needed to run the ship at sea, while the marines could only do the most menial tasks.

Nevertheless St Vincent augmented the role of the marines. They were known as the Royal Marines from 1802, and soon formed their own artillery regiment to operate the guns of bomb vessels. Later they formed battalions for service on shore, for example in Spain and America. St Vincent took good care of recruiting, sending officers round Britain and setting up stations in Malta and Italy. It was never necessary again to send army regiments afloat as part of the crews of ships.

RACIAL ORIGINS

The lower deck of the Royal Navy was far from homogenous in its racial and national composition. In 1801 the *Caledonia* had 585 seamen, including 304 English, 154 Irish, 45 Scots and 21 Welsh. Ten more came from the islands of Shetland, Man and Guernsey. There were 16 North Americans and six West Indians plus three men for the Spanish West Indies. There were Frenchmen, Portuguese, Russians, Germans and Italians, with an isolated Pole, African and Chinaman. The marines were less mixed, but included Germans, Dutchmen and Swedes.[36]

Black and mixed race men were found on board ship in some numbers, and the attitudes to them were less rigid than they became later. The *Bellerophon*, for example, included several men of mixed race. The racial composition was very important to those involved and was described by Marryat, who had served in the West Indies:

> …the progeny of a white and a Negro is a mulatto, or half and half – of a white and a mulatto, a *quadroon*, or one quarter black…I believe a white and a quadroon make a *mustee* or one eight black, and the mustee and the white the mustafina, or one-sixteenth black. After that they are *whitewashed*, and considered as Europeans. The pride of colour is very great in the West Indies…[37]

A marine on guard duty ashore, 1815. From a print by J Stadler, published by Colnaghi.
(NMM PW 4247)

Negroes are often seen in prints and paintings of the period without any patronising or insulting note, as members of messes or gun crews doing their duty or being accepted as messmates. However they tended to be restricted to duties as servants or cooks, unless they did something outstanding. A typical cook's assistant is described by Basil Hall, 'behind him stands his mate, generally a tall, glossy, powerful Negro, who, unlike his chief, has always a full allowance of limbs, with a round and shining face...'[38]

Marryat's creation Mesty in *Mr Midshipman Easy* is treated with a good deal of sympathy. Once a prince in Africa, he has far more intelligence and character than any of the common seaman, though he is capable of great cruelty and has little moral sense, by European standards. As an escaped slave, he enlisted in a man of war where 'he found that the universal feeling was strong against his colour, and that on board a man-of-war he was condemned, though free, to the humblest of offices' – as a servant in the midshipman's berth, '...only tink, Massa Easy – I boil kettle, and prince in my own country.' Marryat himself was lukewarm in his opposition to slavery and this is reflected in one exchange between Easy and Mesty:

'Well,' replied Jack, 'at all events that is better than being a slave.'
 Mesty made no reply: anyone who knows the life of a midshipman's servant will not be surprised at his silence.

Eventually, after distinguishing himself as 'Jack's sheet anchor' during weeks of detached service, he is promoted to ship's corporal, though the villainous boatswain mutters of Jack, 'I don't talk about equality, damme – no nor consort with niggers.'[39]

Captain Frederick Chamier is ambiguous in his comments on Negro behaviour while the ship is in danger. On one hand, 'The blacks...began to manifest considerable uneasiness when they heard the unusual roar of strange sounds; and it was with some difficulty and gentle violence that they were made to continue their work. They toiled sullenly and silently, until a flash of lightning struck the ship and ran along the decks …the blacks hid their faces in their hands, and threw themselves on the deck, roaring and howling as dismally as the wind, creating a confusion quite beyond description.' Yet in the end their labour was essential in saving the ship, 'had they not been on board, the Arethusa would have sunk.'[40]

WOMEN ON BOARD

Apart from the women who came on board when the ship was at anchor, women often lived on board warships, although this was expressly forbidden by Admiralty regulation. Some were the wives of the standing officers, the boatswain, gunner and carpenter, and their presence was tacitly accepted, as their numbers were naturally small, and they were likely to be mature, and useful on board. But many more were carried in some ships. A very small number disguised themselves as men to follow husbands or lovers, but this was rare. Far more lived openly on the messdecks, eating part of the men's rations and often finding a role as nurses or cooks. This was acceptable for soldiers who were serving board ship in the 1790s, for regulations allowed six wives for every company of a hundred men. It was not allowed for sailors and marines, though in the 1790s this regulation was completely flouted. The *Goliath* at the Battle of the Nile seems to have had a particularly large number, and Captain Foley went so far as to record the names of four of them on the muster books (for victuals but not wages) after they lost husbands in the battle. The Admiralty reaction to this is not known.

It was unthinkable for a woman to wear anything but a dress in those days, which might cause some difficulty with the ladderways in a ship, as one of Marryat's characters found:

> "Upon my word, Mrs Trotter, you must be conscious of having a very pretty ankle, or you would not venture to display it, as you have, to Mr Simple…"
>
> "My dear Trotter, how cruel of you not to give me warning; I thought that nobody was below. I declare I'm so ashamed."[41]

There seems to have been a major cultural shift after about 1800, for very few women are noted aboard ship after that. At Trafalgar the British sailors were surprised to rescue a woman called Jeanette from one of the French ships, and to clothe her they had to resort to the costumes used for amateur dramatics. A few months later William Robinson of the *Revenge* noted that, '…our crew, consisting of six hundred and upwards, nearly all young men, had seen one woman on board for eighteen months, and that was the daughter of one of the Spanish chiefs, who made no stay on board…'[42] Clearly women were not common on board ships at sea during that period.

DESERTION AND MUTINY

Once in the Navy, seamen's discontent might overflow from mere grumbling into desertion or mutiny. Desertion was rife, and it was said that 42,000 men ran between 1793 and 1801. This formed part of a vicious circle, in that captains were often reluctant to allow shore leave and the morale of the men became worse. Seaman would find every opportunity to desert, perhaps while taking an officer ashore in a boat, or stealing a boat themselves. Few could swim, but those that could often took the opportunity. In 1811 Robert Hay and his companion strapped seven bladders to their backs to carry them ashore from a guardship at the Nore.

The other outlet for grievances was mutiny, which had always been present on a small scale. A great wave of mutiny began towards the end of the American War and reached a peak in 1797, when two major British fleets mutinied at Spithead and the Nore. In the first case they had some success and were given concessions including a pay rise; in the second the mutiny was eventually suppressed and some of the leaders were hanged. Apart from minor acts of disobedience by individuals, there were two main kinds of mutiny. Spithead was essentially a naval strike. The ships were in harbour and the crews simply refused to raise anchor or obey their officers. Other mutinies were more revolutionary, in that the officers were overthrown and the ships taken over. Classic cases of this kind included the *Bounty* mutiny of 1789, in which her captain, William Bligh, and his supporters were put into an open boat; and the *Hermione* mutiny of 1797, in which the officers were massacred and the ship surrendered to the Spanish. Such mutinies were more common on small ships, especially those on service far away from the main fleet.

Even Captain Marryat, a naval officer himself and generally conservative in most matters, allows his characters to see that the Spithead mutineers of 1797 had a case:

> Doubtless there is a point at which endurance of oppression ceases to be a virtue, and rebellion can no longer be considered a crime: but it is a dangerous and intricate problem, the solution of which had better not be attempted. It must, however, be acknowledged that the seamen, on the occasion of the first mutiny, had just grounds of complaint, and that they did not proceed to acts of violence until repeated and humble remonstrance had been made in vain.[43]

In another, albeit fictional, case he uses the term 'justifiable mutiny', a remarkable expression for any naval officer to use.[44]

For all his grievances and faults, the British seaman (or the foreign seaman in British service) was one of the country's greatest assets. More than any other single factor, he allowed the great victories in the wars with France. He was little rewarded for his efforts.

The mutineers at the Nore as seen by the conservative press, taking over the great cabin of a ship and turning Britannia upside down. The French and the Parliamentary opposition are alleged to be at the bottom of it. Published by S Fores. (NMM PW 3899)

CHAPTER 5

TECHNIQUES

SEAMANSHIP AND ROPEWORK

Seamanship is as central to naval fiction as it was to the success of the Royal Navy. In the real world there were officers whose grasp of seamanship was shaky, but in fiction they only appear as villains, or are confined to the margins. The hero of naval fiction is perhaps an instinctive seaman like Jack Aubrey, or a mathematical, calculating one like Hornblower, but there is no doubt about his ability to get the very best out of his ship in any conditions of wind and weather. Of course seamanship is essential to any user of the seas, but in a powered ship its main function is to keep the ship out of trouble. In the age of sail it was all part of making the ship go, manoeuvring it in a tight corner, or keeping it stopped in safe and relatively comfortable circumstances. It was also far more important in the highly competitive circumstances of wartime, especially in an age when society had high expectations of naval officers, and crews had a lust for prize money.

Oddly enough, nineteenth century writers make rather less of seamanship. They are very good at describing the social life on the decks of a ship, but seamanship is taken for granted. Perhaps this is because they, as professional seamen, learned it at a very early age. Perhaps it is because most of them are describing their time as junior officers, when they rarely had a chance to handle the ship in conditions which were at all difficult. Like all seamen they tend to despise those who fail to understand their art, but Marryat, for one, makes light of the difficulties in learning it. Midshipman Easy, despite his inexperience, has no difficulty in sailing a ship to Gibraltar with a tiny, mutinous and barely competent crew. Nor is he worried about navigation, '…for you know the land was on our left side all the way coming up the Mediterranean: and if we keep it, as it is now, on our right, we shall get back again along the coast.'[1] Forester, on the other hand, makes his hero admire the skill of the seaman in glowing terms. In *A Ship of the Line* he 'yearned and hungered for men, more passionately than a miser desired gold, or a lover his mistress.'[2] He admires the skills of his topmen, believing that landsmen would pay good money to see tricks like theirs in a circus.

Seamanship began with the rigging of a ship, and it involved the ordinary seaman in ropework, taking in sail and hauling on ropes. For the officer of the watch or the captain it meant deciding how to deploy the sails to best effect, to make good speed, carry out a quick manoeuvre or keep the ship safe in a storm. It was quite a new word in the Great Wars with France, and is first noted in Tobias Smollett's works in 1766. Perhaps a word had not been needed before that – the art was taken for granted by the members of the profession, but it was too arcane to be explained to outsiders. The ordinary seaman did not use the word very much, though he understood the concept very well. It included the knowledge which he took

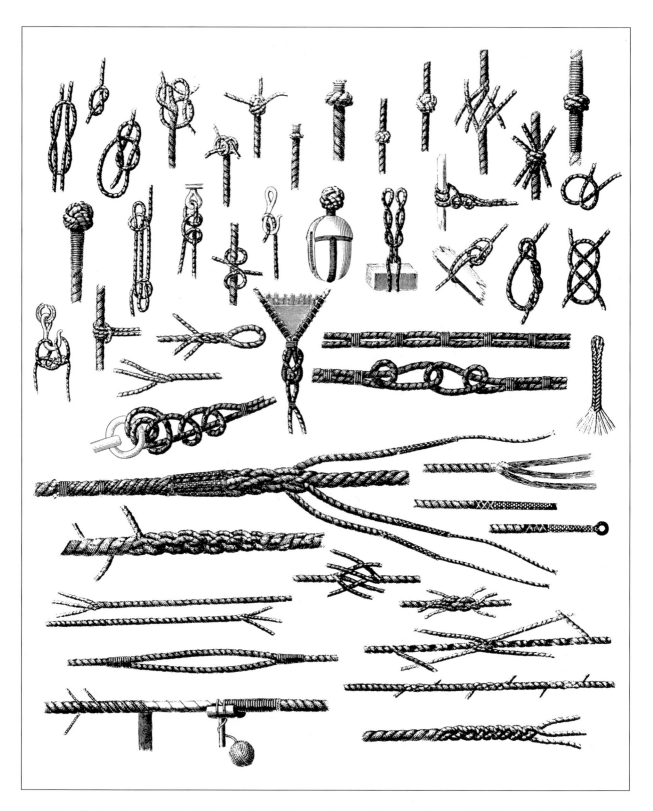

A selection of knots and ropework, showing knots, bends and hitches near the top and more complex ropework in the centre. On the bottom left is worming parcelling and serving, in which shrouds and other parts of the standing rigging have the gaps between the strands filled up by a smaller line. Paper or parcelling is then wrapped round it, and a light rope is twisted tightly round the whole thing. (From Rees' *Cyclopeodia*, 1819)

for granted, of how to live on board a ship, to climb the rigging, to take in sails and steer the ship. It included skills like ropework and knot-tying, casting the lead, rowing a boat and hauling on ropes. His officer was at least familiar with these things, if not quite so expert; but he tended to see seamanship in its higher sense, the operation and control of a ship, getting the best out of a vehicle and a fighting machine in any conditions of wind, tide and sea.

Understanding nautical jargon was as important as anything else, for the seaman virtually had his own language, often using common words with unfamiliar meanings, as Peter Simple found on his first introduction to the sea:

> "Captain of the foretop," said he, "up on your *horses*, and take your *stirrups* up three inches." – "Ay, ay sir" (I looked up and could see no horses)…
>
> "Let me see, sir: I've one *sister*, the other we split in half the other day, and I think I have a couple of *monkeys* down in the storeroom – I say, you, Smith, pass that brace through the *bull's eye*, and take the *sheepshank* out before you come down."
>
> And then he asked the first lieutenant whether something should not be fitted with a *mouse* or only a *Turk's head* – told him the *goose-neck* must be spread out.…In short, what with *dead-eyes* and *shrouds*, *cats* and *cat-blocks*, *dolphins* and *dolphin strikers*, *whips* and *puddings*, I was so puzzled with what I heard, that I was about to leave the deck in absolute despair.[3]

A new boy seaman, whether rating or a potential officer, would start by learning his way around the rigging, and how to do the numerous knots and splices required by his profession. In the older terminology the word 'knot' had a more specialised meaning as, 'a large knob formed in the extremity of a rope…'[4] and this is perhaps reflected in modern usage, as in 'a knot in one's stomach.' But more recently two of the best known pieces of ropework, the reef knot and the bowline, had been accepted in the general term, which now included 'the fastenings by which one knot is joined to another.'[5] The bowline (not to be confused with the rope of that name which held one edge of a square sail forward in the wind) was described by Steel:

> Hold the end of a rope in the right hand, and the standing part in the left; then pass the end under the standing part in the left hand and over through the bight; then bring it over the standing part, and pass it again through the bight, and haul tight.[6]

The famous reef knot was used, as its name suggests, to tie the reef points of a sail together; users were warned, 'in making, observe to pass both parts of the rope on one side, in the bight of the other, thus; turn up one end, and form a bight, and put the other through the bight; take it round underneath, and pass it through the bight again.' Fortunately almost noone had to learn ropes by words alone and most were instructed by an experienced seaman.

In addition there were bends, used to fasten one rope to another, or to an anchor, such as the sheet bend, fishermen's bend and Carrick bend. There were hitches which formed a loop at one end of a rope to attach it to another object, such as a loop, cleat or bollard. These included the magnus hitch, the rolling hitch, the timber hitch, Blackwall hitch and the midshipmen's hitch. Then there were splices to join two pieces of rope in a more permanent manner, such as the long splice, short splice, tapered splice and the cont splice. More experienced boys would go on to learn how to fit the strops on blocks using splices, how to worm, parcel and serve rope for shrouds, and how to do decorative ropework such as mouses and Turk's heads. He would learn how to make rope ladders, nets and rope fenders. He would go on to learn the application of all these works in the appropriate paces in the rigging of the ship.

SAIL HANDLING

JACK AUBREY
COMMANDS

Though sailors knew nothing about the theory, a sail operates as an aerofoil section, using exactly the same principle as an aircraft wing. It is slightly curved in its cross section, and as the air passing over it on one side becomes more dense than on the other, creating a pull forward. This is translated into two components by the modern physicist, one pulling the sail sideways and known as lift, and the other, drag, pulling it backwards. Because the hull of the ship produces much more resistance to a sideways movement than a forward one, most of the force is used to push the ship forward, though some sideways movement, known as leeway, has to be tolerated on most points of sailing. The art of the seaman was to set the sails in such a way to give the ship the desired motive power. This required teamwork between the officers who decided how the sails should be set and the seamen who used their not inconsiderable skills to handle the sails. The most skilled of these, the topmen, worked mainly in the rigging.

A daring young seaman, like Marryat's Peter Simple, could find his way through the rigging as second nature:

I had become from habit so extremely active, and so fond of displaying my newly acquired gymnastics, called by the sailors "sky-larking," that my speedy exit was often prognosticated by the old quartermasters, and even by the officers. It was clearly understood that I was either to be drowned or was to break my neck; for the latter I took my chance pretty fairly, going up and down the rigging like a monkey. Few of the topmen could equal me in speed, still fewer surpass me in feats of daring activity. I could run along the top-

The principles of sailing, showing how the sail acts like an aerofoil section when on the wind, or like a stalled aerofoil with the wind behind. It produces both sideways and forward motion, but the former is restricted by the shape of the ship, and is known as leeway.

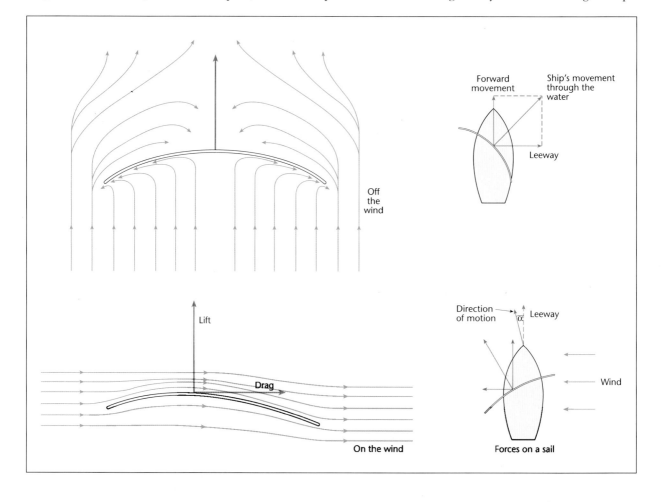

Sailors reefing topsails in windy
conditions. A studding sail
boom has been lashed to the
shrouds to make space.
(NMM PW3760)

sail yards out to the yard-arm, go from one mast to the other by the stays, or down on deck in the twinkling of an eye by the topsail halyards; and, as I knew myself to be an expert swimmer, I cared little about the chances of being drowned.[7]

A landsman visitor to the *Gibraltar* in 1811 described the topmen at work:

When it is necessary to loose sails, either for the purpose of drying them or getting under sail, then the word is given…to 'Lay out, etc.' When the lieutenant supposes that all is ready for letting the sails fall he calls out 'Are you ready forward? Are your ready on the main? Are you ready abaft'. If the midshipmen in the three tops answer in the affirmative, he then sings out 'Trace out, let fall' and immediately every sail drops at the same moment…[8]

When out of use for a short time a sail could be hauled up. This was quite a simple procedure, for the ropes needed to haul it up – the clewlines, buntlines, slablines, clew garnets and so on, mostly led down to the deck. In the case of topsails or topgallants the yard was lowered some way down the mast to take some of the wind out of the sail, then the crew below hauled on their various ropes. But a large part of the sail would still hang loose between the various lines and in bad weather it was necessary to secure it more firmly. Men went aloft and 'laid out' along the yards with their feet on the footropes hanging below, and their breasts balancing them on the yards. Each hauled up the piece of the sail directly below him and gathered it within itself as neatly as possible, and then they took pieces of rope known as gaskets and tied them round the sail and the yard. The sail was now furled.

The size of an individual sail could be reduced by reefing it. Men on deck lowered the yard and hauled at the reef tackles attached to the sides of the sails at an appropriate level, while the topmen mounted the mast and laid along the yards to tie the reef points together over the top of the yard:

…the first lieutenant orders the bosun to 'Pipe all hands to furl sails.' They then come on deck and there wait for the word. In the meantime the midshipmen stationed in the tops

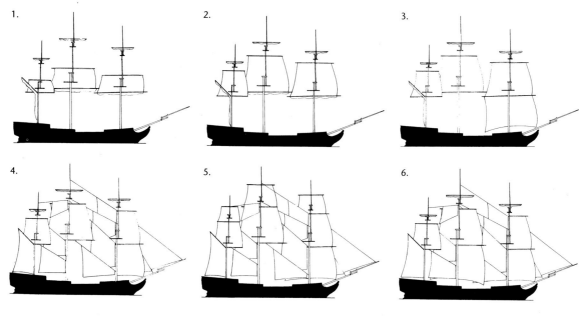

The amount of sail carried in different conditions.

1. Reefed topsails, in strong winds
2. Topsails only, but without reefs
3. Foresail set
4. Jibs and staysails set
5. Topgallants set in fair weather
6. Main course set in squally weather
7. All sail set, in light breezes

take their places. The next word is 'Man the rigging.' This is obeyed by the man ascending the first ratlines of the shrouds and there staying till the lieutenant sings out 'Away aloft.' When they have got into the tops they wait again for the last word, 'Lay out and take in ___ reefs.'…This is done with a rapidity which astonishes the stranger who first beholds it.'[9]

It required a good deal of care and skill, as Captain Riou instructed his officers:

The forecastlemen are to attend the reef tackles, topgallant sheets and topsail lifts, and the captains are to be very attentive to these ropes when hoisting and lowering the sail. It is to these two men that the fore topmen are to look for their security in lying out, by the yard being down by the lifts and the reef tackles sufficiently hauled out. The captain of the starboard watch is likewise to observe that the starboard halyards are hauled taut and belayed in the waist as soon as the yard is down and before the men are out on the yards.[10]

The officer of the watch had to decide how much sail to set in different circumstances. According to the Mediterranean Fleet orders of 1793, all sail, including the fore-and-aft staysails, jobs and driver, would be set in light breezes. In slightly stronger winds the main course would be the first to be furled. If it was squally the uppermost sails, the royals, would be taken in, then the fore and aft sails. In strong winds the topsails would be the only sails set, and in gales they would be reefed to reduce their area. In storms, if time permitted, the yards and upper masts would be taken down to save topweight, and no sails would be set; the ship would run at the mercy of the wind, 'under bare poles'.

SHIP HANDLING

Though the officer of the watch was expected to hand over control to the captain and master in difficult situations, he often had to take effective action before his superiors could be called on deck. Captain Riou ordered his officers to sail into the wind if in any doubt, as that would tend to stop movement:

When sailing on a wind, if any danger suddenly discovered ahead, or in the case of any other ship being very near, and rapidly advancing to cross on the other tack, it requires coolness and seamanlike judgement to prevent an accident; for on those occasions a moment lost or a mistake made is irreparable; but it is strongly recommended in almost every case to put the helm down, as the surest method of avoiding danger.[11]

Captain Griffith enjoined officers to employ the men sparingly and to use better man management:

If only a rope or two to be coiled down, how common the order, 'Send the afterguard aft'? Up come 20 or 30 men, to be sent down again, 'not wanted.' Thus the idle want of thought brings men into scrapes. They are so frequently called when not required, that when they really are the doubt, do not come and incur displeasure. Precisely the boy and wolf in the fable. An officer of judgement will frame his order to suit the occasion. 'Send three or four men aft' is as easily said as the other and its good effects will soon be seen.[12]

A ship in a chase, or in a hurry to get in station, would naturally set as much sail as possible consistent with safety, and that is the circumstances which most interests the writers of naval fiction. But in fact most ships spent the largest part of their time in fleets or escorting convoys, when their speed was not needed. Often they had to slow down deliberately to keep station, and for this the mizzen topsail was essential. It was one of the smallest of the square sails and its pulling power was quite small (though it was useful for training boys in sail handling). Its main purpose was to slow the ship down as necessary, for it was often braced round to back it, putting the wind on the other side. This was the equivalent of a touch on the brake when the ship looked like overtaking the one in front, and was often used in the approach to battle.

A ship could be stopped in the water for a short period by heaving to, bracing the sails so that some were backing and some were filling and the effects cancelled one another out. It was useful in many ways – to allow ships to communicate with one another, to stop and search a suspected ship, to wait for friendly ship to catch up or to invite battle against an enemy. There were two means of doing it. The foresails could be backed, or braced round so that the wind came on the opposite side, counteracting the effect of the main and mizzen; or the main could be backed to counteract the fore and mizzen. Heaving to saved a good deal of labour in stowing the sails, but it did not stop the ship moving with the current and a certain extent with the wind, so it could only be used for short periods and in the open sea.

The points of sailing of a square rigged ship, showing how the yards are progressively braced at a greater angle to the direction of motion as the ship comes closer to the wind. (From Burney's *Dictionary*)

105

Catharpins, as beloved by Jack Aubrey. They were used to tighten the shrouds, which allowed the yards to be braced round harder when sailing close to the wind. The ropes used to tighten them, marked W, are the swifters, used to 'bowse-in' or tighten the shrouds. (From Darcy Lever's *Young Sea Officer's Sheet Anchor*)

THE POINTS OF SAILING

In general the sails were set with their yards at about 15 degrees to the direction of the wind, so that they would have maximum effect. Since the yards could only be braced to about 40 degrees from their position square across the line of the ship, the ship could only sail within about two points, or 22½ degrees, into the wind, or in other words six points (67½ degrees) from the direction of the wind. This was known as sailing close-hauled. If the ship was to sail at about 90 degrees to the wind, or with the wind on the beam, the yards could be braced round slightly so that the ship was sailing large, or free, with a good deal of room for manoeuvre in either direction. As the wind drew more and more behind the ship, the yards were braced round yet more. With the wind some way astern, or quartering, the ship was on one of its most efficient points of sailing. With it dead astern, or sailing before the wind, it was rather less efficient. The sails tended to operate, in modern terms, like stalled airfoils and produced less lift, while one sail would mask another, so some, such as the main course, might be furled to prevent this.

All large ships of the age were square rigged, with the sails hung from yards placed in front of the masts. This was useful for sailing in favourable winds, but it limited the amount which the yards could be angled, or 'braced' round to catch the wind. They would eventually meet the shrouds, which would constrain their movement at about 45 degrees from athwartships. One way of dealing with this was to pull the shrouds together at this point, generally at the level where they were joined by the futtock shrouds. These were the catharpins so beloved of Jack Aubrey – 'small ropes serving to brace in the *shrouds* of the lower masts behind their respective yards, for the double purpose of making the shrouds more tight, and of affording room to draw the yards in more obliquely, to *trim* the sails for a side wind, when they are said to be close-hauled.'[13] A rope called a swifter was led alternately through blocks on the shrouds on each side then hauled tight. The effect of this was marginal, and allowed the ship to sail a few degrees closer to the wind, but that could be crucial in a chase.

Though a ship could therefore point more than 20 degrees into the wind, this was not the full story, for in any conditions but the most favourable, the wind would also push it sideways. The underwater shape of the hull was designed to counteract this, presenting a long and deep surface against the sideways pressure. But the effect of this was undermined by the drag created by the masts, yards, sails and rigging, not to mention the great extent of hull above water, especially in a three-decker. Leeway would tend to increase with the strength of the wind, and in a strong breeze, with the topsails reefed, it would amount to two points, so that any attempt to sail against the wind was neutralised. In a strong gale, with the courses taken in, there would be at least six points, or 67½ degrees, of leeway and at best the ship would sail 45 degrees away from the wind. Every seaman dreaded being trapped in a bay with a contrary wind, for unless he could anchor the ship would be driven onto the shore and wrecked.

TACKING AND WEARING

It was often necessary to turn a ship to bring the wind on the other side. This was most common in the process of beating to windward, when the ship tried to reach a point almost dead upwind of it. The only way in the open sea was move from one tack to another, a process known as tacking. There were two ways of getting the wind from one side or the other, either by presenting the bow or the stern of the ship to the wind.

Presenting the bow to the wind, also known as tacking, was generally the quickest and the most efficient, as the ship only had to travel through 135 degrees rather than 225. A sailing warship had a great deal of momentum and a deep underwater hull, so a large amount of force was needed to drive it through the eye of the wind. Every sail in the ship had to be repositioned at exactly right moment, so a great deal of skilled work was required. In his *Young Sea Officer's Sheet Anchor*, Darcy Lever describes the modern 'expeditious' method of tacking. The ship was assumed to be heading north on the starboard tack, that is with the wind coming over her starboard side. The seamen were called to their stations and the ropes were prepared to haul taut on the windward or weather side, or cast loose on the lee side; 'the Weather Braces stretched along, the lee Tacks, *weather* Sheets and *lee* bowlines hauled through the slack.' The ship was gradually turned into the wind with the cry of 'The helm's a-lee'. The sheets of the forward sails were

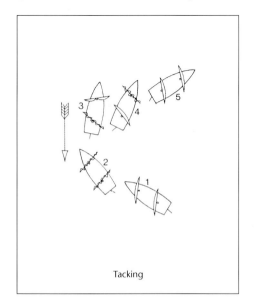

Tacking

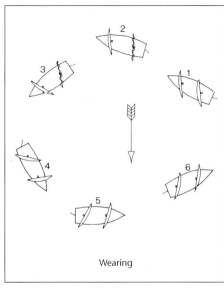

Wearing

Tacking and wearing. Tacking – 1) building up speed by bearing away 2) turning into the wind; sails shivering 3) forward sail backed; after sail braced round 4) after sail filling on new tack, gaining steerageway 5) forward sail braced round and filling. Wearing – 1) Starboard tack 2-3) after sail brailed and yards braced in 4) fore sail squared; after sail braced up for new tack 5) fore sail braced up for new tack 6) port tack.

let go to take the power out of them, while the main and mizzen sails began to back, as the wind came on the forward side of them. The order was given 'mainsail haul' and the main and mizzen yards were smartly braced round to the opposite side, tending to turn the ship's stern to port. The ship turned through the eye of the wind, almost stationary in the water and requiring little helm at this stage. As the wind began to fill the main and mizzen sails, the order 'Let go and haul' was given to bring the fore yards round to the same tack and the ship began to gather headway. As the operation was completed she took up a new course heading south-east, having changed through 135 degrees.[14] In light winds or heavy seas there was always the risk that the ship would fail to come round through the wind, would 'miss stays.' If she became stuck she was said to be 'in irons', like a seamen with his legs restrained.

Wearing, or veering, was the opposite procedure, turning the stern towards the wind. It was necessary when the winds were too light or the sea was too rough to allow tacking. Wearing took much longer than tacking and needed much more space, but it did use the natural momentum of the ship, rather than arresting it as in tacking. The main technique was to keep the foresails filled so that they would carry the ship ahead of the wind. The main and mizzen sails were either hauled up, or 'shivered' - braced so that their yards were pointing into the wind, neutralising their effect.

Some operations, including tacking and wearing, could be performed with all hands if speed was necessary, or they could be done with the duty watch, perhaps with the help of the 'idlers' who did not keep watch. In the *San Domingo* in 1812, each part of the crew was allocated duties for 'Tacking ship with the watch':

> Main brace – Marines, after the lee main clew garnet is risen
> Main topsail brace – Main Topmen, after the weather main clew garnet is risen
> Main topgallant brace – Second Captain of the Poop Afterguard
> Main topmast backstays – One part of the Main Topmen below
> Crossjack braces – Poop Afterguard
> Mizzen topsail braces, mizzen topgallant braces – One part of the Mizzen Topmen…[15]

ANCHOR WORK

Warships rarely came alongside a pier or a jetty in the days of sail, except for essential maintenance work which could not be done any other way. Apart from the difficulty of manoeuvring alongside a quay in variable or unfavourable winds, there was always the danger that the ship might be stuck there indefinitely by a wind blowing it onto the quay. When at rest ships were usually at anchor in a place which provided a certain amount of shelter from the prevailing wind, but also allowed the ship to get out again in most wind conditions.

The basic principle was that the anchor would be dropped into a suitable sea bottom, preferably mud or sand rather than rocks. One or other of its flukes would bury itself in the bottom, retaining it in place. It was essential that the pull on the anchor was horizontal, so a large amount of cable (usually three times the depth of water) had to be paid out to ensure this. Ships could anchor in water up to 40 fathoms or 240 feet deep, and each cable was 120 fathoms long to allow this. A ship would swing with every tide if moored by a single anchor, forming a circle with a radius equal to the length of cable, which meant that it required a good deal of space. It was also possible to use two anchors set in different directions, a process known technically as mooring. This greatly reduced the space needed for an anchor berth, but it required care to prevent the two cables from becoming tangled, resulting in hard work for the crew and the embarrassment of a 'foul hawse.'

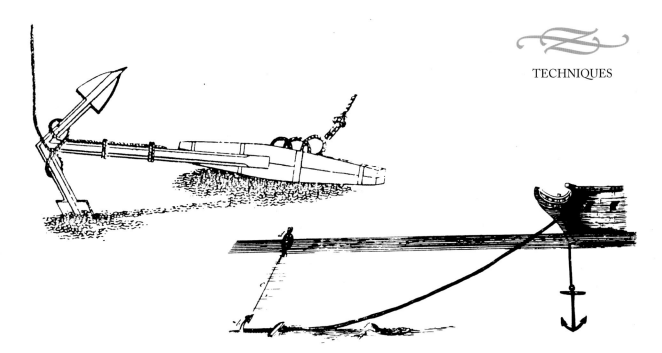

Apart from fighting and tacking quickly, the raising of anchors was the operation which required the largest participation from the crew. Since the cable itself was too thick to wrap round the capstan, an endless rope called a messenger was used to link the two. The process of raising anchor is described by seaman Robert Wilson. It starts when the ship is moored with two anchors, which are raised one at a time:

An anchor with one fluke about to bury itself in the sand on a pull from the cable, to the right. A ship at anchor with an anchor buoy, showing the amount of cable needed in a typical situation.
(Burney's *Universal Dictionary of the Marine*, 1815, Falconer's *Universal Dictionary of the Marine*, 1780)

> …the carpenters get the bars shipped in the capstan and pin and swift them; the topmen (except about 30 or 40), afterguard and Marines man the bars. The messenger is brought to one of the cables, those at the capstan heave round, while about 30 of the topmen not employed there pay out, or slack out, the other cable to allow the ship to near the anchor of that cable they at the capstan are heaving in. Those topmen are called the veering cable men; when there is enough slack, they move up to the capstan and assist to purchase or weigh the anchor. As the cable comes in, it is coiled in a tier snugly by the Quarter-masters and some of the forecastlemen; they are called tierers'. A few of the foretopmen clap on the nippers, the boys move along with them as the cable goes aft, the maintopmen take them off, and the boys carry them forward again…[16]

The heaviest part of the work came when the cable was vertical and the anchor had to be broken out of the mud; then it had to be hauled up vertically until it broke surface. The block and tackle from the cathead was lowered and a hook was attached to the anchor ring. The anchor was raised the rest of the way to the cathead by means of this tackle. After that its lower end was raised until the shank was vertical and the anchor was stowed in that position. When that anchor had been raised, work began on the next, while the topmen went aloft ready to loose sails. When that was complete the ship was sailing, 'under weigh.'

As well as its function in holding the ship stationary, anchors could be used in an emergency to turn the head of the ship through the wind, when danger threatened and it was impossible to tack in any other way. Box-hauling was a kind of 'three point turn' by which a ship was turned round in a very confined space by backing and filling its sails. Club-hauling involved dropping an anchor to help turn the ship's head and then cutting it loose; 'this is never had recourse to but in perilous situations, when it is expected that the ship will miss stays'.[17]

SIGNALS

Ships had to communicate with one another and the shore for various reasons; to pass on intelligence and exchange news, to exchange social communication and to transmit operational orders. If winds were light and the sea was not too rough it was possible to send a boat from one ship to another. To pass on routine messages, such as small changes in the standing instruction, the admiral might order each ship to send a midshipman on board the flagship. Captains might be taken across for an operational conference, a method much favoured by Nelson. Simpler messages could also be passed by hailing though a speaking trumpet, which was not difficult in quiet conditions but much harder with the noise of battle or storm.

The most sophisticated means of signalling, and the only one which was useful in the heat of battle, was by flags. The system had started by using standard flags, such as the red ensign and union flag, and hanging them at specific places in the rigging, and drawing attention to them by firing a gun. In the early 1780s several officers developed new signal codes using specially designed flags and this remained a common theme for inventors over the years – Captain Marryat produced his own method for merchant ships in 1817. During the eighteenth century it was not possible to spell out words by signal flag; a combination of several flags gave a pre-arranged message, such as 'Form in order of sailing by divisions' or 'Anchor as convenient.' Sir Home Popham's code, developed in 1800-3, could be used to spell out actual words, though most signals were still pre-arranged ones, or two letter combinations which spelt words. Thus when Nelson sent his famous signal 'England expects that every man will do his duty' on the approach to the Battle of Trafalgar in 1805, the only word that had to be spelt out was 'duty'. But in practice Nelson only needed signals during the approach. In the battle itself each captain was left to make his own decision about where to engage, unlike the older style of battle where the fleet attempted to manoeuvre as in a quadrille.

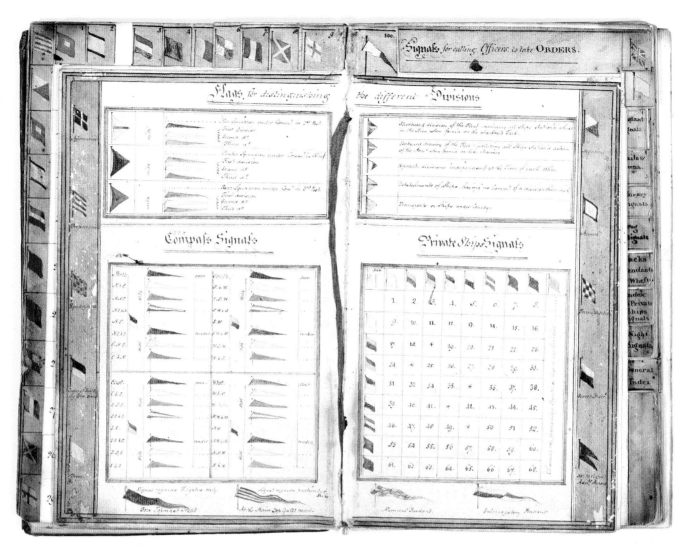

A page from a signal book used by Nelson's fleet during the Nile Campaign, showing signals used to distinguish different parts of the fleet, and individual ships. (NMM D 8796)

In fog or dark, signals could also be made by lights hung from frames, or by firing guns in sequence; though obviously the range was much more limited. There were no specialised signal officers or men. The job went to a senior lieutenant in a flagship, or a midshipman in a private ship.

COASTAL NAVIGATION

There were three main ways of steering the ship, as instructed by the navigating officer. The simplest was to aim at a point on land, though this had its dangers if a tide was sweeping the ship sideways. The second was to steer by the wind. If the ship was close hauled, the helmsman was simply told to keep as close to the wind as possible while keeping the sails full – 'full and by.' Thirdly, when the wind was free and there were no obvious navigational marks, or their use would be misleading, the helmsman was given a compass course to steer.

Each ship had a pair of compasses fitted in a wooden binnacle just in front of the steering wheel, marked in 32 points, from the cardinal ones of north, south etc, down to southeast by south and so on. These too could be divided into quarters so in theory if not in practice it was possible to steer a very accurate course. There was a light between the two compasses for night sailing. As well as its use in steering the ship, the compass could be used to take bearings on points on land, or fixed points in the sea, to establish the ship's position.

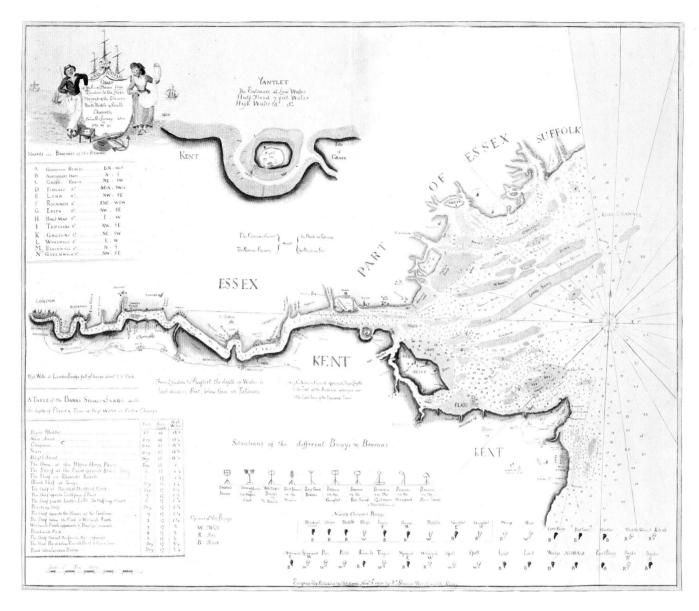

A chart of the Thames estuary, produced by Richard Stanier in 1790. It includes tidal information and pictures of the various beacons and buoys which marked the channels. (NMM B 7431)

The coastal navigator relied on what he could see and identify on land, and to a limited extent on marks in the sea. Great lighthouses like the Eddystone (rebuilt in 1759) were still quite rare. As well as marking a dangerous group of rocks, the lighthouse could be used to take compass bearings. Floating buoys or static beacons were often used to mark the channel in well-used rivers and harbours, but there was no way of lighting them for use at night, and the system of marking varied from place to place.

In the eighteenth century captains and masters supplied their own charts, which they bought or acquired from various sources. They were mostly based on the Mercator projection, which reduced the curved surface of the globe to a flat surface. Most masters were familiar with the approaches to naval ports like Plymouth and Portsmouth without charts, but official ones were produced. For more obscure places the navigator often relied on privately printed charts, from firms like Mount and Page. In distant waters he might acquire foreign charts, for the French were the leaders in this field for much of the eighteenth century. It was only chance that, on the approach to the Battle of the Nile in 1798, Captain Foley in the leading ship had a reasonably accurate French chart of Aboukir Bay, which helped him in his decision to go inshore of the French line. The Admiralty Hydrographic

Department was founded in 1795, and its initial aim was to collect examples of the work of chartmakers, as well as commissioning new surveys. By 1808 it was common to issue the master of each ship with a box of charts for the area he was expected to operate in.

The navigator often relied on transits, on getting two points on land in line to give a very accurate position line. If he had to keep outside a line like this, it was known as a clearing line. Such lines were marked on charts, and many of them were well known to masters with local knowledge. In unfamiliar or poorly charted ports the ship would pay a local pilot, who was exempt from impressment unless he ran the ship aground.

The lead line was essential for finding the depth in shallow waters. According to Captain Riou's orders:

> When the ship is in 20 fathoms water, or sailing on such a course as to render it possible that she may come into such depth of water, a leadsman is instantly to be with his line clear in the weather chains and whenever he has got bottom or that the ship is in hand-line water, another leadsman to be called for, for the opposite chains. These two men are to be relived every half hour and they are upon that occasion to heave the lead in the presence of and to give the line to, the men who relieve them, informing them of the depth of water the ship is in.[18]

OCEAN NAVIGATION

In the open ocean, the seaman had two main ways to find his position. He could calculate it from what had happened in the past, working out the effect of the course and speed of the ship, leeway and tidal and other currents. There was a log-board near the steering wheel, where the officer of the watch recorded the course steered by compass every half hour. Speed was measured by dropping the log line over the stern at regular intervals. A piece of wood, the log itself, was attached to a line which was wound round a reel. When the log was in the water the line was let go and it was timed for a precise period by hourglass. At the end of that the line was stopped and the length which had run out was measured. Distances along the line were measured by a series of knots, hence the term knots for speed. Leeway could be measured with some difficulty, by checking the wake of the ship against the direction in which its head was pointing. Finally, tidal streams were added to the equation, based on the knowledge that came from charts, pilot books, almanacs and previous experience.

It was an inaccurate process, because none of the factors was easy to measure. A helmsman often could not maintain a steady course in light or unfavourable winds. The speed was at best an average, not the actual distance run. Furthermore, there were many inaccuracies in the making and use of log lines. In 1805 Francis Austen found that the line in the *Canopus* was eight inches too long and he had to apply a correction to this.[19] Leeway was difficult to measure, and precise information on tidal streams was rarely possible. The process of dead reckoning, as it was known, was useful if no other means were available, for example when the sky was overcast for weeks at a time; but it was rightly mistrusted as a way of giving a precise position.

This left the seaman with astronomical navigation, based on sun, moon or stars. Provided the skies were clear it was relatively easy to find the latitude of a ship, its distance north or south of the equator. The navigator could take a series of sights of the sun round about noon and find the highest one, which was obviously noon itself. His tables would tell him how high the sun was above the equator that day, and it was a matter of simple arithmetic to find the latitude. By the 1790s most navigators used the sextant to measure such angles. It was made of brass and could measure very accurately an angle of up to 120 degrees. The older quadrant was made of

wood and could only measure up to 90 degrees, but it was still used by old-fashioned officers.

Longitude was of course the problem that had worried navigators and naval administrators for more than a century. Since the earth is constantly moving, any calculation of position to the east or west required precise timekeeping. By the time of Captain Cook's first voyage (1768-71), the lunar method had been devised. This involved measuring the angle between the moon and a particular star, and carrying out a very complex calculation.

The other and simpler solution was already well advanced by the tine Cook returned. John Harrison had almost won his long battle with the Board of Longitude and his chronometer was now accepted as a means of measuring time very accurately, despite all the hazards and ups and downs of service on a ship. Yet it was not universal in the 1800s. Naval ships going on foreign service had to apply for one, and not all did. The 76-gun *Donegal*, for example, evidently did not have one during Nelson's chase across the Atlantic in 1805.

Unlike the sun to the north or south at noon, the moon and stars are not likely to position themselves due east or west of the ship at convenient times, so a more complex calculation was needed to find the longitude. Essentially it involved the celestial triangle, whose points consisted of one of the poles, the position directly under the celestial body in question, and the position of the ship. The angle between the ship and the celestial body was measured by the sextant, and that between the celestial body and the pole could be found in tables. Ideally a navigator would take bearings from three stars at once to get an accurate position; or he might use that day's noon sight, adjusted for known movement since then, to give one of his position lines.

Every officer kept a detailed log book, recording the courses steered, the position of the ship at noon that day, and any other 'remarkable occurrences.' The master's log had the most navigational detail, and it is clear that the officers, including the captain, copied from one another to get a consistent result, for the logs had to be sent to the Admiralty before the officer could claim his pay. In theory all officers were trained in navigation as midshipmen, but in practice many soon forgot most of it, and left the details to the master.

The skills of seamanship, navigation and shiphandling could only be learned by long practice at sea, not in the classroom or on a simulator as in a twentieth century steam navy. The British naval policy of control of the sea, exercised through blockade, ensured that plenty of this practice was available, and this was what gave the Royal Navy the edge in the wars with France. The techniques of seamanship added many new words and phrases to the English language, such as 'to the bitter end', referring to the anchor cable and 'sailing close to the wind.' But much of the seaman's specialised vocabulary – futtocks, catharpins or box-hauling – retains its mystery to the landsman, even the less dedicated reader of naval fiction, though they add much to its atmosphere.

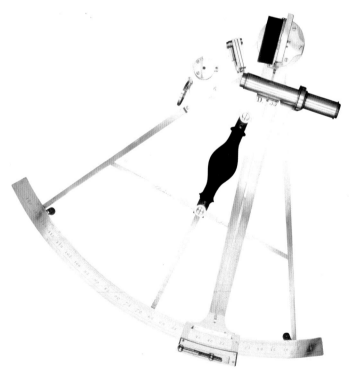

A sextant, circa 1770, showing the telescope near the top, and the accurate graduations on the curved scale below.
(NMM C 8745)

CHAPTER 6

LIFE AT SEA

Officers and seamen were quite used to the fact that the general public, despite the enormous prestige of all things naval, had little understanding of their way of life. Jane Austen describes a dinner party for Captain Wentworth:

> There was a general ignorance of all matters naval throughout the party; and he was much questioned, and especially by the two Miss Musgroves…as to the manner of living on board, daily regulations, food, hours, &c.; and their surprise at his accounts, at learning the degree of accommodation and arrangement which was practicable, drew from him some pleasant ridicule, which reminded Anne of the early days when she too had been ignorant, and she too had been accused of supposing sailors to be living on board without anything to eat, or any cook to dress it if there were, or any servant to wait, or any knife and fork to use.[1]

Life on a ship of war, a community of several hundred people largely isolated from the shore and from other ships, was as complex as any on land.

WATCHES

Until the rules were changed in 1805 the ship's day began officially at 12 noon, when the officers took a sight of the sun to help establish their position. Naval seamen were traditionally arranged in two watches when at sea. Apart from a minority of 'idlers' such as craftsmen and servants who worked mainly in the daytime, the ship's company was divided into two halves and one was on duty at any given moment, day and night. Since a watch lasted for four hours, the majority of men never had more than four hours continuous sleep at sea and often they only had four hours one night in two.

Partly because fleets were spending longer times at sea, a three-watch system was introduced in many ships. Reports from St Vincent's fleet in 1797 show that six ships out of eleven were at three watches. Nelson's *Vanguard* used the three-watch system during the Nile campaign in the following year. After 1800 there was a reaction against the three-watch system. On taking command of the *Otter* sloop in 1809, Captain Willoughby found the men in three watches, which he regarded as part of a general slovenliness. 'Agreeably to the general line of discipline and arrangement I placed the men at watch and watch, obliged them to two changes of linen in the week and to keep their berths and the ship in general clean and wholesome.'

In a two-watch system the men were not expected to be at work for all of the time when on night watch. In the frigate *Amazon* the officer of the watch was expected to keep the men 'awake and in motion', but they were allowed to relax and indeed entertainment such as fid-

115

A model of a galley stove, with its funnel leading out through the decks. The main cooking for the crew was done by boiling in the copper kettles, the lids of which can just be seen on the top, behind the funnel. The ovens are to the left. The front of the stove contains the turnspit and the grill, mainly used for cooking for the officers. (NMM D 3996-2)

dling was positively encouraged. In a three-watch system the men could be kept active during their night watches in order to prevent illness, because they were well enough rested at other times:

all the watch will then be enabled, and should be required, to walk the deck, which will prevent them from lying down on the damp deck or in wet places; a practice that does more injury to the constitution of seamen than at the moment can be imagined; and which, when a ship's company is at two watches, it is scarcely possible to prevent.

Naval ships were better manned than merchantmen, so often the work was less strenuous. While the *Revenge* was at anchor in the Downs in 1805 John Powell wrote:

We keep watch the same here as at sea, ie four hours up and the same down. I am in the starboard watch so that when the larboard watch is on in a morning we can sleep till 7 or 8 o'clock and sometimes longer, which I could not do in an Indiaman. We have very little work to do and plenty of men to assist when any work is to be done. Some days we have but little to do but on others nobody would believe that is unused to the sea what a hurry we are all in. As a proof of it, last Monday I ate one part of my breakfast upon deck, another in the mizzen top and finished it on the mizzen topsail yard.

Any relaxation depended on the attitude of the officers, and the seamen of the *Eurydice* complained in 1796:

we are to holystone the decks from 4 o'clock in the morning until 8, for if a man should rest he is kicked in the face and bleeds on the stone, and afterwards made to wash the stone from the blood and then reported to the captain and flocked [flogged?] for no provocation, unless by our lieutenant report to be conceive other grievous complaints which are too tedious to mention.

THE MORNING

The ship's day began four in the morning, according to William Robinson of the *Revenge*:

They then come on deck again, pull off their shoes and stockings, turn up their trowsers to above their knees and commence *holy-stoning* the deck, as it is termed....here the men suffer from being obliged to kneel down on the wetted deck, and a gravelly sort of sand strewed over it. To perform this work with their bare knees, rubbing the deck with a stone and the sand, the grit of which is often very injurious. In this manner the watch continues till about four bells, or six o'clock; they then begin to wash and swab the decks till seven bells, and at eight bells the boatswain's mate pipes to breakfast.[2]

Mealtimes varied slightly, though with a fleet they were often dictated by the flagship, '...at

eight o'clock in the morning the drums beat off and a pennant is hoisted at the masthead of the commodore's ship; the same again at 12; for it is always the etiquette in a squadron that the senior commanding officer should make the hours of breakfast and dinner.'[3] One man from each mess had already drawn the stores from the purser's steward and taken it to the cook. Now he got the cooked food from the ship's galley and took it to his mess. The seamen had half an hour to an hour for breakfast, then the working day began in earnest. The men would perhaps exercise the great guns or the small arms, or practice various sailing manoeuvres, or carry out maintenance work on the rigging and hull. At midday the officers took their bearings on the sun for navigation, and hands were piped to dinner immediately afterwards. This was the main meal of the day, lasting up to an hour or an hour and a half. The men were issued with their first alcohol of the day – beer in home waters, wine or brandy in the Mediterranean and rum in the West Indies. They feasted on a stew of salt beef or pork, with meatless or 'banyan' days twice a week when they ate cheese or peas. Ship's biscuit, or unleavened bread, made up a large part of the diet. The men relaxed and told stories among their best friends on board, though some social isolates found it difficult to be accepted in a mess.

A deck scene on the East Indiaman *Deal Castle* in 1775, though not unlike what would be seen on a naval ship. Officers promenade the deck and a seaman tends the rigging. An awning has been rigged to protect the officers from the sun. The helmsman is to the right and livestock can be seen in the form of chicken coops and a goat. By Thomas Hearne. (NMM 1201)

AFTERNOON AND EVENING

Work resumed in the afternoon, until four o'clock when the afternoon watch ended. The next watches were only of two hours each, as this would ensure that the men, in either a two watch or a three-watch system, did not have the same watch every day. They were known as the dog watches, because they were 'cur-tailed,' according to Jack Aubrey's awful joke. At eight o'clock in the evening, the first watch began. The off-watch officers and men retired and the ship was left in the hands of the duty watch for the next four hours. To the poet Thomas Downey this was the moment of contentment:

> Mild evening closes round. The watch is set.
> In peaceful slumber, some their toils forget:
> While those on deck appointed to preside,
> Conduct the silent course along the tide
> Until in turn relieved: then lingering wears
> The warning light, and rising moon appears.

Captain Robert Clarke of the Royal Marines was more cynical. 'So much for the happiness of a sea life – and the poetical falsehoods of that villain Downie!!!'[4]

The rest of the crew now retired to their hammocks. Each of these had been rolled, with the bedding, into a tight cylinder and stowed in nettings in racks round the upper decks of the ship. Now they were got out by their users and carried down to the lower decks. Sometimes this could lead to farce. One evening in May 1804 the *Victory* was blockading Toulon when Nelson spotted something under the foresail and went to investigate. At the same moment the Boatswain piped the order to take the hammocks below. 'One of the main topmen who had hauled his hammock out of the netting swinging it over his shoulder came in contact with his lordship's head and laid him prostrate on the deck.' The seaman restored the admiral to his feet and apologized profusely, protesting he was not aware of anyone behind him. Nelson replied, 'My man, it was not your fault, it was my own. I ought to have known better than to stand in your way.'[5]

Each man had a space allocated for his hammock below decks, at least 14 inches wide, though petty officers and captains of parts of the ship were allowed more and were 'not to be pinched.' Each hammock was 'a piece of hempen cloth, three feet wide, gathered together at the two ends by means of a clew, and slung horizontally under the deck, forming a receptacle for a bed for the sailors to sleep in.' A ship of war never seemed more crowded than at night-time, when several hundred men would sling their hammocks together. This was slightly mitigated at sea, when nearly half the men were on duty at any given moment.

After less than four hours sleep the seamen, except idlers, would be woken up to take over the deck. The middle watch, from midnight to four in the morning, was the least popular of all. According to Basil Hall:

> …certainly it is a plague of the first order, to be shaken out of a warm bed at midnight, when three hours of sound sleep have sealed up our eyelids all the faster….It is a bitter break too, to have four good hours sliced out of the very middle of the night's rest, especially when this tiresome interval is to be passed in the cold and rain, or, which is often still more trying, in the sultry calm of smooth, tropical sea, when the sleepy sails, as wet with dew as if they had been dipped overboard, flap idly against the masts and rigging…with notes so monotonous that, the bare recollection of their sound almost sets me to sleep, now.[6]

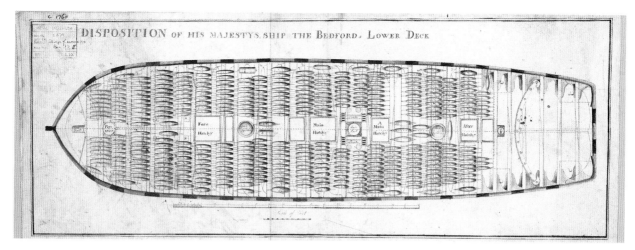

After that the ship's day began again, with a regularity which could become extremely monotonous over the months and years. There was a little variation during the week – Thursdays and Sundays were used for the inspection of clothing, and on the Sabbath there was usually some kind of religious service, and the reading of the Articles of War once a month. The daily work might also vary, with perhaps great guns one day and boarding and small arms the next. But there was a 'uniform sameness, day after day, and month after month', as Nelson put it during two years blockading Toulon.

The hammocks on the lower deck of the 74-gun ship *Bedford*, in service from 1775-1817. The aftermost space, to the right, is unusable for hammocks because of the sweep of the tiller, but it contains small officers' cabins in the corners. The first four tiers of hammocks, in red, are for the marines. (NMM D 4647)

SHIP ORGANISATION

Most naval ships had crews of 200 men or more. The officers often had a different watch system from the crew, so did not have them same men under the every day. There was a danger that contact between officers and men would become very distant and impersonal. The answer was the system of 'divisions', by which each of the lieutenants had a party of men under him for welfare and administrative purposes, subdivided into groups under midshipmen. Admiral Lord Howe's orders of 1776 gave a fairly concise account of the system. 'The petty officers and seamen of the ships' companies are to be formed into two or three divisions, according to the complements and classes of ship, and subdivided into squads with a midshipman appointed to each, who are respectively to be responsible for the good order and discipline of the men entrusted to their care.'

The most important reason for regulating the crew was the need to maintain their health. Sir Gilbert Blane, the Physician of the Fleet under Admiral Rodney in 1780, wrote, 'I hardly ever knew a ship's company become sickly which was well regulated in point of cleanliness and dryness. It is the custom in some ships to divide the crew into squads or divisions under the inspection of respective officers, who make a weekly review of their persons and clothing....This ought to be an indispensable duty in ships of two or three decks.'

To Victorian historians, all this concern for order, health and discipline was highly laudable. But to the seaman it seemed like an assault on his few liberties. In the past, officers had hardly cared what seamen did as long as they turned out for duty when needed. But from the 1780s onwards, the seaman found his own space greatly reduced. Washing was done outside his normal working hours, without any provision for soap or even fresh water. He was obliged to supply himself with a minimum quantity of clothing, bought from the purser's monopoly in the slop chest and paid for out of the man's own, very limited earnings. Admiral Patton was aware that the seamen were forced to spend their own money on clothing and that they resented any regulation:

119

…an idea has always prevailed among seamen that the service of their country does not confine them with regard to the mode of their dress, according to the custom in armies, and it is by them deemed injustice to deprive seamen of the disposal of their own money…

Patton was against a single system of discipline:

One ship is necessarily totally separated and unconnected with any other ship; that it is impossible to bring the real state of the internal discipline under the review of any superior officer not embarked in that ship; that naval service removes ships to such a distance as puts them beyond all control of any power whatever; that ships, which are of great value and immense importance, may be with ease transferred, with all their tackle and ammunition, from one state to another…

To Archibald Sinclair the idea of theoretical discipline was anathema. Captains who wrote treatises on ship administration, he claimed, 'did little or no good, as it was well known in the service that their ships were in the worst possible order.'[7] Marryat was not sympathetic to those who tried to impose too much 'interior discipline' on their ships. Captain Hawkins' order book for the *Rattlesnake* was intended mainly to clear the captain of responsibility and put most of it on the first lieutenant.[8]

Up to about 1800, it was an article of faith that the washing of decks was good for keeping the ship clean, and the men occupied. This was taken very seriously, as in a petition from the crew of the frigate *Blanche* in 1795:

In the first place, we are employed from morning to two or three of clock in the afternoon washing and scrubbing the decks, and every day our chest and bags is ordered on deck, and not down till night; nor ourselves neither even so particular as to wash the decks with fresh water, and if we get wet at any time and hang or spread our clothes to dry, our captain throws them overboard.

In 1797 Sir John Jervis recommended that 'the decks and sides of the ships of the fleet be washed every evening as well as morning during the summer months'. But by 1801 Admiral Keith was or the opinion that 'The custom of washing the decks of ships of war in all climates in every temperature of the air, and on stated days, let the weather be what it may' had become 'universally prevalent to the destruction of the health and lives of valuable men.' He rescinded the orders issued by St Vincent, and ordered that the lower deck be washed not more than once in fourteen days.

Seamen often had difficulties with cleaning their clothes and persons, though it was not the fact of cleaning which was at issue, but the inadequate means available to do it and the punishments for failing to comply. In the *Reunion* in 1795 the men wrote:

'Captain B also obliges us to wash our linen twice a week in salt water, and put two shirts on every week, and if they do not look as clean as if they was washed in fresh water he stops the person's grog for three or four days.'

Which has the misfortune to displease him in the above and if our hair is not tied to please him he orders it to be cut off.

If such petitions do not occur after 1800, it is perhaps because seamen got more used to the need for cleanliness, or officers provided more fresh water or soap for doing it. Even in 1811 however, Phillip Patton was aware of the need for a captain to 'explain himself on this matter publicly, showing the necessity of orderly cleanliness'. He discounted this obsession with the appearance of seamen:

It is not to be expected that the vanity of personal appearance by which armies are in some measure managed can have any sensible effect in regulating the companies of ships. Seamen cannot be made the objects of an admiring crowd and are, from their previous education and changes of situation from merchants' to the King's service, and from their country's to the service of trade, incapable of being modelled so as to imbibe military ideas. Or, if these ideas could be introduced, it is impossible they should prevail without destroying the enthusiasm of seamen, who must always be less exposed to danger from the enemy than from the inconstancy of the atmosphere and the instability of the ocean. This want of security and state of uncertainty seem to render seamen in a great measure incapable of the order and uniformity of land forces; and the services in many respects quite dissimilar.[9]

CONTACT WITH THE SHORE

Seamen had no right to shore leave, and officers often forbade it for fear of desertion. The men of the *Canopus* petitioned the Admiralty in 1806. 'Like other people we cannot after three years toil have the satisfaction of a walk on shore, when we see people of other ships constantly passing us.' In the *Prosperine* nine years earlier, the captain created a kind of hostage system to prevent desertion, '…the smallest indulgence of liberty is obtained by one shipmate hazarding himself to the powers of a court martial, or otherwise punished as the captain thinks proper. If the person obtaining liberty does not return, his bondsman suffers the above.'[10]

Seamen were, however, allowed to keep in contact with friends and family by means of letters, with cheap rates of postage. A literate seaman like John Powell of the *Revenge* was able to make some money by writing letters for his comrades, though he jibbed at forging a marriage certificate for one of their 'wives.' Women were allowed to come on board while the ship was in port, usually rowed out to an anchorage in small boats. According to Admiralty Regulations only the wives of seamen were allowed, but this rule was rarely enforced, except by the evangelical Captain Gambier, who made himself very unpopular. But many of the women were local prostitutes and William Robinson of the *Revenge* describes their coming on board:

> On the arrival of any man of war in port, these girls flock down to the shore, where boats are always ready; and here may be witnessed a scene, somewhat similar to the trafficking for slaves in the West Indies. As they approached a boat, old Charon…surveys them from stem to stern, with the eyes of a bargaining jew; and carefully culls out the best looking, and the most dashingly dressed.
>
> After having moored our ship, swarms of boats came round us; …a great many were freighted with cargoes of ladies, a sight that was most gratifying, and a great treat….So soon as these boats were allowed to come alongside, the seamen flocked down pretty quick, one after the other, and brought their choice up, so that in the course of the afternoon, we had four hundred and fifty on board.[11]

Ships were completely chaotic when women came on board. Chamier's first impression of the lower deck in harbour included 'dirty women, the objects of sailors' affections, with beer cans [sic] in hand' who 'were everywhere conspicuous.'[12]

On overseas stations the men were often given shore leave. In home waters, with the greater temptation and to abscond, this was much rarer. Instead, boats were also allowed to come alongside the ships at anchor to trade with them. In June 1805 the 74-gun *Revenge*

anchored for a week at the Downs to await a favourable wind to take her down the English Channel. Local traders were allowed to come on board by boat and John Powell found plenty more dishonesty around him:

> Any inexperienced person may be taken in by a set of abominable wretches like them when the men received their money they were ready to tear themselves to pieces to buy them new things. One man belonging to another ship had received one hundred pounds and getting drunk the next morning he lost it all every farthing. On the day appointed for payment about two hundred jews came on board bringing with them all sorts of slop, watches, hats, rings, lockets, telescopes etc. It was exactly like a fair. There was also provisions of all sorts to be sold together with gingerbread and cakes which many of the men were fools enough to buy. One man gave eight guineas for a watch and the next morning he found it was good for nothing. Another gave thirty shillings for a hat that was not worth 12, so that's the way that they are always so poor or they usually are. One man got his pocket picked out of twenty six pounds and marine got a flogging for robbing his messmate of six and twenty shilling, but that is only a specimen of their tricks. As for me, as soon as I got mine I locked it up.

He indulged himself in buying a cake and some soap for four shillings. 'I have got the character of a miser and credit of having plenty of money for they are all very sure I did not spend it and must have it.'

ENTERTAINMENT

Shipboard life had many long periods when very little happened beyond a rather sterile routine. Both officers and men had to rely on their own resources for recreation and entertainment. Chaplain Mangin describes the scene in a wardroom.

> ...several [officers] still linger behind, for the various purposes of writing letters, playing backgammon, fencing, singing (with laudable energy of voice and a thorough contempt for music) practising on a violin, or German-flute...A subaltern of Marines, very much devoted to 'the pursuits of literature', may indulge himself by trying to spell through a newspaper of three weeks date...[13]

Robert Clarke, captain of marines in the 74-gun *Swiftsure*, had two overriding interests as his ship escorted a convoy across the Atlantic in 1815. He desperately wanted to get hold of some fine wine for the mess, and was disappointed when the ship was not allowed to stop at Madeira. Then he tried and failed to make contact with a ship in the convoy which he believed was carrying wine to sell. In the meantime he devoted himself to reading, getting through a book every two or three days and producing a critique of Sir Walter Scott's *Rokeby*. Books were important to officers, who usually had some kind of privacy to read them. Captain Hall, a Scot and a writing man himself, thought that Sir Walter Scott, the literary superstar of the day, was 'perhaps the foremost man of all the world'.[14]

Music was perhaps the most important recreation of both the officers and the lower deck. Some captains formed ships bands, with varied results. According to Frederick Hoffman of the *Minotaur*:

> Our gallant and would-be musical captain consulted us all respecting harmonious sounds, but alas! we were weighed in the musical balance and found wanting. This, however, did not discourage him. Nine of the crew came forward with three of the marines, offering

A popular print of a 'milling match' below decks, with the men's waists tied to the ends of a sea chest to prevent too much damage being done, and an officer looking on. Women are shown prominently, if not sympathetically, and black seamen as part of the crew. (NMM B 3848)

themselves as candidates for the band. The captain, after having consulted one of the sergeants of marines, who played the hautboy, whereto anything might be made of the men who had come forward as musicians, it was determined *nem. con.* that a pease-barrel should be manufactured into a big drum, that two ramrods should be metamorphosed into triangles, that the two bassoons and the hautboy taken in the French frigate should be brought into action without loss of time, that the marine and ship's fifer, with the marine drummer, should be drilled with the others, under the direction of the sergeant, and a horrible confusion of unmusical sounds they made for more than six weeks. The skipper was in his glory, and everyone else amazed. Some of my messmates prayed for them heartily, particularly the first lieutenant, who thought the captain musically mad. The mids declared they never would be respectable enough to be called a band, but would be bad enough to be called a banditti, as they looked more like brigands than musicians.[15]

Otherwise the lower deck made its own entertainment. A visitor to HMS *Gibraltar* in 1811 noted:

It is ridiculous to hear the sailors lie and sing in their hammocks of an evening. The chant the most dismal ditties in the world and the words be ever so merry, yet the tune is one and the same, namely 'Admiral Hosier's Ghost.' They never seemed to dance with any spirit unless they had an old black to fiddle to them, of the name of Bond.[16]

In an age when people both afloat and ashore were reliant on their own resources for entertainment, story-telling took on a special place, and this was true at sea even more than anywhere else. Experienced sailors naturally had a great fund of stories from past experience, and the ability to tell them well (and perhaps without too much repetition) made for a good mess-

123

Seamen dancing below decks to a fiddler. Yet again the height between decks is greatly exaggerated. This print was done in 1832, so it is not certain that seamen painted the name of the ship on their shirts during the wars. From *Journal of a Landsman...* London, 1832 by James Hore.
(NMM D 4575-12)

mate and therefore a popular man. Stories even had their market value. In *Peter Simple* a seaman cites the precedent of Boatswain Chucks and asks to be paid with a glass of grog for telling a yarn to an officer.[17] But the influence on nineteenth century naval writing was far greater than that. It is perhaps no coincidence that the Navy of the Napoleonic Wars produced a fine crop of writers, led by Marryat. It was not just because post-war unemployment gave them plenty of time. They had picked up the habit of story-telling from the men under their command and Captain Gascock's *Naval Sketch Book*, for example, is largely and unashamedly a collection of lower deck yarns in what the author believes is the language of the lower deck.

(Scene – Galley of a Cruiser)

WHAT! – your *trafflyggar*-tar? That breed's gone by, my bo – few are now seen in the service – your present race are another set o' men altogether – as different, aye, as different as beer and bilge-water – They're all for *larning* now; and; and yet there's never one in a thousand as larns his trade – and what's worse nor all, they're all a larnin' from sogers to rig as lubberly as lobsters.[18]

Marryat's works are generally closer to the novel in form, but each is essentially a collection of yarns, some even told in direct speech by members of the crew.

DISCIPLINE AND PUNISHMENT

Writing in an age when naval discipline was formal and strict, C S Forester put these thoughts into the mind of Horatio Hornblower. He remembered the Biblical centurion who 'said to a man go and he goeth' and he believed that the Roman army and the Royal Navy were identical in discipline. Captain Marryat, who was there, saw things differently. His

Boatswain Chucks believed that his men needed 'stimilis' in the form of his cane to make them move. 'It is not here as in the scriptures, 'Do this, and he doeth it.' (by the bye, that chap must have had his soldiers in tight order); but it is 'Do this, d—n your eyes', and then it is done directly.'[19]

Informal punishments inflicted by petty and warrant officers were common in 1800. Boatswain Chucks had a 'persuader' made out of three rattan canes twisted into one, know as the trio *juncto in uno* – echoing Nelson's famous *menage a trois* with Sir William and Lady Hamilton.[20] Such punishments figured largely in seamen's complaints, and they tended to be restricted over the years. When Captain Keats wrote the orders for the *Superb* in 1803 he was barely tolerant of informal punishments. 'The boatswain and his mates conformable to the old custom of the service are to carry rattans, but they are to be used with discretion.' By 1811 Captain Cumby of the *Hyperion* was totally opposed: 'The highly improper practice of what is called starting the men, is most peremptorily forbidden; punishment shall only be inflicted by order of the Captain, to whom alone the Lords Commissioners of the Admiralty have thought proper to delegate that power.' This may have reflected the general situation, because according to Captain Corbett of the *Nereide*, 'an idea has crept in and is gaining head, that the punishment they call starting is not legal.' A court martial in 1809 reprimanded him for issuing his petty officers with sticks of an excessive size, but tacitly recognised its legality. The reduction in starting may have done something to reduce the day to day brutality of the seaman's life, but it also tended to raise the stakes for him - if punishment was only by order of the captain, it was likely to be more formal and severe, probably a flogging. William Robinson describes the procedure:

The Sailor's Description of a Chase and Capture. It shows something of the comradeship of messdeck life, and the importance of story-telling in the sailor's culture. It shows a black seaman accepted as part of the mess. (NMM 7233)

Seamen in irons awaiting trial and punishment, guarded by a marine, with mess life going on around him. One is disgruntled with his condition, the other is merely bored. (NMM PAD 0157)

About eleven o'clock, or six bells, when any of the men are in irons, or on the black list, the boatswain or mate are ordered to call all hands; the culprits are then brought forward by the master at arms….All hands now being mustered, the captain orders the man to strip; he is then seized to a grating by the wrists and knees; his crime is then mentioned, and the prisoner may plead, but, in nineteen cases out of twenty, he is flogged for the most trifling offence or neglect.

Not everyone agreed with Robinson's assessment. A visitor to the *Gibraltar* in 1811 had the opposite view. 'I could not but observe how very seldom the men were punished and that they were never disgraced at the gangway but for some willful fault.'[21]

Captain Thomas Bladen Capel of the *Phoebe* was taking no chances of sparking a revolt, a few years after the great mutinies:

In time of punishment the Marine Guard to be under arms on the quarterdeck, the marines paraded on the gangways, the officers to be in uniform, the mates and warrant officers in the waist to mix with the people and a lieutenant to attend in the outer rank to see no irregularity committed and every person … attentive during punishment and any irregular behavior among the people to be immediately reported.[22]

William Robinson describes the punishment of running the gauntlet, usually awarded for theft from comrades. In an environment where the bonds of trust were often reinforced by battle, a thief destroyed morale, as each man became suspicious of his colleagues. In that case the lower deck had no sympathy for the prisoner, and exacted full vengeance.

The criminal is placed with his naked back in a large tub, wherein a seat has been fixed, and his hands lashed down his sides: this tub is secured on a grating, and is drawn round the decks by the boys, the master-at-arms with his drawn sword pointing to the prisoner's breast. The cavalcade starts from the break of the quarter-deck, after the boatswain has given the prisoner a dozen lashes, and the ship's crew are ranged round the decks in two rows, so that the prisoner passes between them, and each man is provided with a three yarn knettle; that is, three rope yarns tightly laid together and knotted. With this, each man must cut him, or be thought implicated in the theft.

Flogging round the fleet was the cruellest of all punishments, worse than death in the opinion of many, including Marryat. It was awarded by court martial, often for desertion.

A launch is fitted up with a platform and shears. It is occupied by the unfortunate individual, the provost-marshal, the boatswain, and his mates, with their implements of office, and armed marines stationed at the bow and stern. When the signal is made for punishment, all the ships in the fleet send one or two boats each, with crews cleanly dressed, the officers in full uniform, and marines under arms. These boats collect at the side of the ship where the launch is lying, and the ship's company are ordered to mount the rigging, to witness that portion of the whole punishment which, after sentence has been read, is inflicted upon the prisoner. When he has received the allotted number of lashes he is, for the time, released, and permitted to sit down, with a blanket over his shoulders, while the boats, which attend the execution, make fast to the launch and tow it to the next ship in the fleet, where the same number of lashes are inflicted with corresponding ceremonies;- and he is thus towed from one ship to another until he has received the whole of his punishment.

A seaman is about to be flogged, when another owns up to the offence. Marines stand guard on the quarterdeck as a deterrent, the officers, including two very young midshipmen or volunteers, are to the left. The crew stand informally to the right. (NMM PU 1077)

The results were usually permanent. 'During the later part of the punishment, the suffering is dreadful; and a man who has undergone this sentence is generally broken down in constitution, if not in spirits, for the remainder of his life.'[23]

THE HAZARDS OF THE SEA

Life was short in the early nineteenth century, by modern standards; infant mortality, diseases and occupational hazards all took their toll. The seamen's profession was one of the most dangerous and adventurous of all, and he accepted that he might well be the victim of a shipwreck some day. John Wetherell claimed to have been wrecked a dozen times in merchant ships and warships, on a dozen ships, though his editor, C S Forester admitted he 'never could resist the temptation to embellish his narrative.'[24] In the years from 1793 to 1799, 2967 merchant ships were lost through shipwreck, compared with 3639 to enemy action. Among warships, it is estimated that 152 were lost through shipwreck from 1793 to 1801, compared with 62 by enemy action.[25] The maximum strength of the navy during this period was 864 ships, not all of which were in commission. Ships were unpowered and solely dependent on the vagaries of the weather, and there were no forecasts beyond the experience and observation of the officers. Though philanthropic societies were beginning to address the problem, there were very few lifeboats and even fewer means of rescuing ships in distress. A wooden ship could catch fire, or it would break up very quickly on rocks, or more slowly if it was pounded on a sandbank.

One of the most celebrated events of the age was the saving of the *Guardian* under Lieutenant Edward Riou. She was originally a 44-gun ship, converted in 1789 to carry stores

The *Guardian* close to sinking
among icebergs.
(NMM PAD 6024)

and a few convicts to the recently founded colony of New South Wales. After leaving Cape Town, on Christmas Eve she found herself in a thick fog among several 'islands of ice' in latitude 43 degrees 30 minutes south. Riou was not alarmed and tried to find small pieces of ice to supplement his water supplies. He relaxed until he heard 'the helm move instantaneously with unaccustomed velocity to one side or the other.' He rushed on deck to find the ship in very thick fog, and difficult to manoeuvre in light winds. She seemed to enter a cavern between icebergs and Riou's eyes focussed on the jib-boom, the extreme forward point of the ship, to judge its distance from the ice. The whole frame of the ship shook as she hit a berg, though the damage turned out to be less than Riou had expected and the hull seemed largely intact. Things got worse when the rudder was torn away. The first impact had caused several leaks and the pumps were rigged to get the water out. The sails were wrecked by a sudden gust of wind, and guns, stores and even anchors had to be dropped overboard. Riou established teams of men to take turns in the gruelling task of operating the chain pumps, to at least prevent the water from gaining in the hold. He began to prepare one sail after another for 'fothering' – covering it with a mixture of ashes, cinders and chopped rope yarns and lowering it carefully under the leak in the hope that it ~~would~~ the yarn would be drawn into the hole to plug it. But on Christmas day the water was nearly at the level of the lower deck beams, one of the pumps broke and the crew was approaching exhaustion. If anything he was in a more desperate situation than Captain Cook in 1770, when the *Endeavour* was grounded and holed on the Great Barrier Reef. At least Cook was in a warm climate and land, however hostile, was not far away.

Discipline began to collapse, the spirit room was broken open and there was a 'rage for the boats' among the drunken crew, who wanted to abandon ship although they were many miles from land and a long way from the nearest trade routes. This was not Riou's intention. He was a man of great strength of character and was perhaps the first to believe that the captain should be the last to leave a sinking ship. Later he would 'reprobate in the strongest terms the idea of a captain of a man-of-war forsaking a ship to save his own life, while a single man remained behind to whom he could by possibility be useful, or indeed under any other circumstances, to quit a ship in distress and leave his crew to perish.' Riou allowed those who wanted to get into the boats, and resolved to save the ship with the remainder of his men. The next two months were an epic of toil, danger, isolation, leadership and suspense. More sails were fothered with limited success. Several rudders were improvised but the ship never steered properly. One day after a superhuman effort, pumping would almost clear the hold; the next, the water would be back again in greater volume than ever. It was almost impossible to navigate as there was no accurate way to measure the speed. The remaining crew came close to mutiny and exhaustion, but there were no more boats for them to escape in. At last, on 22 February, the Cape of Good Hope was sighted and six whale boats towed the ship, now reduced to 'little more than a floating raft', into harbour.[26]

A different kind of horror occurred on 16 March 1800 when the great 100-gun *Queen Charlotte*, flagship of the Mediterranean Fleet, caught fire off Leghorn:

> I made for the ward-room door, upon opening which, a dense volume of thick black smoke drove me back, half-suffocated and bewildered. I ran to the weather-quarter gallery; and there, O God! what a sight burst on my view! The flames that rose from the quarterdeck, and gave it the appearance of the crater of a volcano, had just reached the mainsail; their glare was reflected strongly on the agitated faces of hundreds of men assembled on the forecastle…

The 46-gun frigate *Alceste* on fire off Pulo Leat near Sumatra in 1817, during a failed diplomatic mission to China, showing how fiercely a wooden ship burns. The incident was used by Patrick O'Brian in *The Nutmeg of Consolation*. (NMM PAF 8549)

The sea was covered with struggling sailors; the few boats that ventured near, under a heavy fire, which the guns, that were all shotted, sent forth, were full to sinking....I plunged into the water, and struck out for the launch.

'There is no room, we cannot take you in,' said many voices for the boat. 'Keep off, at your peril!' said a discordant one, as I grasped the gunnel of a well-filled boat, and a heavy blow broke two of the fingers of my right hand, and made me relinquish my hold...

I was roused from my torpid state by the blowing up of the after magazine, which detached the whole of her stern-frame from the body of the now splendid luminary, that gave the idea of a world in conflagration. She now majestically raised her bows high in the air, with her tapering lofty masts, and submerged her stern, going down gracefully in the 'deep deep sea.'[27]

Though officers and men had different views of the pleasures and rewards of life at sea, they shared equally in the dangers and hardships.

CHAPTER 7

ENEMIES AND ALLIES

The Royal Navy had many enemies and relatively few allies for most of its wars against France. At one time or another between 1793 and 1815, Britain was at war with France, Spain, the Netherlands, Denmark, Russia and the United States. Also during the same period, the British fought on the same side as the Swedes, Russians, Spanish, Prussians, Austrians and Turks but this left less impression on the British historical memory. In land warfare the British often needed friends. In 1798 the government craved an alliance with Austria as the key to victory. Co-operation with Spanish guerrillas in the Peninsular War, or with the Prussians at Waterloo, was vital to success. At sea the British were less dependent on allies, even when they had them. It was rare for foreign ships to exercise with the British fleet (though the Portuguese did so with the Channel Fleet in 1794) and it was unknown for them to serve together in battle. Portuguese ships of the line, for example, were sent out to join Nelson in the Mediterranean in 1798 but (like many of the British ships sent out), they failed to join him until after the Battle of the Nile had settled the issue. The image of Britain alone against European tyranny for almost the whole of the wars was perhaps not completely accurate, but it is one that suits the purposes of naval fiction. The British were far more aware of foreign navies as enemies than allies.

THE FRENCH NAVY

Most naval fiction, of both the nineteenth and twentieth century varieties, is set between 1800 and 1815, when the main enemy was Napoleon Bonaparte rather than the French Revolution. Perhaps this was because the enemy, in the form of a dictator and alleged tyrant, was one that the twentieth century could understand; perhaps it was because the Royal Navy was more professional in these years, or because its operations ranged even wider over the seas. The Corsican first attracted notice as an artillery major during the siege of Toulon in 1794. He went on to conquer northern Italy, much to the discomfort of the British Mediterranean Fleet. He abandoned plans to invade Britain by sea in 1798, and instead led a combined operation to capture Egypt, during which his fleet narrowly escaped defeat and capture by the young Nelson. But the great British admiral eventually found his warships at anchor in Aboukir Bay and devastated them, leaving Bonaparte's army trapped in Egypt. The general abandoned them and sailed home, evading British patrols. He became First Consul

and virtual dictator of France, and then crowned himself emperor in 1804. He had an amazing capacity for administrative work, great skill in battle and huge charisma among his followers. He fought in more than fifty battles in his lifetime and reformed the political and administrative systems of France and most of the countries he conquered. He had an insatiable appetite for ever greater power and was indifferent to the casualties his wars might cause, which made him a dangerous force in Europe.

Napoleon Bonaparte is barely mentioned in nineteenth century naval fiction, which deals with officers and seaman who often show great professional skills but have little passion against the enemy. For twentieth century writers, particularly Forester and O'Brian, the emperor looms much larger. Forester wrote in a time of dictators, before, during and after the Second World War. There are obvious parallels with Stalin, as the authoritarian successor to a great revolution; and with Hitler, who conquered most of Europe and planned to invade Britain. Forester was certainly impressed with Napoleon's vindictiveness and ruthlessness, and has him try to execute Hornblower (perhaps drawing inspiration from Napoleon's persecution of Sir Sidney Smith); but there was no suggestion that he committed crimes against humanity on anything like the scale of the twentieth century dictators. The British government had similar attitudes; when he was defeated it sent him into exile rather than trying him for overthrowing the French government or for war crimes.

In the case of Patrick O'Brian's Stephen Maturin, Bonaparte is more like Stalin than Hitler. He is a tyrant, the betrayer of the French Revolution and the oppressor of much of Europe. Although Maturin is an Irish intellectual of liberal persuasion, he is prepared to devote not only his medical skills, but his life, his discretion and his formidable intellect to secret and vital work against the Corsican.

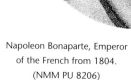

Napoleon Bonaparte, Emperor
of the French from 1804.
(NMM PU 8206)

Despite his unique skills as a soldier and an administrator, his island birth and his many near brushes with the British navy, Bonaparte was always defective in his understanding of sea power. He failed to understand that a fleet was different from an army, far more dependent on wind and weather, and therefore better controlled by the officer on the spot than from a distance. His peremptory instructions to his admirals were not helpful, and led directly to the defeat at Trafalgar. Furthermore, he failed to see that the French fleet, despite the best efforts of its officers and men, was inherently inferior to the Royal Navy.

By the time of the Revolution, the French navy was quite satisfied with the successes of its recent past. True it had not defeated the British in a full-scale fleet battle for almost exactly a century, but it had suffered only two clear-cut defeats itself. In 1759 the Brest fleet was driven into Quiberon Bay and largely destroyed; and in 1782 Admiral Rodney rather reluctantly broke the French line at the Battle of the Saintes in the West Indies, to achieve a decisive victory which saved what was left of the British Empire after the American colonies had defected. Apart from that, the French could look on the American War as a success. Their intervention had done much to secure the position of the rebels ashore, for example when they drove the British fleet off from the Chesapeake and caused the surrender of their army at Yorktown.

The Revolution interrupted the progress of the French navy. Most of the officers were from aristocratic backgrounds and the majority of them fled during the Reign of Terror. Naval officers cannot be improvised as easily as army officers, for the sea is not man's natural environment. There were three ways to find new officers; by promoting petty officers, by

taking on experienced merchant seaman, or by training new ones. None of these was entirely satisfactory. A petty officer had no concern with navigation, ship handling or tactics and did not convert easily to an officer. A merchant seaman was skilled in getting his ship from A to B with the minimum of risk, and had none of the daring required in a naval officer. It took years to train an effective officer from scratch, and it was all the more difficult if there was no corps of experienced officers as teachers and models. A naval officer requires a peculiar combination of skill, courage and zeal for the state which was difficult to achieve. One or two of these elements was not enough, he needed all three to be effective.

Another solution was to employ officers connected with the old regime and of doubtful loyalty, and employ revolutionary officials to supervise them, rather like the political commissars of a later revolution. Such men had some success in fitting the fleet out and preparing it for battle, but were worse than useless in the fight itself. They were virtually extinct by the time Napoleon had completed his rise to power.

Admiral Pierre Villeneuve, who was defeated by Nelson at Trafalgar, was a product of his times, just as much as his great adversary. He entered the Marine Royal as a cadet at the age of 15 and was one of the few officers who did not go into exile as the Revolution became more extreme. He prospered in a navy which needed to maintain an active campaign with a large fleet, but was short of experienced officers and at the beginning of the wars in 1793 he was already a captain at the age of 29. He was a rear-admiral and third in command of Admiral Brueys' fleet in 1798, when it was attacked by Nelson at anchor in Aboukir Bay. He failed to move up in support of the rest of the fleet, and kept up a desultory fire for several hours during the night, until he finally made a decision to escape with the two remaining ships of the line and two frigates. At the time this was regarded as a success, saving something from a disaster, but it was ambiguous to say the least, as were most of Villeneuve's efforts. In strong contrast to Nelson, Villeneuve was by nature a pessimist 'always ready to credit unfavourable news.'[1]

The French navy was further disrupted by the effect of the Revolution on the crews. The discipline of ships often broke down, unpopular officers were hounded out and the seamen sometime joined forces with rioters ashore. This phase was quite short as new officers imposed discipline and the natural professionalism asserted itself, at least when the fleet was at sea.

The French navy also had natural disadvantages. The country was essentially a land power with three frontiers to defend and the north-western one had no mountains as natural defences. The army was always the main weapon of both defence and aggression for France, whereas for the British an army was needed to win wars, but not to avoid losing them. Secondly, the French had a deep interior and were less dependent on sea trade than the British. They had perhaps 60,000 merchant seamen to form a reserve for the navy, whereas the British had at least twice that number. The French had to keep fleets at both Toulon and Brest, and this division led to strategic and tactical difficulties.

For all its problems, the French navy was growing in skill and confidence by the late 1790s. Its only setback in a fleet battle was at the Glorious First of June, but the vital convoy had escaped and they claimed it as a partial victory. Their allies, the Spanish and Dutch, had been defeated at St Vincent and Camperdown, but that did not reflect on the French. All this changed in a single night when Nelson destroyed the Mediterranean Fleet at the Battle of the Nile, in one of the most decisive battles of all time. It was not just the loss of a dozen ships. French confidence and morale was shattered and would never fully recover.

Throughout the last century or so the French had developed a tactical doctrine which was very different from that of the British. They could never realistically seek control of the sea

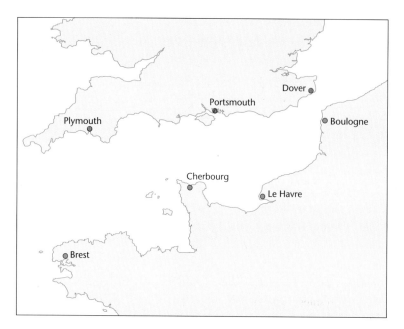

The English Channel showing British and French naval bases.

as the British did. Therefore they adopted the doctrine of the all-important 'mission', the idea that the specific task of a particular group of ships was more important than any abstract control of the sea. British power could not be broken, but it could be circumvented in many ways. A fleet or a squadron could reinforce armies or attack colonies in the West Indies or in India. It could support rebels in Scotland or Ireland or, in the ultimate maritime operation, threaten an invasion of the south of England while the fleet's attention was elsewhere. The British were obliged to spread their forces round the world to avert such a threat, as well as expending large amounts of resources in blockading French ports.

There were many French writers on naval tactics, during the eighteenth century. In general they produced rather sterile, formal systems which were little used in practice. The French remained devoted to the line of battle, even when Nelson's tactics made it vulnerable. As he prepared for the battle of Trafalgar, Admiral Villeneuve was aware that his ships could only form line of battle, which was exactly what Nelson wanted them to do. In more detailed tactics, the French tended to fire their guns high in order to damage their opponents' rigging and allow an escape. This was consistent with their doctrine of the primacy of the mission, but it also meant that British casualties were often remarkably light in action.

One of France's problems was the lack of suitable bases on the Channel Coast. There was no equivalent of Spithead, Plymouth Sound, Torbay or the Downs where a large fleet could assemble and wait in relative safety. The closest large base was at Brest, which was a very good position in many ways, controlling as it did one side of the entrance to the Channel and also threatening the Atlantic; but it was some way from any suitable invasion beach in England, and even within France it was rather isolated, at the end of a rather poor peninsula, some way from the industrial regions of France. Much of its supplies had to come by sea, which gave the British many opportunities to disrupt it. Brest was the main French port in the wars against Britain. It was well sited for the French strategy of launching a force which might strike anywhere, and potentially it could control the entrance to the English Channel. It had a good anchorage in Brest Roads and was well equipped with building slips, dry docks, storehouses, barracks and the other naval facilities. Along the Channel coast, Boulogne was a very inferior base, with a tiny harbour which could only be used at certain states of the tide.

Rochefort had been founded by Louis XIV in the seventeenth century, but the Sun King's powers were not enough to make it a satisfactory site. It was close to the good anchorages in the Basque Roads behind then islands of Oleron and Re, but the dockyard was too far up the narrow, winding River Charente. Rochefort was well equipped and had a strategic position on the French Atlantic coast but it had difficulty dealing with the largest ships and was always a poor third to Brest and Toulon.

Toulon was in many ways the premier naval base of any country in the Mediterranean. It had strong fortifications, a full range of facilities including the only dry docks in the sea and anchorages just outside, but according to Captain Brenton of the British navy, 'it falls infinitely short of Portsmouth, either as a harbour or depot, or of Spithead as an anchorage.'

French shipbuilding had been innovative in the second quarter of the eighteenth century, as the navy revived from near-extinction with no pre-conceived opinions and many good ideas. The builders evolved two types of warship which remained pre-eminent in the early nineteenth century, the 74-gun ship of the line and the frigate. In the 1790s they still produced fine ships with good sailing qualities, though rather weak in their construction. Most were built in the great dockyards at Brest, Rochefort and Toulon. But French ship design, though highly efficient, had become stereotyped by the time of the Revolution. The plans of Jaques-Noel Sane were adopted as standard in the 1780s, and from that time nearly all major ships were built to them. There was nothing wrong with the designs themselves, but the new system signified that administrative convenience took precedence over innovation. The French navy produced no new ideas in ship design or fitting during the Revolutionary and Napoleonic period, though it copied the two big ideas of the British, carronades and coppering.

The French fleet had 241 ships in 1792, including 83 of the line and 77 frigates. It had quite rightly abandoned the intermediate types used by the British, such as the 64 and 50-gun ship, and it had never gone for small three-deckers such as the 98. It had a few very large flagships of three decks and 120 guns. It had several 80-gun ships, and these were very effective as fighting ships and flagships. Its main strength, as in other fleets, was in the 74-gun ship. It also had a strong force of frigates, rising to a peak of 101 in 1795. During the invasion project of 1803-5 it built numerous small craft intended to carry troops to England, though the practical value of many of these was extremely doubtful.

The French relied on compulsion to raise their seamen, as did all the European navies. Compared with the British press gang, the *Inscription Maritime* seemed a model of modernity and efficiency. By a law of 1796 the seamen were divided into four classes – unmarried men, widowers without children, married men without children, and men with families. They were called up in turn to serve with the fleet for a fixed period, though men over 50 were exempted. In fact the system was far less efficient in practice and subject to numerous evasions. The French also built up a corps of long-service seamen-gunners, who acted as dockyard guards in peacetime and formed the nucleus of crews when war started. The revolution-

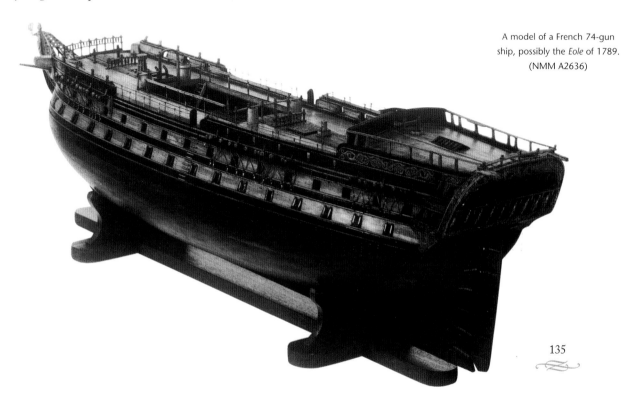

A model of a French 74-gun ship, possibly the *Eole* of 1789. (NMM A2636)

ary government abolished the corps in 1793 but it revived in the 1800s. It was a far-sighted move, anticipating the route taken by the British Navy later in the nineteenth century, but at the time it was too little to compensate for the relative weakness of the French navy.

The French remained formidable opponents through all their tribulations. They spent far too long in port and this affected their seamanship and tactical confidence, but they were quite skilled in the detailed techniques of fighting at sea, and fought back with determination which sometimes bordered on the fanatical. But their lack of sea practice meant that their ships were always less manoeuvrable in battle than the British and their technique consisted of what Lieutenant Senhouse described at the Battle of Trafalgar as 'the greatest passive gallantry'. Each ship operated like an artillery battery ashore, rather than a weapon which could be manoeuvred and pointed. In such circumstances defeat was inevitable, at Trafalgar and in numerous squadron and single-ship actions.

THE SPANISH NAVY

The Spanish were allied with the French for much of the eighteenth century through family ties, and they were subordinated to them for much of the period of the Great Wars, until they revolted in 1808. There was much French influence on their navy, though in fact their needs were closer to the British. They had a large colonial empire to defend, including most of Latin America and the Phillipines. This meant that their ships had to be spread thinly through the oceans of the world. They were rather less vulnerable to land invasion than the French, though this did not stop the Spanish army being a very powerful and proud service.

The Spanish officer corps, in contrast with the revolutionary French, had the highest ideas of aristocratic honour, and these were respected by conservative British officers like Nelson. There was no doubt about their personal courage, but their skills in seamanship were always questionable, due to lack of practice. In naval manning, the Spanish had the worst of both worlds. They did not have a large pool of merchant seamen like the British, or a modern system of recruitment like the French. They had more than 50,000 merchant sailors in 1787, but most of these were from the coasting and fishing trades; despite the great empire, they had less than 6000 deep-sea sailors.

The total quantity was declining, and reached 40,000 by 1808. Either the real number of seaman was being reduced, or many were evading naval service by becoming 'vagabond mariners' outside government control. After 1796 the government attempted to fill out the crews with a levy of non-seamen, often men 'as bereft of clothing as they were laden with vices.'[2] Things were little better in 1805, and Villeneuve complained of the Spanish ships under his command, 'What is essentially lacking in this Squadron is seamen and the funds to supply them with clothing; it is very distressing to see such fine ships manned with herdsmen and beggars and having such a small number of seamen.'[3]

The Spanish had naval bases at Cartagena in the Mediterranean, La Carraca near Cadiz, El Ferrol to the north-west and Guarnizo near Santander on the northern coast. Overseas, their greatest base was at Havana in Cuba. They produced some very good ships, largely by combining British and French traditions and adding something of their own. In the eighteenth century they attracted many British and Irish Roman Catholic émigrés, often debarred from employment in the dockyards of their own country. One of these, Matthew Mullan, designed the famous *Sanitssima Trinidad*. The French influence was led by Jean-Francois Gautier who had earned the trade at Toulon. The native Spanish shipbuilding school was headed by Jose Romero y Landa, who was Director of Engineering in the 1790s. For timber the Spanish had the resources of Cuba, where many fine ships were built.

For all the quality of their shipbuilding, the Spanish were not as good as the French in identifying the best lines of development. Like the British they relied too heavily on small two-deckers, perhaps because they could be built in large numbers to spread round the empire. Like the French they looked towards large three-deckers, but they tended to build upwards rather than outwards. While the French developed the 120-gun three decker, the Spanish built the largest ship of the day, the *Santissima Trinidad*. She was eventually rebuilt with more than 130 guns on four decks, which made her a rather clumsy sailer.

THE UNITED STATES NAVY

The United States Navy, in its original form, was a product of the War of Independence (1775-83). Originally the rebellious colonies relied on privateers to harass British shipping, but in 1775 the Scots American John Paul Jones commissioned the first ship of the Continental Navy, and went on to have considerable success against British shipping. The navy lapsed after the war, as many navies did in those days. But the Americans already had an extensive foreign trade in their own ships, and these were vulnerable in other people's conflicts. Each western nation had to protect its own trade against belligerent powers and Barbary corsairs, and the Americans were no exception. George Washington signed a Navy Act in 1794, authorising six very large frigates, the first of which were launched three years later. There was a 'quasi war' with France, and the new navy had its first success in 1799, when the *Constellation* defeated the French frigate *L'Insurgente*. It is perhaps no coincidence that most American wars since then have begun with an attack (sometimes spurious) on American ships, for example the *Maine* in 1898, Pearl Harbour, and the Gulf of Tonkin incident which started their involvement in Vietnam. In 1804 the American frigates took part in attacks on the Barbary coast, adding the famous phrase to the US Marines anthem, 'to the shores of Tripoli.'

In a sense the American strategic and political problem was the opposite of that of the French. They had plenty of experienced seaman, but a population which was famously averse to taxation, and a state structure which was deliberately weak. There were two views on the purposes of the American navy. One group held that it should be a coast defence force, kept as cheap as possible, and with this in mind a fleet of rather unseaworthy gunboats was built to defend the individual ports. To others it was intended to defend seaborne trade, whether off the coasts of North Africa or breaking an enemy blockade of their own ports. Success in single-ship actions in the early stages of the war of 1812 gave the country much greater confidence in its navy and it was seen as a force which could also hit back at the enemy. Secretary of the Navy Jones outlined the policy in a circular to captains in February 1813:

> Our great inferiority in naval strength, does not permit us to meet them on this ground without hazarding the precious germ of our national glory. – we have however the means of creating a powerful diversion, and of turning the scale of annoyance against the enemy. It is therefore intended, to dispatch all our public ships, now in port, as soon as possible, in such positions as may be best adapted to destroy the commerce of the enemy, from the Cape of Good Hope, to Cape Clear, and continue out as long as the means of subsistence can be procured abroad, in any quarter...
>
> Cruizing singly, will also afford to our gallant commanders, a fair opportunity of displaying their judgement, skill and enterprise, and of reaping the laurel of fame, and its solid appendages, which so extended a field of capture, without impairing the means of continuing the persuit, cannot fail to produce.[4]

In July 1813 the British Admiralty warned captains 'That they do not conceive that any of His Majesty's Frigates should attempt to engage, single-handed, the larger class of American Ships, which, though they may be called Frigates, are of a size, Complement and weight of Metal much beyond that Class, and more resembling Line of Battle Ships.'[5]

The Americans were clever, innovative and experienced shipbuilders. They experimented (like the British) with ships with sliding keels, and considered the highly dangerous practice of using red-hot shot at sea. They were already in the process of developing the forerunners of the two types – the schooner and the clipper ship, which would be the main types of sailing ship in the second half of the nineteenth century. They had numerous rivers to provide good shipbuilding sites. They had almost infinite supplies of timber by European standards. Though the British tended to regard American timber as generally inferior to Baltic supplies, this did not stop the use of the very best in warship building. When cannonballs appeared to bounce off the sides of the USS *Constitution* in battle with the *Guerriere*, she gained her immortal nickname 'Old Ironsides.'

In warship design, the main American innovation was simply in size. Even more than the French they were the inferior naval power in a war with Britain and they went far further in developing ships which could run away from anything they could not fight. Mainly they concentrated on the traditional frigate, which was already more than fifty years old. They made them larger than the British or French models, but the only major change in layout was to deck over the open waist, creating a 'spar-deck', so called because it protected the gun crews from falling spars in a fight. Samuel Leech, who was captured in HMS *Macedonian* in 1812, had no doubt about the differences:

> On being taken on board the enemy's ship, I ceased to wonder at the result of the battle. The *United States* is built with the scantling of a seventy-four gun-ship, mounting thirty long twenty-four pounders…on her main deck, and twenty-two forty-two pounders, carronades, on her quarter deck and forecastle, howitzer guns in her tops, and a travelling carronade on her upper deck, with a complement of four hundred and seventy-eight picked men….She was larger in size, heavier in metal, more numerous in men and stronger built than the *Macedonian*.[6]

Diagrams comparing the sizes of a British 18-gun brig and its American equilavent, and a British 38-gun frigate and an American 44, from William James's *Naval Occurrences of the Late War…* London, 1817.

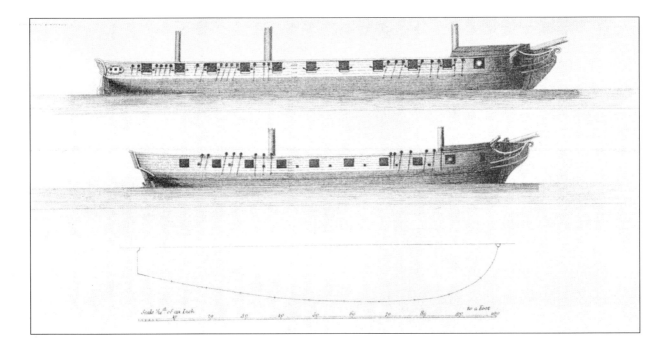

In 1813 the Americans began to carry this shipbuilding policy yet further, by ordering four 74-gun ships of the line. As might be expected, they were much bigger and better armed than their British equivalents. None was ready for the war of 1812, but in future years they would cause considerable rethinking of British ship design. The Americans also created a navy to fight the British on the Great Lakes.

The Americans had a large merchant fleet in proportion to their population, and offered relatively good wages to their naval seamen, so they were almost unique in the period in having no need for impressment or conscription. According to Samuel Leech of the Royal Navy:

> Many of our hands were in the service against their will; some of them were Americans, wrongfully impressed, and inwardly hoping for defeat:...On the other hand, the crew of our opponent had all shipped voluntarily for the term of two years only (most of our men were shipped for life.) They understood what they fought for; they were better used in the service. What wonder, then that victory adorned the brows of the American commander?[7]

It was also believed that many British seamen took service with the Americans and provided a core of battle experience. According to a dialogue recorded by Captain Marryat:

> "Your impressment," said the American, "fills our ships. Your seamen will not stand it; and for every two men you take by force, rely on it, we get one of them as a volunteer."
>
> Peters violently dissented from this proposition, and appeared angry with Green for making the assertion.
>
> "I see no reason to doubt it," said Green; "I know how our fighting ships as well as traders are manned. I will take my oath that more than two-thirds have run from the British navy because they were impressed..."[8]

The number of British sailors in the American navy was perhaps exaggerated. The British could only find four on board the *Chesapeake* after her capture, though of course there might well have been others who had no motive to reveal themselves. Those identified included for example, 'John Pearce 21 years of age had been about 7 months in the Chesapeake, was born

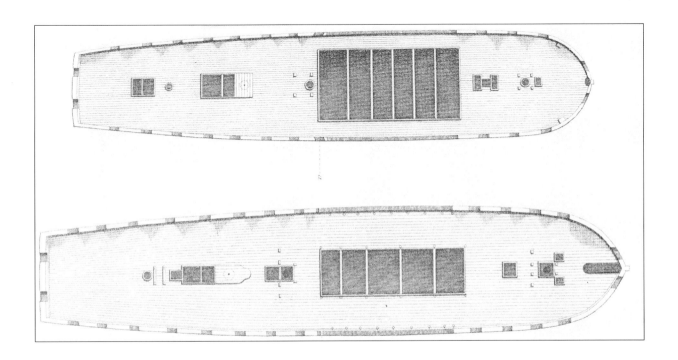

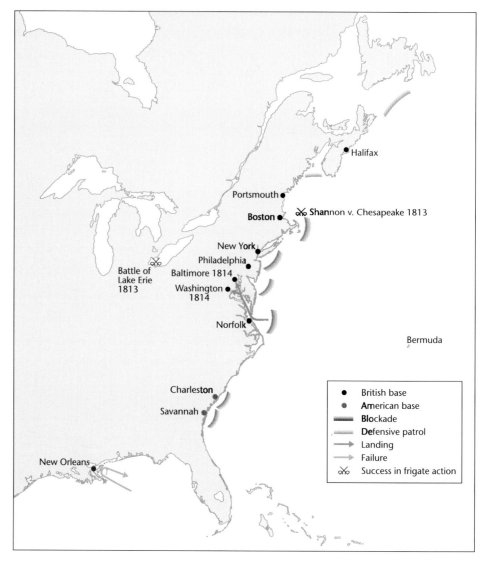

Legend	
●	British base
●	American base
▨	Blockade
▨	Defensive patrol
→	Landing
→	Failure
⚔	Success in frigate action

The seaboard of the United States in 1812, showing American ports and the British blockades.

in Ipswich in England, which he left 10 years since in the *Frances & Joseph* English merchant ship belonging to London which he left soon after his arrival in Philadelphia after being a considerable time in the coasting trade he shipped onboard the *Chesapeake* last September."[9]

C S Forester carefully avoided the War of 1812 in his Hornblower books. One of his reasons for sending his hero to the Baltic in 1812 was the fear that he might end up attacking Washington, for he was writing during the Anglo-American alliance of World War II. Patrick O'Brian treated the matter differently. From *The Fortune of War* onwards, the Americans are the most common and formidable enemy that Jack Aubrey faces. Their eccentricities, as seen from a British viewpoint, are highlighted, but they nearly always appear as noble and brave opponents, with none of the viciousness which Maturin encounters with the French secret service. However the war of 1812 was surprisingly bitter for those who took part in it. Captain Frederick Chamier wrote:

> That this war, or rather the means by which it was carried on, was disgraceful to a civilised nation, no man doubts now. Because, forsooth, some savages, or perhaps men dressed on degree better than savages, commence a system of barbarity and desolation in the north; we pretending to be the most civilised nation on the face of the earth, must imitate their ravages in the south; because, in Canada, some huts and hovels were burnt, we in the Chesapeake

were to burn and destroy some noble mansion, desolate some magnificent estate, and turn a land of plenty and prosperity into a bleak desert of starvation and misery.[10]

Though prisoners were on the whole well treated by both sides, there was some retaliation after prisoners on board HMS *Ramillies* tried to blow the ship up. Captain Hardy had one of them put in irons as an example, which caused the Americans to do the same with a British prisoner.[11]

OTHER NAVIES

The Dutch navy had been a world-beater in the seventeenth century and during the Third Anglo-Dutch War (1672-4) it had fought the combined forces of Britain and France to a standstill. It began its decline soon after that, partly because warships were getting too big to operate from the shallow Dutch harbours, partly because the rising power of France meant that they had to devote much of their defence effort to land warfare. The Dutch remained excellent sailors and ship designers, closer to the sea than even the British at the height of their maritime power, but they no longer had ships, or a state structure, which allowed them to develop as a world naval power. Their ships were small because of the difficulties of navigation. They had no three-deckers and few 74s, and their line of battle was mostly made up of obsolete 64s. They had naval bases at the Den Helder to the north of the country where the mainland ended, and to the south at Hellevoetsluis and Vlissingen. They fought determinedly in their only fleet battle, against Admiral Duncan at Camperdown in 1797, but were heavily defeated and never fully recovered. In later years they provided many of the ships of Napoleon's invasion force.

The Danish navy was quite innovative in its shipbuilding practices, producing, for example, a new type of stern for the *Christian VII*. Danish shipbuilders used features of both British and French design, but tended to favour the French. The navy used the 74-gun ship quite extensively. It was defeated by Nelson at Copenhagen in 1801, but losses on that occasion were not heavy, and many officers attributed the defeat to a misguided offer of a truce by the Crown Prince. Copenhagen itself was attacked much more heavily by the British in 1807, and most of the modern ships in the Danish fleet were destroyed or captured. As always, the British feared the ships of a weaker naval power falling under the control of the French.

The Swedish navy was even more innovative than the Danes. Its greatest figure was the naval architect Fredrik Chapman, the son of an English immigrant from Yorkshire. The fleet had a relatively small force of ships of the line, but an extensive gunboat navy using rowing craft designed by Chapman, to take part in the amphibious campaigns, which were common in conflicts with Russia. The Swedes combined technological innovation with social conservatism; their naval officers were part of the military and were expected to wear spurs, much to the amusement of other navies. The main base was at Carscrona to the south of the country. Due to Sweden's erratic internal politics the country was neutral, an ally and a nominal enemy of Britain at different periods after 1808.

The Russian fleet had been founded by Peter the Great at the end of the seventeenth century, and he travelled in England and the Netherlands to find out about shipbuilding and naval practices. His successors did not travel, but they were equally reliant on foreign ideas and personnel to keep their fleet operational. British officers, including Sir Charles Knowles, Sir Samuel Bentham and Sir Sidney Smith from Britain and John Paul Jones from the United States, were recruited to the Russian navy, and even Nelson is said to have consid-

ered emigrating during a low period in his career in the early 1790s. The Russians had a large fleet, with 82 ships of the line in 1801, but few of these were operational. They also had a gunboat navy, though less innovative than the Swedish one. They had good bases in the Baltic at Kronstadt and Reval, with smaller fleets in the Black Sea, the Caspian and Siberia. The main problem was the low technological base of Russia, and the lack of trained seamen. The peasants who were recruited lived miserable lives and had low skills and morale. Nevertheless the Russian fleet tried to break out of the confines of the Baltic and Black Sea, operating in the North Sea in 1795 and the Mediterranean in 1798, in alliance with Britain but with limited success. The Russian fleet was much more effective in 1807 when a squadron under Vice-Admiral Seniavin was co-operating with Sir John Duckworth (1748-1817) of the Royal Navy against the Turks. It was the Russians who defeated them at Lemnos and practically destroyed the Turkish fleet.

The Portuguese navy was one of the few that spent more time as an ally than as an enemy of Britain. It was quite small for a country with an extensive Atlantic coastline, with a dozen ships of the line and about 15 frigates in 1798. In that year it sent four 74-gun ships to aid Nelson after the Battle of the Nile, but he was not impressed and wrote, 'I never expect any real service from that squadron.' His friend Sir William Hamilton though that their commander, the Marquis of Niza, was 'sensible that the command he has is above his ability.'[12] To Britain the base at Lisbon was more important than the Portuguese Navy, particularly as a means of protecting British trade.

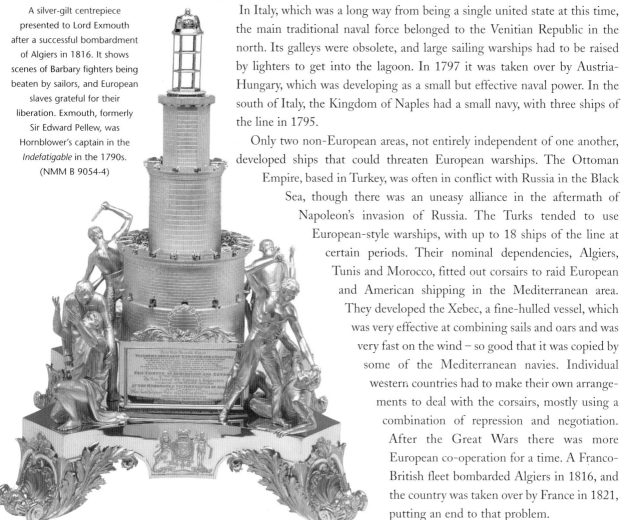

A silver-gilt centrepiece presented to Lord Exmouth after a successful bombardment of Algiers in 1816. It shows scenes of Barbary fighters being beaten by sailors, and European slaves grateful for their liberation. Exmouth, formerly Sir Edward Pellew, was Hornblower's captain in the *Indefatigable* in the 1790s. (NMM B 9054-4)

In Italy, which was a long way from being a single united state at this time, the main traditional naval force belonged to the Venitian Republic in the north. Its galleys were obsolete, and large sailing warships had to be raised by lighters to get into the lagoon. In 1797 it was taken over by Austria-Hungary, which was developing as a small but effective naval power. In the south of Italy, the Kingdom of Naples had a small navy, with three ships of the line in 1795.

Only two non-European areas, not entirely independent of one another, developed ships that could threaten European warships. The Ottoman Empire, based in Turkey, was often in conflict with Russia in the Black Sea, though there was an uneasy alliance in the aftermath of Napoleon's invasion of Russia. The Turks tended to use European-style warships, with up to 18 ships of the line at certain periods. Their nominal dependencies, Algiers, Tunis and Morocco, fitted out corsairs to raid European and American shipping in the Mediterranean area. They developed the Xebec, a fine-hulled vessel, which was very effective at combining sails and oars and was very fast on the wind – so good that it was copied by some of the Mediterranean navies. Individual western countries had to make their own arrangements to deal with the corsairs, mostly using a combination of repression and negotiation. After the Great Wars there was more European co-operation for a time. A Franco-British fleet bombarded Algiers in 1816, and the country was taken over by France in 1821, putting an end to that problem.

CHAPTER 8

THE NAVY IN ACTION

The wartime aim of the Royal Navy was to seek and exploit control of the sea – unlike other navies, which tended to look for gaps in British control rather than try to break it. Control could be gained in two ways – by destroying or capturing enemy fleets, ships and naval resources, or by confining them to their harbours. More specifically, the navy had several major tasks, of which the most important was naturally to guard the homeland from invasion. It protected British trade, of several kinds – strategic goods such as timber, tar, munitions and military stores which were necessary to run the war; necessities such as coal for London, without which the capital would freeze in winter; and luxury goods such as tobacco, tea and spices, providing a high rate of profit which helped to finance the war. The navy had to deny the use of the sea to enemy commerce, whether strategic or commercial, which it might do in tandem with private men of war in the business for profit. In a very complex situation after the Berlin Decrees of 1806, it attempted to open the ports of Europe to British trade, or to close European ports which followed the decrees. The navy could mount expeditions against enemy colonies, as it did many times, while its control of the sea prevented the enemy from doing the same thing. The navy could maintain diplomatic links and carry out intelligence activities on any of the coasts of the world. Finally the navy could land armies on enemy-held shores, or support allies who were fighting the French, such as Spanish guerrillas. For all this the Royal Navy needed a variety of ships, techniques and tactics.

The navy did not always have to fight to achieve all its aims. A war might be averted and a potential enemy deterred by rapid mobilisation of the fleet, as happened for example during a diplomatic crisis with Spain in 1790. An enemy fleet might be prevented from leaving port by a blockading force outside. A raid on a convoy might be prevented by the apparent strength of the escort. The essence of naval strategy was to deploy limited resources around the oceans of the world, to create the maximum effect. Yet fighting was not just a theoretical possibility for the Royal Navy. It took part in thousand of individual combats over the years and it was fully trained and experienced in fighting at every level – from the individual gun crew to the commander-in-chief of a great fleet.

FLEET ORGANISATION

There were half a dozen main fleets during the Great Wars. At home, the North Sea Fleet guarded the coast between Portsmouth and Shetland, and blockaded the enemy ports on the

143

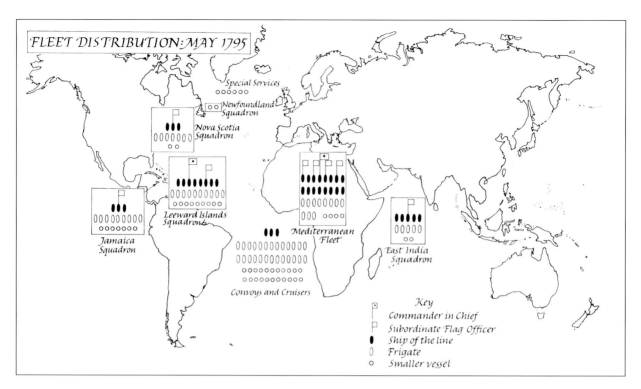

FLEET DISTRIBUTION: MAY 1795

Special Services
Newfoundland Squadron
Nova Scotia Squadron
Leeward Islands Squadron
Jamaica Squadron
Mediterranean Fleet
East India Squadron
Convoys and Cruisers

Key
Commander in Chief
Subordinate Flag Officer
Ship of the line
Frigate
Smaller vessel

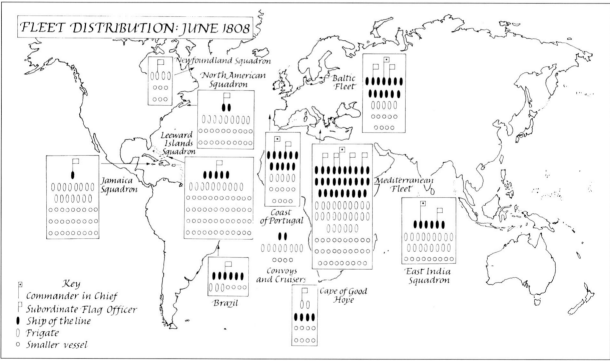

FLEET DISTRIBUTION: JUNE 1808

Newfoundland Squadron
North American Squadron
Baltic Fleet
Leeward Islands Squadron
Jamaica Squadron
Coast of Portugal
Mediterranean Fleet
Convoys and Cruisers
East India Squadron
Cape of Good Hope
Brazil

Key
Commander in Chief
Subordinate Flag Officer
Ship of the line
Frigate
Smaller vessel

The distribution of ships of the Royal Navy in May 1795 and June 1808, showing the increasingly worldwide role as well as the concentration on places like the English Channel.

opposite sides. It was divided into several squadrons, usually based in the Downs off Kent, in the Thames Estuary, at Yarmouth and at Leith in Scotland. It had a small core of ships of the line, but operated mainly frigates and smaller craft as the main defence against enemy invasion. The Channel Fleet was based at Portsmouth and Plymouth and its main role was to blockade the French at Brest, with subsidiary forces off Rochefort, Ferrol and other ports where a fleet might be based. It was one of the principal striking forces of the navy, with up to 47 ships of the line and 25 other ships. Its boundaries stretched as far south as Cape Finisterre in Spain and it was a detachment of the Channel Fleet under Sir Home Popham that raided

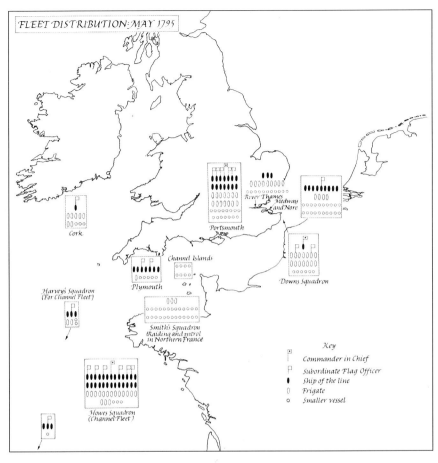

FLEET DISTRIBUTION: MAY 1795

River Thames
Medway and Nore

Portsmouth

Downs Squadron

Cork

Channel Islands

Plymouth

Harvey's Squadron
(For Channel Fleet)

Smith's Squadron
(Raiding and patrol
in Northern France)

Howe's Squadron
(Channel Fleet)

Key
Commander in Chief
Subordinate Flag Officer
Ship of the line
Frigate
Smaller vessel

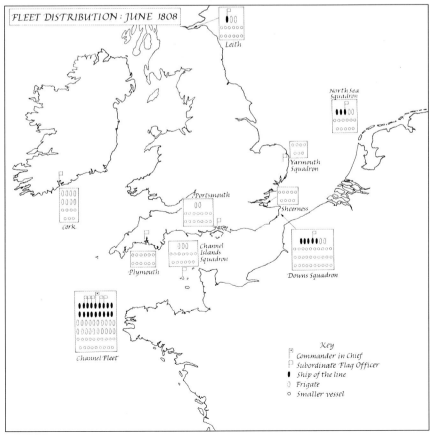

FLEET DISTRIBUTION: JUNE 1808

Leith

North Sea
Squadron

Yarmouth
Squadron

Sheerness

Portsmouth

Cork

Channel
Islands
Squadron

Plymouth

Downs Squadron

Channel Fleet

Key
Commander in Chief
Subordinate Flag Officer
Ship of the line
Frigate
Smaller vessel

the French and co-operated with Spanish guerrillas in 1812. But in general the Channel Fleet was not popular with sailors. Chamier wrote of his ship's transfer from the Mediterranean:

> …we became one of the "Channel-gropers" (as they dignified ships on the home station): henceforth we were to buffet the Bay of Biscay, instead of the smooth Mediterranean, and to have the benefit of all the fogs, snow-storms, gales of wind, mists, rains and squalls – instead of the delightfully even climate, the sun-shining days, the star-sparkling nights of our late station.[1]

There were smaller squadrons under the admirals at Portsmouth and Plymouth, and a force in the Channel Islands, one in the south of Ireland, as well as groups assembled for particular purposes, such as Sir Sidney Smith's force of 29 ships, intended to raid the northern French coasts in 1795, and Sir Home Popham's force which took the Cape of Good Hope in 1806, and then went on to an unauthorised and unsuccessful attack on the Spanish in the River Plate. There were also some ships on 'particular services' under the direct orders of the Admiralty, though these were rather less common that readers of naval fiction might imagine.

Baltic fleets were intermittent in the early stages. One was sent under Sir Hyde Parker and Lord Nelson to attack the Danes at Copenhagen in 1801. Another under Admiral Gambier bombarded the Danish capital in 1807 and captured a large proportion of their fleet. The following year a regular fleet was formed under Sir James Saumarez, and it remained in the sea for the rest of the war, though much of it had to withdraw during the frozen winters.

The Mediterranean Fleet was in many ways the best command of the navy. It was equal in status and power with the two home fleets, but more independent. It was also a very difficult force to command, with many foreign powers of varying degrees of friendliness to deal with, and tenuous supply links with home. It was enough to wear out St Vincent in the 1790s, and drive Cuthbert Collingwood to an early grave in the next decade. Its first task was to contain the enemy fleets in Toulon and Cadiz, and that took up the main body of the fleet; but at any given moment it had many other ships involved in convoy escort, diplomatic missions, transport of troops and raids on enemy commerce or shore installations. The Mediterranean Fleet peaked in 1812, with 29 ships of the line, the same number of frigates and 26 sloops.

On the other side of the Atlantic, there were two main fleets in the West Indies. The Jamaica station, based at Port Royal, was mainly concerned with convoy escort. The Leeward Islands station had moments of great activity, for example when Sir John Jervis led the capture of enemy colonies in the area in 1794-5, and strategic importance when Nelson pursued the French Mediterranean Fleet there in 1805; but it was never quite as important as it had been in previous wars. The North American station had bases at Halifax and Newfoundland. For most of the time it was naval backwater, until the War of 1812 brought it into prominence. It included sixty ships in 1813.

The geographical title of a fleet was not to be taken too literally. For example, Jervis took the Mediterranean Fleet out of that sea in 1796, but it retained its title; Nelson went even further for very different reasons, when he took it across the Atlantic in pursuit of the French.

By later standards, commanders-in-chief had very small staffs. The most important staff officer was the captain of the fleet, an experienced captain with the status of a rear-admiral. Below him was the flag-captain, who was also the captain of the flagship. He also had considerable duties in running the ship, and in most cases he was a young, inexperienced captain who could not act as a mature adviser. The larger fleets had physicians of the fleet, who provided very capable medical advisers in the persons, of Thomas Trotter and Leonard Gillespie, for example; but they could not contribute much to the strategy of the campaign. Then there was the flag lieutenant, who was the admiral's signal officer. The admiral had a

secretary, who wrote out his letters and did much of his administrative work, with a few clerks under him. There was a master of the fleet, who was the senior navigator. Nelson tended to be particularly casual about staff work and rarely employed a captain of the fleet. His flag captain at the Nile, Edward Berry, was very inexperienced and perhaps takes some of the blame for the dismasting of the *Vanguard* early in the campaign. He chose his flag lieutenant on the *Victory* from among the ship's officers, rather than bringing his own with him. However he did choose some distinguished individuals for other roles on his staff, notably Alexander Scott as his chaplain, translator and part-time spy.

BLOCKADE

Blockade was at the centre of British naval strategy. It was the only way of neutralising an enemy fleet which refused to come out and fight. Cochrane attempted to destroy the enemy in harbour by means of fireships at Basque Roads in 1809, and there were numerous plans to attack the French at Boulogne by means of rockets, balloons and submarines, but these had no effect. Until the advent of the submarine and the torpedo bomber more than a century later, a fleet was generally safe in its harbour behind strong fortifications. It remained a 'fleet in being', always able to threaten the British naval supremacy in any part of the world. Blockade was the only counter to this.

At its starkest, there were two main means of blockade – open and close. The issue was highlighted in the Channel Fleet during the 1790s. Lord Howe and other admirals believed that keeping a fleet constantly off the port of Brest would be too wearing and expensive in men and materials. He kept the main force at anchor off the southern English coast, with frigates to warn if the enemy tried to escape. Apart from the obvious risk that the enemy might evade the blockaders, there was the problem of the morale of the ships at anchor, for it was a notorious fact that the morale of crews tended to decline in these circumstances, and they were far more prone to mutiny than when at sea. The Spithead and Nore mutinies of 1797 both took place among ships at anchor. This was one of the reasons why St Vincent, on taking command of the Channel Fleet in 1800, insisted on keeping the ships at sea as long as possible even in winter, with a policy of 'close' blockade.

St. Vincent's squadron on the blockade of Cadiz in 1798. The town can be seen behind the ships, with the Spanish fleet at anchor to the left.
(NMM PAH 9505)

In fact there were several varieties of blockade, and fleets could be locked up tightly or kept on a loose rein according to circumstances. St Vincent's blockade of Cadiz in the late 1790s was like a cork in a bottle. Nelson's blockade of Toulon in 1803-5 was more like a cat trying to lure a mouse out of its hole. The tactics depended partly on the character of the commander; the fierce determination of St Vincent, the desire for order of Lord Howe, or the implacable lust for battle of Nelson. They also depended on the geographical circumstances. The Brest fleet was the closest French one to Britain and the most dangerous and had to be watched most carefully, while the Toulon fleet, though very dangerous, might be stopped at several stages along the way before it did any damage. The Dutch ports were only accessible for large ships at fortnightly spring tides, so the blockading fleet could spend a large proportion of its time at anchor in home waters. The fleet off Cadiz could anchor in the open waters of the Atlantic, but off Toulon the water was deeper and the ships had to stay mobile.

A strong force of ships of the line was the main strength of a blockade of a naval port. It usually had an inshore squadron of good-sailing two-deckers to meet the first effect of an enemy exit. Frigates were essential in blockade service, whether open or close. In close blockade they provided the first warning of any signs of enemy movement. In open blockade they were even more important. If the enemy came out while the main fleet was away, half the frigates would pursue him while the rest went to make contact with the main fleet.

Blockade was the bread and butter of naval warfare. Whether the time was spent at anchor or under weigh, it was a boring and depressing period with no chance to see the world, few chances of action and often difficult weather conditions. Fleets on blockade often had the greatest discipline problems, and most of the large-scale mutinies. The heroes of naval faction mostly avoided blockade service, though Hornblower found adventure in 1803-5 in the *Hotspur,* the smallest and most active ship off Brest. Jack Aubrey found himself part of the Mediterranean Fleet in the 74-gun *Worcester* in *The Ionian Mission,* though not for long, for the fictional Lords of the Admiralty recognised that he, and his friend Maturin, were far more useful in special operations. But for all its humdrum practice, blockade was a war-winning strategy. In the immortal words of the American naval historian Alfred Thayer Mahan, 'Those far-distant, storm-beaten ships, upon which the Grand Army never looked, stood between it and the dominion of the world.'[2]

THE PROTECTION OF TRADE

The navy had a long-standing and essential duty to protect British maritime commerce, which was the mainstay of the country's finances. The convoy system had evolved over a hundred years since the first French privateer campaign in the 1690. Convoys were enforced by Act of Parliament and any captain ignoring the rules was liable to a fine of up to £1000. Fast ships were allowed to sail independently as 'runners', but the rest were obliged to join convoys escorted by the navy, although the might lose time in waiting for one to leave. There were regular coastal convoys between the main ports along the coast. In the early years of the Great Wars some ports had a small warship permanently attached and the captain was under orders to respect the wishes of the local merchants in taking convoys in either direction. This led to divided command, and after 1798 convoys ran all along the coast on a regular fortnightly service, with ships joining or leaving at ports along the way. During the season there were monthly convoys to North America, and also to India and the West Indies. Baltic convoys left regularly from Longhope Sound in the Orkneys.

There were no specialised convoy escort vessels. Sloops and frigates took it on as part of their normal role, hired or purchased merchant ships were often used, and even ships of the line on the way to foreign stations might be pressed into service. On his way to join St Vincent's Mediterranean Fleet and ultimately win the Battle of the Nile, Nelson's *Vanguard* escorted eleven merchantmen to Lisbon, and in fiction Hornblower's *Sutherland* protected a fleet of outward-bound East Indiaman. The escort of a military convoy might be huge, and a large part of the Channel Fleet went with an East India and other convoys in April 1794; in other cases, a convoy of more than a hundred ships might have a single sloop. If there were several escorts, they were ranged round the convoy, which in theory was formed up in several lines to take up a rectangular space. Escorts paid most attention to the windward side, from which an attack was most likely to develop. Relations between merchantmen and warship captains were often very bad and some captains threatened to press men out of ships that failed to keep station or to obey the orders in the Convoy Signal Book.

How can we measure the Navy's success in the war against British trade? Only a tiny proportion (0.6 per cent) of ships actually in convoys were taken, but enemy privateers were never suppressed, substantial forces always had to be maintained for convoy escort, and merchant shipping was always under threat. An extreme view might suggest that the French *Guerre de course* could never have succeeded anyway, that Britain was not dependent on imports for survival (unlike the twentieth century), and that the attack on trade had no more than a nuisance value, unless the merchant classes were able to force the government to sacrifice principle for financial gain, and to make peace. We can discount this view, because overseas trade brought the wealth which enabled the country maintain a strong army and navy, and to finance the coalitions which eventually won the war. We can measure the defence of trade by its ultimate effects; during the wars, British shipping rose from 1.5 to 1.8 million tons, while government receipts from customs duties more than trebled in the same period.

AMPHIBIOUS OPERATIONS

It is often suggested that amphibious warfare was a new feature in the twentieth century. In fact James's *Naval History* records 68 major landings during the wars, and there were countless minor ones. The largest ones were largely unsuccessful - the operations on the French dock-yards at Toulon and Rochefort, and the landing of nearly 30,000 men at Walcheren in 1807. The smaller ones were generally more successful. Most of the enemy colonies, especially in the West Indies, were captured in the French Revolutionary War, along with key naval bases at Minorca and Malta. In true eighteenth century fashion, virtually all of them were given back or exchanged in the Peace of Amiens in 1801. Most were retaken during the Napoleonic Wars and some, such as the Cape of Good Hope, became permanent British possessions.

Most landings were lightly opposed, because with the short range of guns it was impossible for an army to protect a long coastline. In the West Indies, an island could be isolated by the dominant sea power and taken by a superior force of troops. But it was not always so easy. When Keith landed General Abercrombie's army in Egypt in 1801, a force of 5,500 men was opposed by a French one of 2,000, and suffered 500 army casualties, and nearly 100 naval ones. Despite these losses, the operation was a success.

The techniques of fleet battle were hotly debated in various publications, but amphibious warfare was never talked about in this way. Nevertheless there were techniques of amphibious warfare, which every captain and admiral seems to have learned about. Naturally the operations involved the use of ship's boats, or specially designed flat-bottomed landing craft which could be rowed ashore with troops and marines. It was common to find a beach as far as possible from enemy fortifications and arrange the boats in a line to row ashore, with a small warship at either end. Another common technique was to land ship's guns, often slung under a boat. They were often much larger than anything that could be transported to the site by road, and could have a decisive effect.

Part of the occupation of Diamond Rock, off Martinique in 1805. Using their well-known skills at ropework, seamen hoist a gun to the top of the rock, where it will be used to bombard French shipping approaching the main island. (NMM 2062)

Troops preparing to disembark for the landing on Mauritius in 1810. The campaign is fictionalised in *The Mauritius Command*. (NMM PAF 4779)

A co-ordinated amphibious campaign could have a profound effect on the war on land. In 1812 Sir Home Popham deployed a force headed by two ships of the line on the north coast of Spain. It was a deeply-indented, mountainous coastline, where ships could move far more easily than armies. He began the campaign by landing men and cannons at the village of Lequitio, bombarding a French-held hill fort and fortified convent and capturing them with the aid of Spanish guerrillas. He then raided several positions in the Bilbao estuary and drew out the French troops all along the coast. He concluded with the capture of the port of Santander in July. Wellington was not always appreciative of naval co-operation, but in this case it took the pressure of his army which was in a dangerous position at the siege of Burgos.

CUTTING OUT EXPEDITIONS

A cutting out expedition was defined as one in which the boats of a warship, often under the guns of enemy shore batteries, 'cut out' or captured an enemy ship which was sheltering close inshore or in harbour. It was recognised as one of the most dangerous forms of warfare. One of Marryat's characters claimed that 'there is no service in which, generally speaking, there is so great a sacrifice of life, in proportion to the object to be obtained, as that which is generally termed 'cutting out'.[3]

By the third week of October 1799 the small frigate *Surprise*, under Captain Edward Hamilton, had been blockading Puerto Cabello, on the Spanish Main, for several weeks. Her particular target was the frigate *Hermione*, whose crew had revolted two years earlier, butchered their officers including the notorious Captain Pigot, and surrendered the ship to the Spanish. Now she was moored head and stern under powerful Spanish batteries. Hamilton's plans for a daring attack had been overruled by the Admiral, but now his supplies were running out and he decided not to wait any longer. On the night of the 24th his crews, all dressed in dark clothes, went into the ship's six boats and rowed to the *Hermione* to execute a detailed plan. On the way in they were discovered by Spanish gunboats and the

alarm was raised. Undaunted, the boat's crews stormed on board the frigate and fought a fierce hand-to-hand battle before taking possession of her. The cables were cut, the fore topsail was loosed and the boats took her in tow. The Spanish batteries opened fire as she passed them, but by 2 a.m. next morning the ship was outside gunshot of them and firmly in British possession again. The *Surprise* had only 12 men wounded, and the navy felt it had avenged one of its most alarming mutinies.

The cutting out of the *Hermione* was probably the most famous action of its kind, but it was far from unique. In the same year, 1799, the 36-gun frigate *Trent* and the 12-gun cutter *Sparrow* found four Spanish ships sheltering in a Bay in the west of Puerto Rico, protected by a battery. Marines were landed to neutralise the shore guns and seamen in boats headed for the Spanish ships under cover of the *Sparrow*'s guns. Two of the enemy were scuttled and two captured. Later the 32-gun frigate *Success* chased a Spanish ship into the small harbour of La Selva near Cape Creux. The port seemed undefended and a party of 42 men was sent in by boat. In fact the Spanish did have a small battery on shore, and the ship had a crew of 113 men, but the *Success*'s men prevailed and captured her. Yet again that year, the 18-gun sloop *Echo* chased a French privateer into a Puerto Rican bay. *Echo*'s pinnace and jolly-boat failed to capture her, but they did take a merchant brig carrying cocoa and indigo.

GUNNERY

The single gun was, in a sense, the basic unit of naval fighting. It was the rate of fire of each gun which gave the British much of their superiority in battle, and that in turn was fuelled by the training and the raw energy of the Royal Navy's seamen. The exact rate of fire has never clearly been settled, but a remark by Captain Phillip Broke of the *Shannon* gives some clues of what was expected in a good ship, suggesting that one broadside a minute might be possible.

Captain Riou of the *Amazon* gave detailed orders for the crew of an 18-pounder gun, consisting of ten men and a boy. The gun captain was to stand at the rear of the gun with vent

The cutting out of the *Hermione*
under Spanish guns.
(NMM BHC 0519)

tubes in his hat or pocket. He was 'never to take hold of a tackle fall of handspike or move from the breech of the gun but to secure to take his powder horn, but he is to direct the others to point the gun and never to fire unless he is sure of hitting.' The second captain was to take in the slack of the relieving tackle behind the gun, to prevent it running out again after it had fired. He also carried vent tubes in his hat, but unlike the captain he was free to assist in hauling out the gun. Numbers 1 and 2 in the crew stood closest to the side of the ship and the muzzle of the gun. When preparing for action they opened the gun port by pushing on it. Number 1 took out the tompion which blocked the mouth of the gun, while number 2 placed the rammers and sponge on the deck. When loading, number 1 would 'Take the cartridge out of the box with the wad brought by 3. Load with cartridge and war. Take the shot and wad from 3. Load with wad and shot.' Number 2 would then ram the wads, cartridge, ball and shot down the barrel of the gun. When the gun was being run out 1 and 2 would look backwards toward the gun captain, at the same time taking up the slack on the loose portion of the train tackle. The heavy work would be done by numbers 3, 4, 5, and 6. On their respective sides of the gun, and working as a team, each would 'take hold of the training tackle fall, your eyes fixed on the captain of the gun, always ready to run out and point the gun as he shall direct'. The differential rates of hauling on each side had a certain amount of value in aiming the gun. If any further adjustments had to be made, numbers 5 and

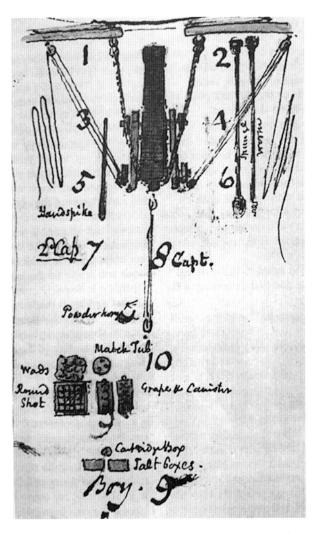

A 18-pounder gun on the frigate *Amazon*. The numbers indicate the positions of the members of the gun crew, and the various tools and implements are laid out. (NMM ER/3/7)

6 would lever it round with the handspike, as required. The captain would prick the cartridge through the touch hole and fit the fuse ready for firing. At the rear of the gun stood one man to look after the wads and shot, and another who was responsible for fetching the powder from the nearest hatchway and for fire precautions. A boy was to 'remain stationary in charge of the salt box given to him' to strew on the deck to prevent slippage, and for use in case of fire. He was to pass on the powder brought to him by number 10, and 'never to permit any man not belonging to his gun to take his powder, or deliver his box to any other person'. When the gun was fired it was allowed to recoil inboard and then was restrained by its tackle. Number 2 sponged it out and the process began again.[4]

Early defeats in the War of 1812 caused British admirals to stress the importance of gunnery practice:

> Their Lordships trust that all the Officers of His Majesty's Naval Service must be convinced that upon the good discipline and the proper training of their Ships Companies to the expert management of the Guns, the preservation of the high character of the British Navy most essentially depends, and that other works on which it is not unusual to employ the men are of very trifling importance, when compared with a due preparation (by instruction and practice) for the effectual services on the day of Battle.…Officers should earnestly endeavour to impress on the minds of the men that the issue of the Battle will greatly depend on the cool, steady and regular manner in which the Guns shall be loaded, pointed & fired…[5]

THE ORDER OF BATTLE

Even more than the gun, the ship was the basic unit of any naval action. It was made up of many teams, such as the individual gun crews, and it might itself for a small part of a large fleet. But the ship was the indivisible unit of naval power. In land warfare units might be split up and the initiative might rest with junior officers, NCOs or individual men; in naval warfare the ship was supreme. This meant that the captain had a unique role in battle. He stood on the quarterdeck in action, where he could see the sails of his own ship, her movement through the water and the position of the enemy. His main task was to bring his ship into battle to the best advantage. Beside him stood his first lieutenant, who would take over in the event of the captain's incapacity, and the master who would advise on the manoeuvres of the ship. He had two or three midshipmen beside him to carry messages to the various parts of the ship. The officers stood in an exposed position, particularly on a frigate which had no poop to offer a certain amount of shelter. They set an example of coolness under fire, and at Trafalgar Lieutenant Roteley, a young marine officer in the *Victory*, remembered his father's advice, 'Louis, you will soon be in battle…whatever you do, be sure to keep your head erect in battle, never bow to a Frenchman's shot, it is folly, for when you hear the ball's whistle you are safe, the ball has passed harmless before you can hear it.'[6]

The boatswain took charge of the forecastle, while each of the gun decks had two lieutenants in command, one forward and one aft. Each had a number of midshipmen under him, commanding a group of perhaps four guns. Each gun crew included men with subsidiary duties who might be called away if needed − firemen, pumpers, boarders or sail trimmers − but this was not a system that worked well in practice. Officers, such as Captain Hallowell of the *Swiftsure* at the Nile, knew that once the men had started fighting it was very difficult to get them to leave their guns. Many years later, Lieutenant Rotely told a naval audience, 'I need not inform a seaman of the difficulty of separating a man from his gun.'[7]

Below decks, a large team worked in the magazines. According to the quarter bill of the *Goliath* in 1805, this would number thirteen, many of them skilled men from the gunner's crew, working in the main magazine making up cartridges and passing them to the decks above. The ship's cook was stationed in the light room to tend the lantern there. The after magazine was used for storage rather than making up cartridges. Inside it were the cooper and one of the men who worked in the hold. Outside in the passage, to pass the cartridges along, were the barber and 'Jack in the dust', the purser's assistant. The schoolmaster tended the lantern in the light room and a ship's corporal handed up the cartridges. The men of the carpenter's crew were stationed in vital points close to the waterline of the ship to carry out emergency repairs, and there was at least one man in each vacant compartment to report on any danger of fire or leaks.[8]

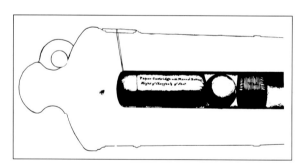

The interior of a loaded cannon as drawn in 1796, showing flannel cartridge, ball and wad. It was more common to place another wad between the cartridge and the shot.

BOARDING

Boarding was of course the oldest naval tactic of all; apart from ramming it was the main one in the days before large cannons. It had been in decline for several centuries as fleets tended to rely more and more on their guns, often fired at relatively long range as the ships fought in formal line of battle. Boarding was reserved for the final stage of a battle, after the enemy was virtually defeated. It was the new commanders of the Revolutionary Wars − Nelson and Cochrane − who brought boarding back as a tactic which could swing a fight

Gun crews on the quarterdeck
of a ship in action, from an
anonymous book of drawings.
(NMM PAD 8487)

one way or the other. At St Vincent, Commodore Nelson took the crew of the Spanish 80-gun *San Nicolas* by surprise when he personally led a boarding party to take the ship. He then crossed her to take the 112-gun *San Josef* in the same fashion. The fleet nicknamed it 'Nelson's patent bridge for boarding first rates' but Lady Nelson was less impressed. On his promotion to rear-admiral she implored him to leave boarding to captains.

To carry this out, sailors were armed and trained with cutlasses and pistols. Captain Edward Riou had strong views on how the cutlass should be used:

> Eagerness and heat in action, especially in a first onset, ought never to be the cause of a man putting himself so much off his guard…as to lift his arm to make a blow with his cutlass. 'Tis folly in the extreme and whoever practices it (however common the practice may be) if opposed to a valiant and dextrous adversary, will certainly fall. But on the contrary by rushing sword in hand, the point straight out and thereby the guard maintained and watching the opportunity of making a thrust, the slightest touch of the point is death to his enemy.[9]

But Riou had little practical experience of boarding, unlike Marryat:

> In most instances of boarding, but more especially in boarding small vessels, there is not much opportunity for what is termed hand to hand fighting. It is a rush for the deck: breast to breast, thigh to thigh, foot to foot, man wedged against man, so pressed on by those behind, that there is little possibility of using your cutlass, except by driving your antagonist's teeth down his throat with the hilt. Gun-shot wounds, of course, take place throughout the whole of the combat, but those from the sabre and the cutlass are generally given and received before the close, or after the resistance of one party has yielded to the pertinacity and courage of the other.[10]

SINGLE SHIP ACTIONS

Single ship action, a battle between two ships of roughly equal force, was the purest form of naval combat. It was far simpler than a great fleet action involving many ships. It was a type of battle which resonated through the ages – the gladiatorial contests of the ancients, Medieval jousting, down to the duels of their own day. Captain Broke of HMS *Shannon* even issued a challenge to the USS *Chesapeake*, promising single combat:

JACK AUBREY COMMANDS

The *Java*, to the left, is partly dismasted by the larger USS *Constitution*, with her foremast falling and her bowsprit tangled up on the American deck. She was eventually forced to surrender after three and a half hours of fighting. By Lieutenant Buchanan and Nicholas Pocock. (NMM A 9308)

As the *Chesapeake* appears now ready for sea, I request you will do me the favor to meet the *Shannon* with her, Ship to Ship, to try the fortune of our respective Flags; to an Officer of your character, it requires some apology for proceeding to further particulars, be assured, Sir, that it is not from any doubt that I can entertain of your wishing to close with my proposal, but merely to provide an Answer to any objection which might be made, and very reasonably, upon our receiving an unfair support.[11]

Like a gunfight in a western, it involved speed in the use of guns. In more modern times is not unlike an international football match, or a boxing contest. Indeed William James's accusations against the Americans in the War of 1812, that they disguised the real force of their frigates for propaganda reasons, reminds one of the Queensberry Rules – it was rather like putting a light heavyweight in against a welterweight. The single ship action can be seen as the highest form of teamwork among the officers and crew of a ship; or as a single combat between two captains. It is no surprise that the single ship action is one of the great staples of modern naval fiction. The *genre* began with the *Lydia's* chase and capture of the *Natividad* in *The Happy Return,* and was revived with the *Sophie* versus the *Cacafuego* in *Master and Commander.*

It has been shown that 'when broadsides were approximately equal, the British ship always prevailed.'[12] Indeed, the British ship could expect to draw when the enemy had a 3 to 2 advantage, and to win when his advantage was less than that. This proportion was not applicable in actions against the Americans in the war of 1812. When the USS *Constitution* defeated the British *Guerriere*, for example, she had a superiority in broadside of almost 3 to 2. When the ships were equally matched, the battle might go either way – HMS *Shannon* defeated the *Chesapeake* when both sides were evenly matched in gun power, though the *Shannon's* crew was exceptionally well trained and led, while the American crew had not had time to work up.

Cochrane's legendary fight with the Spanish frigate *Gamo*, four times the size of his own *Speedy*, involved surprise and daring. Cochrane brought his ship so close to the enemy that 'the whole of her shot must necessarily go over our heads, whilst our guns, being elevated, would blow up her main deck.' Twice the Spanish attempted to reply by boarding, but Cochrane heard the order and the *Speedy* sheered off in time, firing a volley of musketry as he did so. Then, after an hour of fighting, Cochrane put the helm of the ship in the hands

156

Captain Phillip Broke leads his men in boarding the *Chesapeake* in 1813. (NMM PU 5837)

of the surgeon and led the rest of the crew in a boarding party:

> Leaving him therefore for the time both the captain and crew of the *Speedy*, the order was given to board, and in a few seconds every man was on the enemy's deck – a feat rendered the more easy as the doctor placed the *Speedy* close alongside with admirable skill.
>
> For a moment the Spanish seemed taken by surprise, as though unwilling to believe that so small a crew would have the audacity to board them; but soon recovering themselves, they made a rush to the waist of the frigate, where the fight was for some minutes gallantly carried on. Observing the enemy's colours still flying, I directed one of our men immediately to haul them down, when the Spanish crew, without pausing to consider by whose orders the colours had been struck, and naturally believing it the act of their own officers, gave in, and we were in possession of the *Gamo* frigate, of thirty-two heavy guns and 319 men, who an hour and a half before had looked on us as a certain if not an easy prey.[13]

In single ship actions, as in other forms of battle, raking was a key tactic. This meant manoeuvring one's ship so that its broadside pointed towards the bows, or even better the stern, of the enemy. The effect of this could be devastating, knocking guns off their carriages, cutting masts and killing and wounding men in large numbers.

The famous action between HMS *Shannon* and the USS *Chesapeake* was more evenly balanced in most respects. In his challenge before the battle, Captain Broke of the British ship described his armament and crew in some detail. According to William James the *Shannon* had a broadside of 538lbs, the *Chesapeake* had 590; she had 306 men, the American had 376.[14]

When the *Chesapeake* came out of Boston in the afternoon of 1 June 1813, the *Shannon* stood ready to meet her. There was a risk that the *Chesapeake* might pass under her stern and rake her, but the American captain chivalrously declined the opportunity and came alongside the *Shannon*. Captain Broke's crew was perhaps the best trained for gunnery in the world. His guns were loaded alternately, one with two round shot and 150 musket balls, and the next with one round and one double-headed shot, to do the greatest variety of damage to men, hull and rigging. As its opponent slowly came into the field of fire, each gun was aimed and fired in turn, and in most cases a particular gunport on the enemy ship was hit.

When the *Chesapeake* was almost head to wind in the light breezes, and stopped in the water, the *Shannon* was able to rake her diagonally and do considerable damage. The Americans seemed ready to board, though Broke still wanted to exploit his advantage in gunnery; but his headsails were shot away and he lost manoeuvrability. Broke rallied his men on the forecastle, called up the boarders and had the two ships lashed together. He led a party onto the American's gangway. The *Chesapeake's* crew had already been demoralised by the gunfire and Broke took the ship after slight resistance. The *Chesapeake* was taken to Britain in triumph, a success after a long series of defeats. She was broken up and some of her timbers were incorporated in a mill in Hampshire, where they remain to this day.

SQUADRON ACTION

Squadron action, fought between less than about ten warships on each side, were essentially small-scale fleet actions and their tactics provided a microcosm of the larger battles. The Battle of Algeciras, fought on 6 July 1801 off the Spanish coast just across the bay from Gibraltar, had something in common with the Nile in that the enemy, three French ships of the line under Admiral Linois, were anchored in an apparently good position, Rear-Admiral Sir James Saumarez, Nelson's second in command at the Nile, attacked with six ships of the line but the French position really was well chosen this time, among the rocks and shoals of the Spanish coast, and well protected by shore batteries largely manned by seamen. Furthermore the winds were unreliable and HMS *Hannibal* of 74 guns was driven aground and forced to surrender. Saumarez retreated to Gibraltar, but the French victory was far from complete, as their ships had also gone aground.

Neither side believed this was the end of the matter. Saumarez inspired his men to work day and night to get his damaged ships repaired, while the French were joined by five Spanish and one French ship of the line. This combined fleet of nine ships, including three very large Spanish ones, sailed towards Cadiz on the 12th, hotly pursued by Saumarez with five of the line led by the 80-gun *Caesar*. But the French had not repaired their ships fully, and the Spanish were lacking in battle experience and competence. During a night action one Spanish 112-gun ship was set on fire and it collided with another of similar gun power, destroying both. A French 74 was captured. For his triumph against adversity, and for preventing an enemy concentration at Cadiz, Saumarez received the highest honours.

The squadron action at Algeciras, near Gibraltar, in 1801. (NMM PAH 8001)

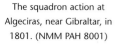

BATTLE TACTICS

To contemporary public opinion, and to historians and naval officers for many generations afterwards, fleet battles were by far the most important feature of naval warfare. Here, of course, the Royal Navy was strikingly successful. There were six great fleet battles, in which the French, Dutch, Danes and Spanish were decisively defeated. Five of these battles took place in the first phase of the great wars, from 1793-1801. This was a much greater rate of activity than in previous wars, which had produced one or two great victories at most.

Since the First Anglo-Dutch War of 1652-4, the line of battle had been the main tactic of fleets in combat. A warship had a large number of guns on its sides and very few firing forward or aft, and it was natural to put the fleet in a single line so that the guns of one ship did not mask those of another. This however was rather a defensive tactic, and it became increasingly difficult to achieve a decisive victory if both sides used it. From the middle of the eighteenth century, British admirals began to move increasingly away from the rigid line of battle, culminating in Nelson's headlong attack at Trafalgar.

One of the first problems faced by any commander was to get his fleet into battle. Fleets could not maintain their battle order for long, and the tended to sail without any particular order until the enemy was sighted. Forming a line could take some time, and Nelson wrote that 'If the two fleets are both willing to fight, but little manoeuvring is necessary, the less the better. A day is soon lost in that business.'[15]

In a purely hypothetical case two fleets would spot one another in the open sea, each would sail as close to the wind as it could to get the weather gage and battle would commence. This never happened in practice during the Great Wars, for two reasons. Firstly, fleets hardly ever met in the open sea, which was too vast for such things to happen by chance. Secondly, in the great majority of cases one fleet or the other would clearly know that it was inferior in material or technique or would try to avoid battle. One tends to associate this feeling of inferiority with the French and Spanish, and indeed it was a vital factor at Trafalgar; but there were also cases where a British force was much outnumbered, as when Admiral Cornwallis, with five ships of the line, retreated very skilfully from a force of thirteen French ships of the line in June 1795.

As a result, battles only took place when the defensive side had to stand and fight. Two of the great battles — the Nile and Copenhagen — were fought against an enemy at anchor. Two more — Camperdown and Trafalgar — were against enemy fleets which were too close

On the left the British fleet begins its attack at the Battle of the Nile in 1798. To the right, the *Culloden* has gone aground on a shoal and the 50-gun *Leander* and the brig *Mutine* stand by her. In the right distance, the *Alexander* and *Swiftsure* approach, having been sent on a reconnaissance of Alexandria. By William Anderson, from information supplied by Captain Thompson of the *Leander*. (NMM PAG 8968)

inshore to escape. The other two – the Glorious First of June and St Vincent – were against enemy fleets which were protecting convoys of great value to the state. Of all these battles only the Glorious First of June was fought out of sight of land, which is why it has a chronological rather than a geographical name.

Many theoretical books were published on naval tactics, mostly by the French. The most influential British writer was the Scotsman Clerk of Eldin, who had no seafaring experience but got all his information from reading and conversation. He put forward the idea that breaking the enemy line was the only way to get decisive results. The evidence is contradictory, but Captain Thomas Hardy later claimed that 'Lord Nelson read Mr Clerk's works with great attention and frequently expressed his approbation of them in the fullest manner; … He most approved of the attack from to-windward, and considered that breaking through the enemy's line absolutely necessary to obtain a great victory.[16]

In the past it had been generally assumed that an attacking fleet needed to be to the windward side of its enemy, to have 'the weather gage'. This offered several advantages. The fleet with the weather gage would have more control of the battle, deciding when to attack and at what range to fight. It would have a clearer view as the smoke was blown away from it towards the enemy. It would be able to launch attacks by fireships or ship's boats towards the enemy. Against this, the fleet on the lee side would be able to deploy its lower guns better, as its ships would be heeling away from the enemy. It would be able to retreat, assuming it was not pressed against a coast. It was generally assumed that the attacking fleet, usually the British one, would try to get the weather gage, while a defensive one would decline it. Clerk, in a rather paradoxical phrase proposed the attack 'from to windward', that is from leeward. The fleet which lost the weather gage would not accept this as in the past, but would break through the enemy line a few ships from its head. This would allow him to use both broadsides as he passed through, against the weak bows and sterns of the enemy.

In reality there were two main means of achieving a decisive victory in fleet battle; by breaking the enemy line or by concentrating one's force on part of his line. Nelson's plans for Trafalgar used both these ideas. In his original plan he would attack in three squadrons, including one under a reliable officer who would choose the place and time to attack. In practice he had fewer ships than expected and used two squadrons. One, headed by Nelson himself, would break the enemy line about a third from its head while the other, under Collingwood, would destroy the portion that was cut off. But neither admiral executed the plan in full. Collingwood rushed too far ahead in his own flagship the *Royal Sovereign* and perhaps suffered unnecessary casualties as a result. Nelson seems to have varied in his aims during the approach, first steering towards the head of the enemy line to prevent their retreat, then going for the centre to attack the flagship. All the leading ships suffered heavy casualties in the early stage of the melee battle which ensued, until the British superiority in gunnery and manoeuvre began to prevail.

Attack in Line Ahead

Larger fleet in
rough line abreast

Smaller fleet in
rough line ahead

Ships tack or wear to
attack cut-off section
of the enemy

Smaller fleet forms
line ahead and
breaks enemy line

Main force cannot
get to windward

Breaking the line, as proposed
by Clerk of Eldin.
(from N Tracy *Naval Warfare in
the Age of Sail*)

SUCCESS IN BATTLE

To examine the British success in fleet actions, it is interesting to look at the statistics over sixty years or so. Ignoring the indecisive battles, such as Toulon and Ushant, we can see certain trends in the victories. Looking at British victories and taking into account the numbers of ships of the line present on both sides, one pattern begins to emerge. Copenhagen is missed out, because it is difficult to assess the floating batteries in the Danish defences, and how they could be equated with ships of the line, but clearly, the trend is for British fleets to win against greater odds. St Vincent is notable in this respect, in that it was the first battle to be won against a clear numerical superiority in favour of the enemy.

Looking at the proportion of ships from the enemy fleet captured or destroyed, the First Battle of Finisterre in 1747 is an extreme case, but its significance is reduced by the fact that the British fleet was much larger than the French one on that occasion. Camperdown is significant in that it was a very decisive victory - a Nelsonian battle without Nelson. Apart from that, the Nile was the really outstanding battle - a crushing victory, which altered the balance of power overnight. This view is shared by French historians – 'Aboukir was such a defeat that the French Navy never had the time to put itself back together again.'[17]

Combining the two factors produces a rather crude measure of success in battle. The enemy force is divided by the British force, and then multiplied by the net loss to the enemy. In this table, First Finisterre is put into proportion, and St Vincent looks much less decisive, because of the small number of ships captured. Trafalgar appears important in two ways - as the culmination in a long process of ever increasing victory, and as the only battle in which numerical inferiority was combined with overwhelming success. Strategically it was less important than the Nile, in that the French had already given up their invasion plans, but this is not to deny the achievement of Nelson and his officers and men.

How great was the effect of Nelson on fleet battles? Overwhelming victory was possible without him, as Duncan showed at Camperdown against the Dutch in 1797, capturing eleven out of sixteen enemy ships. All the famous single-ship actions were fought without Nelson, and most were as successful as any of the great fleet battles. But his influence was decisive at St Vincent, and at the Nile and Trafalgar he achieved a greater degree of success than anyone before or since.

THE EXPERIENCE OF BATTLE

Standing orders usually enjoined silence as the ship approached a battle, but there were whispered conversations, at the very least, as the ships were got ready:

> In such a bustling, and it may be said, trying as well as serious time, it is curious to notice the different dispositions of the British sailor. Some would be offering a guinea for a glass of grog, whilst others were making a sort of mutual verbal will, such as, if one of Johnny Crapeau's shots (a term given to the French,) knocks my head off, you will take all my effects; and if you are killed, and I am not, why, I will

Diagrams showing the success of the British Navy in fleet battles, 1747-1805. Combining the first two graphs shows a steady growth of success against increasing odds, and demonstrates that Trafalgar was truly an outstanding battle, the only one which gave overwhelming victory against an enemy of superior numbers.

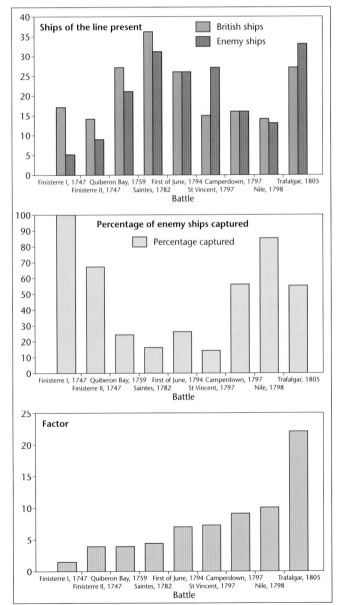

have yours, and this is generally agreed to.[18]

All this changed dramatically once the fight began. Below decks in the *Victory* at Trafalgar, Lieutenant Roteley of the Royal Marines found a scene of horror, with the ship engaged on both sides:

A man should witness a battle in a three-decker from the middle deck, for it beggars all description. It bewilders the senses of sight and hearing. There was fire from above, fire from below, besides the fire from the deck I was upon, the guns recoiling with violence reports louder than thunder, the deck heaving and the side straining. I fancied myself in the infernal regions, where every man appeared a devil. Lips might move, but orders and hearing were out of the question: everything was done by signs.

Despite their great importance to contemporaries and historians, fleet battles figure little in naval fiction. Jack Aubrey, we are told, fought at St Vincent, though there is some confusion about which ship he fought in. At the Nile he was the senior surviving lieutenant of his ship, which entitled him to a rather delayed promotion to 'Master and Commander'. Hornblower was never in a fleet battle, for he was a prisoner or in other theatres when the great battles were fought. Nor do fleet battles play much part in the works of Marryat – he only entered the navy in 1806, after the age of great battles was over. In *Peter Simple*, however, he puts some comments in the mouth of his character:

I am only astonished, seeing the confusion and *invariable variableness* of a sea-fight, how so much could be known. One observation occurred to me then, and I have thought of it ever since with redoubled conviction; this was that the admiral, after the battle began, was no admiral at all: he could neither see or be seen; he could take no advantage of the enemy's weak points or defend his own; his ship, the *Victory*, one of our finest three-deckers, was in a manner tied up alongside a French eighty-gun ship.[19]

The best fictional account of Trafalgar comes in a military novel – *Sharpe's Trafalgar*.

The cockpit of a ship in action, giving some impression of the crowding, chaos, agony and pathos of the scene. (NMM PAD 8484)

A sea fight would also descend into chaos in the individual ship, according to Marryat:

> The first lieutenant is missing; you will find him in the cock-pit – they have just finished taking up the arteries of his right arm, which has been amputated; and the Scotch surgeon's assistant, who for many months bewailed the want of practice, and who, for having openly expressed his wishes on that subject, had received a sound thrashing from the exasperated midshipmen, is now complimenting the fainting man upon the excellent stump they have made for him: while fifty others, dying or wounded, with as much variety as Homer's heroes, whose blood, trickling from them in several rivulets, pours into one general lake at the lower level of the deck, are anxiously awaiting their turn, and distract the purser's steward by their loud calls, in every direction at the same time, for the tin-pot of water, with which he is relieving their agonising thirst.[20]

THE TREATMENT OF THE WOUNDED

Unless they were so seriously injured that they could not be expected to survive, it was the universal practice to carry wounded below to the cockpit. Even Nelson, with his spine shot through, was carried down five decks, by way of steep ladderways, to the cockpit of the *Victory*. Down there was a scene of horror, borne with fortitude by every true seaman. Lieutenant Nicolas visited the cockpit and found a scene beyond his comprehension:

> My nerves were but little accustomed to such trials, but even the dangers of the battle did not seem more terrific than the spectacle before me. On a long table lay several anxiously looking for their turn to receive the surgeon's care, yet dreading the fate which he might pronounce. One subject was undergoing amputation, and every part was heaped with sufferers: their piercing shrieks and expiring groans were echoed through this vault of misery…what a contrast to the hilarity and enthusiastic mirth which reigned in this spot the preceding evening![21]

Even a hardened medical practioner could come close to despair, especially when he was short-handed, like the surgeon of the *Ardent* at Camperdown:

> Ninety wounded men were brought down from the action. The whole cockpit, deck, cabins, wing berths and part of the cable tier, together with my platform and my preparations for dressings were covered with them.
>
> So that for a time they were laid on each other at the foot of the ladder where they were brought down…
>
> Melancholy cries for assistance were addressed to me from every side by wounded and dying, and piteous moans and bewailing from pain and despair. In the midst of these agonising scenes, I was able to preserve myself firm and collected, and embracing in my mind the whole of the situation, to direct my attention where the greatest and most essential services could be performed. Some with wounds, bad indeed and painful, but slight in comparison with the dreadful condition of others, were most vociferous for assitance.[22]

The surgeon's greatest talent in battle was amputation, and there was rarely enough time to assess the condition of a limb properly before cutting it off. Hence the popular image of the sailor, including Hornblower's Captain Bush and the great Nelson himself, lacking at least one limb.

Seamen held their nerve among all the devastation and horror of battle, and they generally prevailed. As a result of fleet battles, single ship actions, and various random captures, the British took or destroyed 570 enemy warships from 1793 to 1801, including 86 ships of the line; they lost 59 vessels, including five of the line.[23]

CHAPTER 9

THE EXPERIENCE OF WAR

The Great Wars with France lasted twenty-two years, with two short intervals, and many of the participants, especially the weary victims of the press gangs, must have despaired about them ever ending. This pattern is repeated in naval fiction. Those who are not fans of it sometimes describe the sagas as 'interminable.' But real battles and real wars do come to an end, at least when they are fought against a specific enemy like a state, rather than a vaguer concept like 'terrorism.'

An individual naval conflict might end in indecision, with one side or the other retreating with acceptable damage. This was deeply unsatisfying situation for British officers and the public. In 1795 Horatio Nelson had his first taste of fleet action when the Mediterranean Fleet met the French off Corsica in March 1795. He was almost the only captain to engage the enemy seriously, turning his ship occasionally to fire broadsides from as little as 100 yards

Nelson captures the damaged
Ca Ira in 1795.
(NMM PW 5872)

into the stern of the damaged *Ca Ira*, resulting in her capture, along with another 74 which attempted to tow her. His superior, Admiral Hotham, stopped the pursuit and told Nelson, 'We must be contented. We have done very well.' Hotham was voted the thanks of both houses of Parliament, but Nelson wrote to his wife, 'had we taken ten sail, and allowed the 11th to escape when it had been possible to have got at her, I could never have called it well done.' This was the basis of Nelson's later beliefs and tactics.

Ten years later Admiral Calder thought he had done very well in driving off the French fleet which Nelson had chased to the West Indies, thus ruining Napoleon's invasion plan. He wrote to his superiors:

> I have had the good fortune to have fallen in with the combined squadrons of Toulon and Cadiz upon their return from the West Indies. The action has been unique, having been fought in a fog at night. I hope your lordship and my royal master will think I have done all that it was possible to have been done. If so, and you should think me deserving of any mark of royal bounty, I beg leave to observe that I have no children, but I have a nephew, the son of an old faithful servant of the crown…to whom I hope His Majesty's royal bounty may extend, if my services may be thought worthy of any mark by His Majesty.[1]

But public and naval opinion was hostile to him, because he had not produced any captured ships. He demanded a court martial, but in the meantime Nelson fought and died at Trafalgar, setting a new standard for naval victory. The unfortunate Calder was reprimanded rather than honoured.

Apart from such unsatisfactory cases, a naval fight would end in victory for one side and defeat for the other. The rewards for victory were high for officers and the penalties for defeat, apart from the obvious ones of death or disablement, were severe.

DEFEAT

If defeat seemed inevitable and heavy casualties had already been suffered it was acceptable for the captain, or senior surviving officer, to surrender the ship. There were no fixed rules about when this could be done. At one end of the scale, a captain who made no attempt at all to resist, except against enormous odds, was risking disgrace. At the other, French officers were sometimes fanatical in their devotion to the cause. At the Nile, Captain Du Petit-Thouars of the *Tonnant* held out for two days after the defeat of all his colleagues except one, though the ship was dismasted at anchor, and surrounded by several British ships. In general, surrender was acceptable after fire had been exchanged, some casualties had been suffered, no relief was at hand and the ship was in such a position, for example dismasted or being raked, that more casualties seemed certain and victory was impossible. A British captain would face court martial for the loss of his ship in any circumstances, though that was in a sense more like a court of enquiry than a criminal trial and often resulted in acquittal with honour.

The decision to surrender was a matter for the captain or the senior surviving officer, perhaps consulting with the other officers where practicable in the chaos of battle. The seamen were not consulted. Samuel Leech describes the process in the *Macedonian* in 1812:

> A council was now held among the officers on the quarter deck. Our condition was perilous in the extreme: victory or escape was alike hopeless. Our ship was disabled, many of our men were killed, and many more wounded. The enemy would without doubt beat down upon us in a few moments, and as she could now choose her own position, would

no doubt rake us fore and aft. Any further resistance was therefore folly. So, in spite of the hot-brained lieutenant, Mr Hope, who advised them not to strike, but to sink alongside, it was determined to strike our bunting. This was done by the hands of a brave fellow named Watson, whose saddened brow told how severely it pained his lion heart to do it....His Britannic Majesty's frigate *Macedonian* was now the prize of the American frigate *United States*.[2]

PRISONERS OF WAR

Having surrendered, the men of the captured ship became prisoners of war, and in the first instance they were usually battened down below under armed guard, for revolts of prisoners were not unknown. Officers were often treated better, and were entertained by their captors. One of the officers of the intransigent *Tonnant*, after her final surrender at the Nile, was taken on board the *Theseus*. He spoke good English and was able to exchange information with his captors about the battle.[3] Surrender implied that the captors would protect the prisoners. After Trafalgar the ships were caught in a great storm and the French officers of the *Algeciras*, seeing that the ship was being driven onto shoals without any help from the British navy, peacefully took back the ship from her prize crew and took her into Cadiz.

On arrival in port, the prisoners were marched under guard to a place of confinement, which might take many days. Marryat's *Poor Jack* was captured and his party of 47 seamen

The Dutch Admiral de Winter hands over his sword to Admiral Duncan after the Battle of Camperdown in 1797. Painting by Samuel Drummond. (NMM BHC 0506)

Prison hulks at Portsmouth, by Daniel Turner. The town and harbour are in the left distance. (NMM BHC 1924)

and guarded by a dozen aged soldiers; he and his companions managed to escape by starting a fire in the church where they were imprisoned overnight.[4] John Wetherell, whose adventures were edited by CS Forester, had no such success:

> The next day the 4th we again began our journey and to our disadvantage we had to travail 27 Miles in rain and a very heavy road, and our guard was not composed of the most humane men in France. They took a dislike to us thro' some of our men being unable to walk fast enough thro the middle of the heavy road; indeed the Serjeant of the guard (Dutch man) said if we did not go faster along he would break his Sword cross some of our backs.[5]

Prisoners' treatment depended on several factors. Officers generally fared far better than the men, for their word of honour was considered worth something and they were allowed to live in lodgings in non-military towns, having given their parole not to escape. The men were usually detained in any place convenient for the authorities. Often this meant old castles of no immediate use to the army, such as Edinburgh Castle in Scotland, Portchester Castle near Portsmouth, or the notorious fortress of Verdun in northern France. Later the British built Dartmoor Prison on an isolated site to keep captured Frenchmen.

One peculiarity of the British system, much complained of by those subjected to it, was to keep prisoners in hulks or old, disarmed warships. It was reported:

> The Medway is covered with men-of-war, dismantled and lying in ordinary. Their fresh and brilliant painting contrasts with the hideous aspect of the old and smoky hulks, which seem the remains of vessels blackened by a recent fire. It is in these floating tombs that are buried alive prisoners of war – Danes, Swedes, Frenchmen, Americans, no matter. They are lodged on the lower deck, on the upper deck, and even on the orlop deck.[6]

There was not much systematic mistreatment of prisoners of war, but they were vulnerable to many hardships, caused by government niggardliness, corruption, disease or petty vindictiveness. In past wars it had been common to exchange prisoners as soon as possible, with priority being given to naval rather than merchant seamen. But after the French Revolution trust between the sides broke down completely and in 1796 it was reported 'The mode in which the present war is carried on, has for a long time prevented the most necessary communication, such as had not ceased to exist between hostile nations at any preceding period. The persons whose lot it has been to suffer most from this interruption, are the prisoners of war on either side.'[7] As a result many men were condemned to long and indefinite periods

of imprisonment. Some adjusted quite well and, for example, made ship models to sell on a local market. John Wetherell describes the occupations of his fellow prisoners. 'some Makeing Ships for Sale; others got work from the people in town, Shoe makers, Taylors, button makers, and chair bottomers; we also had wooden shoe sole and heel makers, barbers, Jews selling old clothes, watches, books, fiddles &c.' He also describes his prison at Givet, near Charlemont. They were guarded

> ...by a Brigadier [corporal] and one Gendarme to each passage which contained eight rooms, and each room 16 men, so that each brigadier had 128 Men in his department. The sick were reported at muster in the morning so that they could be sent to the hospital directly after muster. Bread and rice and beans was served every 4th day; 3lns of bread for 4 days. We also had salt at the same time. Every five days we had wood...[8]

Captain Sir Sidney Smith was an exceptional prisoner. When captured during a raid on Le Havre in 1796, he was in civilian clothes and as regarded as a spy. He was known to have worked with French Royalists and to have tried to burn the town and the fleet at

Sir Sidney Smith in the Temple
Prison in Paris. By Hennequin,
Auguste and Cosway.
(NMM PAF 3568)

Toulon in 1794. He was separated from his other officers and put in the Medieval Temple Prison in Paris. A Royalist officer, Francois de Tromelin was captured with him. He posed as Smith's French-Canadian servant and attracted the amorous attentions of the gaoler's daughter before being released. Smith managed to escape after two years and returned to England in a fishing boat.

It was not normal to imprison enemy civilians on the outbreak of war, but Napoleon did this in 1803, confirming British impressions of his barbarism. When the war with America broke out in 1812, the English lawyer William James happened to be in Philadelphia on passage between Jamaica and Canada. He was imprisoned by the Americans in very light conditions, and even allowed to visit their warships for research. His only real hardship was having to listen to American boast as about the prowess of their ships, particularly when the *Constitution* beat the *Guerriere* in August 1812. James quickly concluded that something was wrong with the American claims, which did not take into account the discrepancy in size between the ships concerned. After his release he produced a book with a detailed refutation of the American version. His more general *Naval History of Great Britain*, first published between 1822 and 1824, has its faults. To the modern mind it concentrates far too much on the action between the ships and fleets and says little about the strategic context which brought them together. Nevertheless it is still an invaluable reference work for writers of naval fiction and non-fiction, giving accurate details of countless fleet and squadron battles, single ship actions, and amphibious landings. Both Forester and O'Brian owe it a considerable debt.

In June 1815 the Duke of Wellington won the Battle of Waterloo and brought the long wars with France to an end. Napoleon fled and on 14 July he surrendered to HMS *Bellerophon*, the leading ship in a squadron blockading Rochefort. Her captain was Frederick Lewis Maitland, and the defeated emperor and the captain talked about the customs of the Scottish aristocracy:

Local boatmen make their fortunes by taking curious passengers out to see the *Bellerophon*, carrying the captive Napoleon, in Plymouth Sound in 1815. Painted by John James Chalon.
(NMM BHC 3227)

He conversed a great deal, and showed no depression of spirits: among other things, he asked me where I was born. I told him, in Scotland. "Have you any property there?" said he. "No, I am a younger son, and they do not bestow much on people of that description in Scotland."[9]

He inspected the ship's marines and commented, 'What could be done with a hundred thousand men such as these.' Maitland took Bonaparte back to Plymouth Sound, where local boatmen made a fortune by taking passengers out to see the hated and feared enemy. Captain Maitland reported to Lord Keith, now in command of the Channel Fleet. He had to break the news to the former emperor that he was to be exiled to the lonely outpost of St Helena.

VICTORY AND ITS REWARDS

Victory in single-ship combat or in fleet or squadron or fleet battle brought many rewards, both material and spiritual. Elation was surprisingly rare, however, mainly because the men tended to be exhausted and traumatised after a long and bloody battle. After Trafalgar, Lieutenant John Yule of the *Victory* wrote to his sister:

> Although my ideas are now a little more collected that they were when I last wrote, they are by no means clear even now, the horrors of an action during the time it lasts and for a short time afterwards make everything around you appear in a different shape to what it did before…the action will be by the nation conceived a very glorious one but when the devastation is considered how can we glory in it? How many orphans and fatherless has it made? How many has it made sad and how few (concerned) has it made glad?[10]

The capture of enemy merchant ships also brought rewards, mostly of the more material kind, in the form of prize money. When captured, an enemy ship, whether warship or merchantman, was sold and the value was divided among the captors, with the lion's share going to the officers. According to the rules at the beginning of the wars, the sum was divided into eight parts. The admiral had one eighth of all the ships captured under his command, the captains had two eights (or three if not under the direct orders of an admiral). The lieutenants had another eighth between them, and another went to the warrant officers. The recognised petty officers, such as craftsman and boatswain's mates, had a further eighth. The last class included the rest of the crew, from captains of tops and corporals of marines, to the most inexperienced landsmen. They shared one quarter between them. In 1808 the system was reformed. A captain now got a quarter, with a share of that allotted to the admiral, the lieutenants remained at an eighth, the junior officers another eighth. The remaining half was divided into shares with different amounts going to midshipmen and senior petty officers, junior petty officers including captains of tops, seamen and finally landsmen and servants.

In a practical example of the old system, the *Pelican* of 18 guns took an American ship running contraband in 1796. The Admiral got £484, though he was not present. The captain received £968, compared with a commander's annual salary of £109. The lieutenants got £161, nearly double their annual salary, warrant officers got £80 compared with a boatswain's pay of £26 in a small ship. The petty officers got £35, the seaman £11/7/9 (£11.39), slightly less than an ordinary seaman's yearly pay of £12/7/0 (£12.35).[11] Prize money, though a useful bonus to an ordinary seaman, was of much greater value to a senior officer, and it could change the life of a captain or admiral, his family and even his descendants. It dominated the thoughts of many officers. It could make the difference between a life of hardship on the fringes of the middle class, and wealth as a country gentleman. In Jane Austen's *Persuasion*, the snobbish Sir Walter Elliot is sarcastic when he finds that an admiral of relatively humble origin is about to take up the tenancy of his country house. "'He would be a very lucky man, Shepherd,' replied Sir Walter, 'that's all I have to remark. A prize indeed would Kellynch Hall be to him; rather the greatest prize of all, let him have taken ever so many before – hey, Shepherd?'"[12]

The taking of a rich prize was one moment of true elation in a naval career. According to Frederick Chamier:

> There are many gratifying moments in life….But to a sailor, "prize-money" is as sweet as "revenge in woman;" and that is saying as much for the feeling, as even Lord Byron could say, from whom I borrow the simile. At the moment of capture I would not have changed my profession for any other in the world. Oh, the joy of legally mistaking the *meum et tuum* – the immense gratification of converting one man's property to one's own use – the having a license to rob and to murder – it's quite delightful! and quite unknown to your sober, virtuous people on shore…[13]

Prize money did have its risks, as Jack Aubrey well knew. A prize ship had to be condemned by a court as lawful prize, in that it was owned by or operating on behalf of the subjects of an enemy power. There were enough dubious neutrals and ships under false colours to make the issue very doubtful in many cases. St Vincent wrote with some exaggeration, 'where one captain makes fortune by the capture of neutrals, ten are ruined.'[14]

Prize money provided a system of rewards and incentive at no real cost to the government, but it had many disadvantages. It could set one officer against another, as when Nelson and St Vincent fought a legal battle over their Mediterranean prize money. It was

One of the Spanish treasure ships blows up during the British attack in 1804, an incident which features in both *Hornblower and the Hotspur* and *Post Captain*. The captors were denied the fabulous sums of prize money because Britain and Spain were not technically at war at the time, and the spoils were deemed Droits of Admiralty. (NMM PW 5685)

partly a matter of chance whether an officer became rich, but it was also a matter of the right appointments and support. An appointment to a frigate was highly valued, and Frances Austen always regretted that he never got one. Orders to go on a 'cruise' against enemy shipping would prove beneficial to both the captain and the admiral who gave the order, but could cause much jealousy among those who were kept on more routine and less profitable duties.

Prize money involved large amounts of cash, and in the atmosphere of the time it tended to breed corruption. Thomas Cochrane was very aggrieved by his treatment by the court in Malta. He found that the marshal and the proctor were in fact the same person, allowing him to make vast profits on other people's ventures:

> In addition to his multitude of fees and charges, the marshal also claimed, and received as his personal perquisite, *one half per cent* on the inspection of prizes, *one per cent* for their appraisment, and *two and a half per cent* on the sale. This, with *one fourth* added as foresaid, made *just five per cent* on all captures for the marshal's perquisites alone, irrespective of his other fees; which, being subjected to no check, were extended according to conscience.[15]

Worst of all, prize money had the potential to distort naval strategy. If captains and admirals were completely cynical about it, they would seek out merchant shipping with valuable cargoes and avoid warships which were less valuable, and might fight back. There were several features in the system to compensate for this, and to encourage officers to take on warships. In purely financial terms, head money was offered for warships only, at the rate of £5 per man of the crew of the enemy ship. After a great victory Parliament might well vote a large sum of money to be distributed among the fleet in the same way as prize money, and often a substantial sum to the commander-in-chief. Promotion was offered too for success against warships, though that had its limitations. The officers who made the most important decisions, Admirals and post-captains, could only be promoted by seniority so it had no direct benefit to them. The first lieutenant of a successful ship was usually promoted, but he had not made the decision to attack. Promotion after a battle was most useful to commanders who needed to make the vital step to captain, like Jack Aubrey in *Master and Commander* and *Post Captain*. In such a case it was very necessary to establish that the success really had been against warships rather than merchantmen or privateers.

The third type of reward was honour, not just in the abstract sense but also in the form of decorations, medals and titles. There were no campaign or gallantry medals until many years afterwards, but captains were often presented with gold medals after a successful battle, and they were often knighted. A successful commander-in-chief would have a peerage, probably an earldom, as with St Vincent after the battle from which he took his name. Nelson fought his first two battles as a subordinate admiral and became only a baron after the Nile, much to his annoyance. He rose one grade to viscount after Copenhagen, and no doubt would have gone on to at least earl, if not marquis or duke, if he had survived Trafalgar; instead his brother became an earl.

A presentation sword given to Sir John Jervis by the City of London after the Battle of Cape St. Vincent.
(NMM D 4861 5-D)

NAVAL OFFICERS – SUCCESS AND FAILURE

George Elphinstone, Lord Keith, was a man who had made a great success of his naval career. Though he never fought in a fleet battle or served on the Board of Admiralty, he greatly improved the economic and social position of himself and his family. He had been born in an ancient and very uncomfortable tower-house on the banks of the Forth, the fifth son of a declining aristocratic family which had lost most of its land in supporting the losing side in several rebellions. According to his own account he was sent into the navy with £5 in his pocket, and his family declined to send him on navigation classes beforehand. By the end of the wars he had made between £100,000 and £200,000 in prize money and built mansion across the Forth form his birthplace. Tulliallan House is now the Scottish Police College.

His fellow Scot Thomas Cochrane had more ambiguous success. He too came from an impoverished aristocratic family, though he was the eldest son and inherited the title. He made vast amounts in prize money from his famous captures, but was imprisoned for alleged stock exchange fraud and dismissed from the navy. He founded the navies of Chile, Peru, Brazil and Greece during their wars of independence and was the first to use steam power in action. He was re-instated as a rear-admiral in 1832 and eventually reached the rank of full admiral at the time of the Crimean War in 1854. Through his writings, according to a modern historian who is sceptical about his veracity, he was the 'posthumous winner' of many battles against the legal system.[16]

Edward Rotherham, captain of the *Royal Sovereign* at Trafalgar and the first British captain to engage in that conflict, ended the war in a far more embittered state. In 1815 he was disappointed not to be made a Knight Commander of the Bath, although he 'had the honour to command the Royal Sovereign who led the British Fleet to Victory, a Victory! too well known by its splendour to require any comment.' He was a regular writer to the newspapers, complaining about many aspects of the naval administration before he died of an apoplexy in 1830. In one of the most chilling passages of his *Growls of a Naval Life* he considered, 'Having been some thirty years at sea setting down to reflect what sort of life you have spent and asking yourself whether you wish to pass such another'.[17]

George Elphinstone, Lord Keith, who made a considerable fortune in prize money and restored the status of his Scottish aristocratic family. (NMM BHC 2815)

There were many embittered lieutenants and other officers who had not done well out of the war, and did even less well in peace. Peter Pickersgill, second lieutenant of the *Revenge* at Trafalgar, complained more than thirty years later that despite promotion to commander in 1810, 'for want of interest, never could obtain a command afloat.' Spencer Smyth, midshipman of the *Defiance,* had seen more action than most. 'I have been engaged in three general battles and at the capture and destruction of 24 ships of the line, 23 frigates, 36 corvettes and brigs and three privateers, besides several more vessels.' He was promoted to commander after the victory against the Turks at Navarino in 1827 but then, 'being without interest, was placed on half pay.' Lieutenant Thomas Chrystie of Fife was aware that 'there would be no chance of promotion for an officer who had little or no interest.' He took service in the merchant navy, complaining that 'the system of favouritism, particularly on account of corrupt Parliamentary reasons, may not continue to blot on the honourable government of this noble country.' Alexander Maconochie, a commander of 1815 and a relative of the Cochranes, turned his attention to penal reform. Commander John Finlayson had been Nelson's signal officer at Copenhagen in 1801, when he turned his blind eye to the admiral's signal. In the 1840s he complained, 'I joined the steam service under the idea of having a preference for a command in my own service, but found interest was wanting and merit or service had no chance, and now like many others growing grey with youngsters stepping over my head.' At the same time Lieutenant John Fullarton of Ayrshire wrote of his past career, 'Nothing but the common occurrences of services. Health broken from climate and hurts received, like a thousand others upon the active list. As Jack says, "not worth a single damn."'[18]

RESULTS OF THE WAR

In the long naval wars as a whole, there were winners and losers too. As they came to an end in 1814-15, and were finished off by the Battle of Waterloo in 1815, the greatest fleet in the world was largely paid off. From 1,009 ships in 1813, the navy had only 179 in 1826 and only a few of these were in commission. From a peak of 145,000 men in 1810-13, parliament voted for 23,000 in 1826. But despite that, Great Britain was clearly established as the world's greatest imperial and naval power, and for most of the nineteenth century she was far further ahead of the others than she ever was in the eighteenth or twentieth centuries. The French recovered from their defeats and remained as rivals, though not very close ones. The Spanish and Dutch never recovered and were reduced to minor naval powers. The Russians retained a large fleet after the wars, but badly maintained and manned. The Americans had a small but very effective force, especially as their new 74-gun ships of the line came into service.

The Royal Navy, despite contrary impressions at the time and among some later historians, remained in the forefront of technological change in the nineteenth century. Lord Melville, First Lord of the Admiralty for nearly twenty years from 1812, is often falsely accused of stating, 'their Lordships feel it is their bounden duty to discourage to the utmost of their ability the employment of steam vessels, as they consider the introduction of Steam is calculated to strike a fatal blow at the supremacy of the Empire.' In fact he did much to promote steam power and wrote in 1823, 'There is every reason to believe from the purposes to which Steam Vessels are now applied that they would be found very useful in the protection of our trade in the Channel.…It will be proper now to provide Steam Engines for at least six vessels…and I therefore desire that you will take the necessary steps for that purpose.'[19]

Geoff Hunt's much-admired cover painting for the author's *Nelson's Navy* of 1989, showing a ship of the line and a frigate off the entrance to Portsmouth Dockyard. A similar scene was used for the cover of Patrick O'Brian's *The Reverse of the Medal*.
(Artist: Geoff Hunt RSMA)

The ironclad *Warrior* was built in 1860 in response to the French *Gloire*, but was considerably larger than her rival and was followed by several similar ships within ten years. At the beginning of the next decade the Royal Navy initiated the end of sail power, when launched the *Devastation*, the first mastless battleship. From that moment the warship was something unrecognisable to the sailor's of Nelson's day.

The old meritocratic navy of the wars became increasingly political and aristocratic as economic constraints began to bite, while middle class expectations were raised in Victorian times. The route to officer rank narrowed and by the end of the century it was only open to those who started a career at Dartmouth College at the age of 13, with political and financial support from a wealthy and well-connected family. It took most of the first half of the twentieth century to open up the career again and produce a navy which fought successfully in an even greater struggle, the Second World War. In the words of one of the most penetrating critics of British strategy, 'Adversity had rescued the Navy from the arrogant complacency bequeathed by the Victorian era, and which had marred its performance in the Great War [ie 1914-18]; had awoken it from the conservatism and torpor of the inter-war years; and had restored it to the bold, hardy, resourceful and highly professional service that it was in Nelson's time.'[20]

THE EFFECTS

The traditions of 1793 to 1815 had a profound effect on the British in the Second World War. The visionary inventions of the early 1800s – the submarine, the rocket, the torpedo and aerial bombardment – were now used to devastating effect and almost succeeded in eliminating the country. Naval fiction about the epoch had revived with C S Forester's publication of the first of his Hornblower books, *The Happy Return*. Winston Churchill read Hornblower at a highly emotional moment, during his first trip out of his homeland for fifteen months, since Britain became a besieged fortress with the Fall of France. On passage to Newfoundland aboard the great but doomed battleship *Prince of Wales* to meet President Roosevelt, he also saw the Alexander Korda film *That Hamilton Woman* for the fifth time. Despite the apparent celebration of adultery, the Prime Minister was moved to tears in view of the ship's officers. As he rose he addressed the company, 'I though this would interest you, gentlemen, many of whom have been recently engaged with the enemy in matters of equal historical importance.'[21] On arrival he telegraphed the minister who had recommended Forester's books – 'Hornblower admirable.' The minister's staff frantically searched the codebooks, thinking this was some secret operation they had not been told about.

Today a long naval war on the scale of either of these great conflicts is highly unlikely, and in any case a naval officer is constantly in touch with his headquarters by radio. He suffers from a glut of information rather than a famine, so the 'man alone' aspect is not very relevant. Perhaps this is why modern novels on international conflict deal mainly with espionage or special operations, where the individual or small group dominates the action. Naval fiction, particularly the books of Patrick O'Brian, is translated into many and unexpected languages, and we can presume that it does not give the patriotic stimulus that Hornblower gave to Churchill and his nation in the 1940s. Yet readers remain fascinated by it. Perhaps, in a world dominated by mass media and instant communication, they hope to discover their own initiative and inner resources in the way that Nelson, Cochrane, Sidney Smith, Edward Riou and Phillip Broke had to do in real life, and Hornblower, Drinkwater, Jack Aubrey and Stephen Maturin did in fiction.

FOOTNOTES

FOREWORD
1 *A Voice from the Main Deck*, 1st Publishing: Whittemore, Niles and Hall, Boston, 1857; Latest Publishing: Chatham Publishing, London, 1999.

INTRODUCTION
1 For instance Thursfield, Lloyd, Bromley.
2 Pocock, *Marryat*, p.9
3 Sternlicht, p.9
4 Lavery, *Shipboard Life*, p.622.

CHAPTER 1
1 *Master and Commander*, p.5.
2 *Persuasion*, p.63.
3 Le Faye, p.215.
4 Cunningham, p.36.
5 Brenton, 2, p.112.
6 *Midshipman Easy*, pp.105-6.
7 Hughes, pp.145-6.
8 Ackerman, p.184.
9 *Post Captain*, p.60.
10 *Hornblower and the Hotspur*, p.299.
11 Sainty, pp.102-3.
12 Lewis, *Health of Seamen*, p.270.
13 *Peter Simple*, p.46.
14 Nicolas, 5, p.341.
15 Nicolas, 6, p.33.
16 Gatty, p.235.
17 *Ibid.*, pp. 163, 293.
18 BL Add 37809, f.384.
19 Gautier, p.273, n.
20 Nicolas, 1, p.149.
21 Macperson, 4, p.535.
22 W James, 3, p.253.
23 Richardson, pp.49-50.
24 *Midshipman Easy*, pp.242, 246.

CHAPTER 2
1 Rolt, p.19.
2 Based on C James, 2, 1811.
3 Chamier, p.191.
4 Harding and Le Fevre, p.189.
5 *Naval Chronicle*, 12, p.34-40.
6 Corbett and Richmond, *Spencer Papers*, 2, p.213.
7 Laughton, *Naval Miscellany*, 2, p.330.
8 Gardiner, pp.153-79.
9 Lavery, *Ship of the Line*, 1, p.107.
10 *Desolation Isalnd*, p.13.
11 Lavery, *Ship of the Line*, 1, p.121.
12 Gardiner, p.90.

CHAPTER 3
1 Smith, 1, p.126.
2 *Persuasion*, p.19.
3 *Ibid.*, p.25.
4 Owen, p.131.
5 Allardyce, pp.11-12.
6 Hall, 1, pp.260, 268.
7 Le Faye.
8 Cochrane, p.10; Raigersfield, p.9.
9 Lewis, *Social History*, pp.62-3, 70.
10 Lavery, *Nelson and the Nile*, p.164.

11 Lewis, *Social History*, p.36.
12 L Faye, p.26.
13 Raigersfield, p.10.
14 H Robinson, pp.220-1.
15 AGC/24/17.
16 *Ibid.*
17 *Midshipman Easy*, p.365.
18 Laughton, *Barham Papers*, 3, pp.389-91.
19 Lavery, *Shipboard Life*, p.264.
20 NMM, WEL/8.
21 Johnson, p.82.
22 Thursfield, p.11.
23 Le Faye, p.32.
24 Tucker, 1, pp.391-7.
25 Marshall, 4, pp.966-69.
26 Cochrane, p.76.
27 *The Happy Return*, 1951 edit, p.11.
28 Lavery, *Shipboard Life*, p.355.
29 *King's Own*, p.134.
30 *Midshipman Easy*, p.225.
31 Lavery, *Shipboard Life*, p.567.
32 *King's Own*, p.134-5, 198.
33 Lavery, *Shipboard Life*, p.496.
34 *Midshipman Easy*, p.83.
35 Quoted in Pocock, p.110 and n.
36 *Peter Simple*, p.103.
37 *King's Own*, p.136-7.
38 Lavery, *Shipboard Life*, p.379.
39 *Midshipman Easy*, p.162.
40 Richardson, pp.121, 140.
41 Lavery, *Shipboard Life*, p.603-5.
42 *The Naval Officer*, p.40.

CHAPTER 4
1 Lewis, *Health of Seamen*, pp.265-6.
2 Chamier, p.118.
3 *Hornblower and the Hotspur*, p.179.
4 Nicolas, 5, p.24.
5 Smith, 1, p.111
6 Leech, p.12.
7 Newnham, p.353.
8 *Poor Jack*, p.134.
9 *Ibid.*, p.137.
10 Hay, p.219.
11 Hall, 3rd series, p.144.
12 *The Happy Return*, 1969 Penguin edition, p.158.
13 *Midshipman Easy*, p.413.
14 Burney, p.352.
15 Bromley, *Manning Pamphlets*, p.165.
16 *King's Own*, p.4.
17 *Ibid.*, p.69.
18 *Poor Jack*, p.132.
19 Grocott, p.144-5.
20 PRO, ADM 1/1508.
21 *King's Own*, p.2.
22 Reproduced in Lewis, *Social History*, p.l7.
23 Hall, 3rd series, p.116.
24 *Midshipman Easy*, p.287.
25 Hall, 2nd series, p.61.
26 Leech, p.20.
27 Hall, p.137; Thursfield, p.254.
28 *King's Own*, p.14.
29 Hall, 2nd series, p.71.
30 Lavery, *Shipboard Life*, p.164.
31 *Ibid.*, p.455-6.
32 *King's Own*, p.22-3.
33 Hall, 2nd series, p.67.
34 *Ibid.*

35 *King's Own*, pp.41, 306.
36 Lavery, *Shipboard Life*, p.451.
37 *Peter Simple*, p.261.
38 Hall, 2, p.60.
39 *Midshipman Easy*, passim.
40 Chamier, pp.105-6.
41 *Peter Simple*, p.26.
42 W Robinson, p.87.
43 *King's Own*, p.1-2.
44 *Peter Simple*, p.450.

CHAPTER 5
1 *Midshipman Easy*, p.128.
2 Lavery, *Ship of the Line*, p.45.
3 *Peter Simple*, p.3.
4 Burney, p.212.
5 Steel, p.122.
6 *Ibid.*, p.138.
7 *Peter Simple*, p.50.
8 Lavery, *Shipboard Life*, p.464.
9 *Ibid.*, p.464.
10 *Ibid.*, p.138.
11 *Ibid.*, p.122.
12 *Ibid.*, p.359.
13 Burney, p.79.
14 Lever, p.76-7.
15 Lavery, *Shipboard Life*, p.347.
16 Thursfield, p.251-2.
17 Burney, p.91.
18 Lavery, *Shipboard Life*, p.146.
19 NMM, AUS, 2b.

CHAPTER 6
1 *Persuasion*, p.58; PRO Adm, 1/396.
2 W Robinson, pp.32-3.
3 Lavery, *Shipboard Life*, p.462.
4 *Ibid.*, pp.465
5 NMM WEL/30.
6 Hall, 1, p.224-5; Lloyd, *Keith Papers*, 1, p.30; Lewis, *Health of Seamen*, p.168.
7 Parsons, p.13.
8 *Peter Simple*, p.437-8; Lloyd, *Keith Papers*, 2, p.412-3.
9 Lavery, *Shipboard Life*, pp.423, 424, 623-4
10 *Ibid.*, pp.434, 426.
11 W Robinson, p.87-8.
12 Chamier, p.10.
13 Thursfield, p.11-2.
14 Hall, 3, p.163.
15 Hoffman, p.109.
16 Lavery, *Shipboard Life*, p.463.
17 *Peter Simple*, p.291.
18 Glascock, *Naval Sketch Book*, 2, pp.57-8.
19 *Peter Simple*, p.103.
20 *Ibid.*, p.74; *Mariner's Mirror*, vol 7, p.345; Thursfield, p.333; PRO Adm 1/5392.
21 Lavery, *Shipboard Life*, p.463.
22 NMM WEL/8.
23 *Ibid.*, p.7.
24 Wetherell, pp.7-8.
25 Grocott, vii.
26 Laughton, *Naval Miscellany*, 2, pp.298-358.
27 Parsons, pp.66-72.

CHAPTER 7
1 Desbriere, p.132.
2 Caral Rahn Phillips, *Mariner's*

Mirror, 87, no 4, pp.420-45.
3 Desbriere, p.96.
4 Dudley, p.48.
5 Dudley, 2, p.183.
6 Leech, p.84.
7 *Ibid.*, p.85.
8 *The Naval Officer*, p.268.
9 Dudley, 2, p.193.
10 Chamier, p.178.
11 Dudley, 2, p.245-8.
12 Lavery, *Nelson and the Nile*, p.240.

CHAPTER 8
1 Chamier, p.150.
2 Mahan, 2, ch. 15.
3 *King's Own*, p.213.
4 Lavery, *Shipboard Life*, pp.172-79.
5 Dudley, 2, p.59.
6 *Nelson Dispatch*, 6-9, 1/99.
7 *Ibid.*
8 Lavery, *Shipboard Life*, p.285-6.
9 *Ibid.*, p.181.
10 *King's Own*, p.218.
11 Dudley, 2, p.126.
12 Lewis, *Social History*, p.377.
13 Cochrane, pp.55-6.
14 W James, 6, p.65.
15 Corbett, *Fighting Instructions*, p.314.
16 Markham, *Letters*, p.398.
17 Acerra and Meyer, p.23.
18 W Robinson, p.43.
19 *Peter Simple*, p.34.
20 *King's Own*, p.44.
21 Hargood, p.286.
22 Keevil and Coulter, 3, pp.58-9.
23 Steel, p.90.

CHAPTER 9
1 Laughton, *Barham Papers*, 3, p.259-60.
2 Leech, p.77.
3 Lavery, *Nelson and the Nile*, p.223.
4 *Poor Jack*, p.257-63.
5 Wetherell, p.118.
6 Dupin, p.41.
7 House of Commons, Accounts and Papers, 1798, Vol XVIII, Report on the Treatment of Prisoners of War, p.60.
8 Wetherell, pp.137, 141.
9 Maitland, p.83.
10 *Nelson Dispatch*, 1995-6, p.398.
11 Hill, p.201-2.
12 *Persuasion*, p.17.
13 Chamier, p.27.
14 Quoted in Hill, p.21.
15 Chamier, p.296.
16 Hill, p.116.
17 NMM SPB/15.
18 BL Addit Ms 38041, John Vincent Barrie, *Alexander Maconachie of Norfolk Island*, Oxford, 1958.
19 Quoted in Lewis, *The Navy in Transition*, p.195.
20 Barnett, p.881.
21 Morton, p.81.

BIBLIOGRAPHY

For more detailed references on many naval points, see the author's *Nelson's Navy: The Ships, Men and Organisation, 1793-1815* first published in London and Annapolis in 1989 and reprinted several times.

MANUSCRIPT SOURCES

National Maritime Museum (NMM);
AGC/24/17
AUS, Austen Papers
WEL/8

British Library (BL);
Additional Manuscripts, especially the
   Nelson papers

Public Record Office (PRO);
ADM/1, captains' letters to the Admiralty

NAVY RECORDS SOCIETY VOLUMES

Julian Corbett (ed), *Fighting Instructions, 1530-1815*, 1905 reprinted 1971
Julian Corbett and H W Richmond (eds), *The Private Papers of George, Second Earl Spencer, 1794-1801*, 4 vols, 1913-24
Sir John Knox Laughton (ed), *The Barham Papers*, 3 vols, 1906, 1910, 1911
Sir John Knox Laughton (ed), *The Naval Miscellany vol II*, 1910
H G Thursfield (ed), *Five Naval Journals*, 1951
Sir Clements Markham (ed), *The Letters of Admiral Markham*, 1904
Christopher Lloyd (ed), *The Keith Papers*, vols II and III, 1950, 1955
Michael Lewis (ed), *The Health of Seamen*, 1965
J S Bromley (ed), *Manning Pamphlets*, 1974
Brian Lavery (ed), *Shipboard Life and Organisation*, 1998

BIOGRAPHIES

Individual, arranged by name of subject;

Deirdre le Faye, ed, *Jane Austen's Letters*, 3rd edition, Oxford, 1995
Basil Hall, *Fragments of Voyages and Travels*, London, 1865
Frederick Chamier, *The Life of a Sailor*. By a Captain in the Navy, 3 vols., London, 1832
Thomas Cochrane, Earl of Dundonald, *The Autobiography of a Seaman*, 2 vols., London, 1860
G L Newnham Collingwood, *A Selection from the Public and Private Correspondence of Vice-Admiral Lord Collingwood*, London, 1828

Alexander Allardyce, *Memoir of Viscount Keith*, Edinburgh and London, 1882
Joseph Allen, *Memoirs of the Life and Services of Admiral Sir William Hargood*, Greenwich, 1861
Robert Hay, *Landsman Hay*, London, 1953
Frederick Hoffmann, *A Sailor of King George*, 1901, reprinted London, 1999
Samuel Leech, *A Voice from the Main Deck*, 1857, reprinted London, 1999
John Vincent Barrie, *Alexander Vincent of Norfolk Island*, Oxford, 1958
Frederick Lewis Maitland, *Narrative on the Surrender of Bonaparte*, 2nd Edition, London, 1826
Sir Nicholas Harris Nicolas, ed, *The Dispatches and Letters of Lord Nelson*, 7 vols, 1844-6, reprinted London, 1997-8
Charles Owen, *No More Heroes*, London, 1975
G S Parsons, *Nelsonian Reminscences*, London, 1843
Tom Pocock, *Captain Marryat, Seaman, Writer and Adventurer*, Chatham, 2000
Jeffery de Raigersfield, *Life of a Sea Officer*, c.1930, reprinted London, 1929
William Richardson, *A Mariner of England: an account of the career of William Richardson from cabin boy in the merchant service to warrant officer in the Royal Navy, 1780-1819, as told by himself*, Colonel Spencer Childers (ed), London, 1908
William Robinson, *Jack Nastyface, memoirs of an English seaman*, rp London, 2002
Alfred and Margaret Gatty, *Recollections of the Life of Alexander John Scott*, London, 1842
J D Tucker, *Memoirs of the Rt Hon the Earl of St Vincent*, London, 1844
John Wetherell, *The Adventures of John Wetherell*, ed C S Forester, London, 1954
Hercules Robinson, *Sea Drift*, Portsea, 1858

Collective;
Richard Harding and Peter Le Fevre (eds), *Precursors of Nelson*, London, 2000
John Marshall, *Royal Naval Biography*, 12 volumes, London, 1823-30

CONTEMPORARY WORKS ON SEAMANSHIP ETC

William Burney, *Universal Dictionary of the Marine*, 1815, reprinted New York, 1970
D'Arcy Lever, *The Young Sea Officer's Sheet Anchor*, 2nd edition, 1819, reprinted New York, 1963

William Falconer, *Universal Dictionary of the Marine*, 1780, reprinted 1970
David Steel, *Elements of Mastmaking, Sailmaking and Rigging*, reprinted New York c.1963 from the 1794 edition

OTHER CONTEMPORARY WORKS

Rudolph Ackermann, *The Microcosm of London*, 1808-10, reprinted as *Ackerman's Illustrated London*, ed Fiona St Aubin, 1985
Edward Pelham Brenton, *The Naval History of Great Britain*, 2 vols, London, 1837
Charles Dupin, *Voyages dans La Grande Bretagne*, 4 vols, Paris, 1825-26
William Glascock, *Tales of a Tar*, London, 1830
Naval Sketch Book, London, 1826
Major Charles James, *The regimental companion: containing the relative duties of every officer in the British Army*, 7th ed, 4 vols. London, 1811
William James, *The Naval History of Great Britain*, 6 vols, London, 1837, reprinted London, 2002
David MacPherson, *Annals of Commerce*, 4 volumes, London, 1805
Adam Smith, *Wealth of Nations*, Oxford, 1976 edition
David Steel, *Naval Chronologist of the Late War, 1793-1801*, London, c 1802

NAVAL FICTION, NOVELS MENTIONED IN THE TEXT

Frederick Marryat;
The King's Own, 3 vols, 1838
Poor Jack, 1840
Masterman Ready, 3 vols, 1841-2
Midshipman Easy, 3 vols, 1836, reprinted,
Peter Simple, 3 vols, 1834
The Naval Officer, or Frank Mildmay, 3 vols, 1829

Patrick O'Brian;
Master and Commander, 1969
Post Captain, 1972
Desolation Island, 1978

C S Forester;
The Happy Return, 1937
Hornblower and the Hotspur, *1962*

OTHER FICTION

Jane Austen, *Persuasion*, rp 1993

COMMENTARIES AND CRITICISM

Arthur Cunningham (ed), *Patrick O'Brian, Some Critical Appreciations and a Bibliography,* Wetherby, 1994

Maurice-Paul Gautier, *Captain Frederick Marryat, L'Homme et L'Oeuvre,* Paris, 1973

Stanford Sternlicht, *C S Forester and the Hornblower Saga,* Syracuse, 1999

OTHER BOOKS

Martine Accerra and Jean Meyer, *Marines et Revolution,* Rennes, 1988

Corelli Barnett, *Engage the Enemy More Closely,* rp London, 2000

Edouard Desbriere, *Projects et Tentatives de Debarquement aux Iles Britanniques 1793-1805,* Paris, 1900-02

W S Dudley, *The Naval War of 1812, a Documentary History,* vol II, Washington, 1992

Robert Gardiner, *Frigates of the Napoleonic Wars,* London, 2000

Terence Grocott, *Shipwrecks of the Revolutionary and Napoleonic Eras,* London, 1997

Richard Hill, *Prizes of War,* Stroud, 1998

Robert Hughes, *The Fatal Shore,* London, 1998

R F Johnson, *The* Royal George, London, 1971

J Keevill and JLS Coulter, *Medicine and the Navy,* 4 vols, London, 1957-63

Brian Lavery, *Nelson and the Nile,* London, 1998

Ship of the Line, 2 vols, London, 1983-4

Michael Lewis, *A Social History of the Navy,* London, 1960

The Navy in Transition, London, 1965

Alfred Thayer Mahan, *The Influence of Sea Power on the French Revolution and Empire,* 2 vols., London, 1892

H V Morton, *Atlantic Voyage,* London, 1943

LTC Rolt, *Navigable Waterways,* London, 1989

J C Sainty, *Admiralty Officials 1660-1870,* London, 1975

PERIODICALS

Mariners Mirror, 1911-, journal of the Society for Nautical Research

The Naval Chronicle, 1798-1818, selection Nicholas Tracy (ed), London, 1998-99

The Nelson Dispatch, Journal of the Nelson Society

GLOSSARY

Aback, the situation of the sail of a ship, when its forward surface is pressed upon by the wind.

Abaft, the hinder part of a ship, or some point nearer to the stern than any given part; as, abaft the foremast.

Abeam, the point at right angles to the keel, opposite the ship's mainmast.

About, the situation of a ship immediately after she has tacked, or changed her course, by going about, and standing on the other tack.

Abreast, synonymous with Abeam.

Adrift, the state of a ship or vessel broke loose from her moorings, and driven without control, at the mercy of the wind, sea, or current.

Afore, all that part of a ship which lies forward, or near the stem.

Aft, After, behind, or near the stern of a ship. See Abaft.

Aloft, up in the tops, at the mast-head, or any where about the higher yards or rigging.

Alongside, close to the side of the ship.

Amidships, the middle of the ship, either with regard to her length or breadth.

Anchor, best bower and small bower, the two stowed furthest forward or near to the bows; the best bower being the anchor on the starboard bow, the small bower the one on the larboard bow; the sheet anchor is of the same size and weight as either of the bowers; stream anchor a smaller one; and kedge anchor, the smallest of all.

An-end, any spar or mast placed perpendicularly.

Astern, behind the ship.

Athwart, across the lay of the ship's course or its keel.

Athwart hawse, the situation of a ship when she is driven by the wind, tide, or other accident, across the stem of another, whether they bear against, or are at a small distance from, each other, the transverse position of the former with respect to the latter being principally understood.

Athwart the fore-foot, is generally applied to the flight of a cannon-ball, as fired from one ship across the line of another's course, but ahead of her, as a signal for the latter to bring to.

Bar, a shoal running across the mouth of a harbour or river.

Bare poles, having no sail up.

Barricade, more commonly called Bulwark, the wooden parapet on each side of the forecastle, quarterdeck, or poop.

Beam;—On the beam, implies any distance from the ship on a line with the beams, or at right angles with the keel: thus, if the ship steers or points northward, any object lying east or west, is said to be on her starboard or larboard beam. See Abeam.

Bear up, or bear away, is to change the course of a ship, in order to make her run before the wind, after she has sailed some time with a side wind, or close hauled.

Beating, the operation of making a progress at sea against the direction of the wind, in a zig-zag line, or traverse; beating, however, is generally understood to be turning to windward in a storm, or fresh wind.

Bend the sails, is to affix them to the yards; bend the cable, to fasten it to the anchor, &c.

Bends, the streaks of thick stuff, or the strongest planks in a ship's side.

Bight, any part of a rope between the ends; also a collar or an eye formed by a rope.

Binnacle, the frame or box which contains the compass.

Birth, a place of anchorage; a cabin or apartment.

Bitts, large upright pins of timber, with a cross-piece, over which the bight of the cable is put; also smaller pins to belay ropes, &c.

Boarding-netting, network triced round the ship to prevent the boarders from entering.

Bow, is the rounding part of a ship's side forward, beginning where the planks arch inwards, and terminating where they close at the stem or prow. On the bow, an arc of the horizon, not exceeding 45 degrees, comprehended between some distant object and that point of the compass which is right ahead, or to which the ship's stem is directed.

Bowlines, ropes made fast to the leeches or sides of the sails, to pull them forward.

Box off, is, when a ship having got up in the wind or been taken with the wind ahead, the head-yards are braced round to counteract its effect, and prevent the ship from being turned round against your inclination.

Braces, ropes fastened to the extremities of the yards to brace them about.

Brails, ropes applied to the after leeches of the driver, and some of the stay-sails, to draw them up.

Break ground, to weigh the anchor and quit a place.

Breeching, a stout rope fixed to the cascabel of a gun, and fastened to the ship's side, to prevent the gun from running too far in.

Bring to, to check the course of a ship by arranging the sails in such a manner that they shall counteract each other, and keep her nearly stationary; when she is said to lie by or lie to, having, according to the sea-phrase, some of her sails aback, to oppose the force of those which are full. To come to is sometimes used with the same meaning; although, more generally, it means to let go the anchor.

Bring up, to cast anchor.

Broach to, is when, by the violence of the wind, or a heavy sea upon the quarter, the ship is forced up to windward of her course or proper direction in defiance of the helm.

Bulkheads, partitions in the ship.

Bumkin, a short boom or beam of timber projecting from each bow of a ship, to extend the clew or lower edge of the foresail to windward.

Cable, a large rope by which the ship is secured to the anchor.

Cable's length, a measure of 120 fathoms, or 240 yards.

Cap, a thick block of elm, with a round hole in the fore part for the topmast to enter, and a square one abaft to receive the lowermast head.

Capstan, a machine by which the anchor is weighed.

Cat-head, a strong bracket projecting from the forecastle on each bow, furnished with sheaves or strong pulleys, and to which the anchor is lifted after it has been hove up to the bow by the capstan.

Chains, or channels, of a ship, those strong projections from the sides to which the shrouds or rigging of each of the lowermasts are secured, by means of wooden blocks, or deadeyes, strongly chained and bolted to the ship's side.

Chess-tree, a piece of wood bolted perpendicularly on each side of the ship just aft of the forecastle to receive the tack of the mainsail furnished with a sheave through which the tack passes, thereby extending the clew of the sail to windward.

Close hauled, the arrangement or trim of a ship's sails when she endeavours to make a progress in the nearest direction possible towards that point of the compass from which the wind blows.

Club-hauling, tacking by means of an anchor.

Coamings, raised borders around the hatchways to prevent water ingress.

Conning the ship, the directions given to the steersman by a superior seaman, termed the quartermaster, or by the captain, officer of the watch, master, or pilot, as the case may be.

Courses, a name by which the fore and main sails, and driver, are usually distinguished.

Crank, the quality of a ship which, for better design or want of sufficient quantity of ballast or cargo, is rendered incapable of carrying sail, without being exposed to the danger of upsetting.

Cutwater, the knee of the head.

Davit, a piece of timber used as a crane to hoist the flooks of the anchor to the top of the bow: it is called fishing the anchor. Also used for raising ships boats.

Driver, a large sail suspended to the mizen gaff: called also spanker.

Edge away, as, when a ship changes her course, by sailing larger, or more afore the wind than she had done before.

Fill, is to fill the sail that has been shivered or hove aback, to bring the ship to.

Fleet, an assemblage of ships of war, to the number of ten and upwards.

Flukes, the broad parts or palms of the anchors.

Flotilla, a fleet of small vessels of war.

Fore-and-aft, the lengthway of the ship.

Forging ahead, to be forced ahead by the wind.

Founder, to sink.

Furl, to wrap or roll a sail close to the yard, stay, or mast to which it belongs, and secure a gasket or cord about it to fasten it thereto.

Gaskets, a piece of plait to fasten the sails to the yards.

Gripe, is when, by carrying too great a quantity of aftersail, a ship inclines too much to windward, and requires her helm to be kept a-weather, or to windward.

Gun-shot, implies, says Falconer, "the distance of the point-blank range of a cannon-shot." With submission, we take a gun-shot distance to mean long, and not point-blank range: if this be correct, a ship is within gun-shot of another when she is within a mile or a mile and a quarter of her.

Haul the wind, to direct the ship's course as near as possible to that point of the compass from which the wind arises.

Hawse-holes, the holes through which the cables pass.

Hawse, is generally understood to imply the situation of the cables before the ship's stem, when she is moored with two anchors out from the bows; viz., one on the starboard, and the other on the larboard bow. It also denotes any small distance ahead of a ship, or between her head and the anchors by which she rides.

Hawser, a small cable.

Heave to, synonymous with bring to. Heaving to an anchor, is when all the cable is taken in until the ship is directly over her anchor, preparatory to its being weighed out of the ground.

Knot, one nautical mile per hour.

Labour, to pitch and roll heavily.

Larboard, a name given by seamen to the left side of the ship, when looking forward from the stern (this term was abolished in 1844).

Large, a phrase applied to the wind, when it crosses the line of a ship's course in a favourable direction; particularly on the beam or quarter: hence, to sail large, is to advance with a large wind, so as that the sheets are slackened and flowing, &c. This phrase is generally opposed to sailing close hauled, or with a scant wind.

Lasking course, is when a ship steers in a slanting or oblique direction towards another.

Lie to, synonymous with Bring to, Heave to.

Looming, an indistinct appearance of any distant object, as ships, mountains, &c.

Luff, the order to the helmsman to put the tiller towards the lee-side of the ship, in order to make the ship sail nearer to the direction of the wind.

Main sheet, a large rope affixed to the lower corner or clew of the mainsail by which, when set, it is hauled aft into its place.

Main tack, another large rope affixed to the same corner of the sail, but to haul it on board or down to the chess-tree on the forepart of the gangway; when set upon a wind, or close hauled, the foresail is furnished with similar gear.

Musket-shot distance, from 300 to 400 yards.

Offing, implies out at sea, or at a good distance from the shore.

Overhaul, to examine; also to overtake a ship in chase.

Pistol-shot distance, about 50 yards.

Plying, turning to windward.

Port the helm, the order to put the helm over to the larboard side of the ship. Used instead of larboard, on account of the affinity of sound between the latter word and starboard.

Quarter, that part of a ship's side which lies towards the stern, or which is comprehended between the aftmost end of the main chains and the side of the stern, where it is terminated by the quarter-pieces.

Rake a ship, is when the broadside sweeps another's decks fore and aft, either by lying athwart her bows or her stern. Rake means also the inclination of the masts, bowsprit, stem, or sternpost.

Reef, to reduce a sail by tying a portion of it to the yards with points.

Ride, to be held by the anchor cable.

Round to, is when going large or before the wind, to come round towards the wind by the movement of the helm.

Ship the tiller, &c., is to fix it in place.

Slipping the cable, unsplicing it within, a buoy and buoy-rope having been previously affixed to it, to show where the ship has left her anchor.

Splicing, the mode by which the end strands of a rope are united.

Spring, to anchor with a, is, before letting go the anchor, to cause a smaller cable or hawser to be passed out of a stern or quarter port, and taken outside of the ship forward, in order to be bent or fastened to the ring of the anchor intended to be let go, for the purpose of bringing the ship's broadside to bear in any given direction.

Spring, a mast, yard, or any other spar, is when it becomes rent or split by an overpress of sail, heavy pitch or jerk of the ship in a rough sea, or by too slack rigging.

Squadron, an assemblage of ships of war less than ten in number. See Fleet.

Stand on, keep on the same course.

Starboard, the right side of the ship, when the eye of the spectator is directed forward, or towards the head.

Stay, to stay a ship, is to arrange the sails and move the rudder, so as to bring the ship's head to the direction of the wind, in order to get her on the other tack.

Steer, to manage a ship by the movement of the helm.

Tack, is to change the course from one board to another, or to turn the ship about from the starboard to the larboard tack, or vice versa, in a contrary wind.

Tant, or taunt rigged, means when a ship is very lofty in her masts. All-a-tanto, is said when a ship, having had some of her masts struck, has rehoisted them.

Taut, a corruption of tight.

Thrum a sail, is to insert in it, through small holes made by a bolt-rope-needle, or a marline-spike, a number of short pieces of rope-yarn or spun-yarn, in order, by the sail's being drawn over a hole in the ship's bottom, to assist in stopping the leak.

Tow, to draw a ship or boat forward in the water, by means of a rope attached to another vessel or boat, which advances by the effort of rowing or sailing.

Unmoor, is to reduce a ship to the state of riding by a single anchor and cable, after she has been moored or fastened by two or more cables.

Unship, is to remove any piece of timber, wood, &c., from the place in which it was fitted.

Wake of a ship, is to be immediately behind or in the track of her. It also means when a ship is hid from view by another ship.

Warp a ship, is to change her situation by pulling her from one part of a harbour, &c., to some other, by means of warps (ropes or hawsers), which are attached to buoys, to other ships, to anchors sunk in the bottom, or to certain stations on the shore, as posts, rings, trees, &c. The ship is then drawn forward to those stations, either by pulling on the warps by hand, or by the application of some purchase, as a tackle, windlass, or capstan.

Weather a ship, headland, &c., is to sail to windward of it.

Weather gage, implies the situation of one ship to windward of another when in action, &c.

Wear, or veer ship, is to change her course from one board to the other by turning her stern windward.

Weigh, is to heave up the anchor of a ship from the ground in order to prepare her for sailing.

Work a ship, is to direct her movements, by adapting the sails to the force and direction of the wind. To work to windward is a synonym of beat, tack, turn to windward, &c.

INDEX

Page references in *italics* are to illustrations.